MW01592894

The
Pool Care
Handbook

An illustrated guide to DIY pool care, including water chemistry, maintenance, troubleshooting, and more.

·

Swim University
A Division of Ace Media, LLC.
2525 Arapahoe Ave. Unit E4 PMB 512, Boulder, Colorado 80302-6746
www.SwimUniversity.com

Printed in the United States of America

Author: Stephanie Halligan
Technical Editor: Rita Ray
Cover and Interior Design: Matthew Giovanisci

Table of Contents

1

~~~

INTRODUCTION
Our Pool Care Principles

INTRODUCTION
Our Pool Care Principles

We know how frustrating it is to feel like you're wasting time and money on taking care of your pool and how, despite all that work, you can't seem to keep your water clear.

Whether you're new to pool ownership or need help troubleshooting a problematic pool, the Pool Care Handbook is the ultimate guide to help keep your pool sparkling clean throughout the year.

In this guide, you'll learn how to:

- Keep your water chemistry balanced without wasting time or money.
- Prevent algae and cloudy water.
- Maintain sparkling clean pool surfaces with minimal effort.
- Understand your pool equipment and plumbing, inside and out.
- Easily troubleshoot water and equipment issues when they arise.
- Open, close, and maintain your pool without hiring help.

Pool Care Principles

Our method for simple pool maintenance is based on Swim University's 3 Cs of pool care: **Circulation, Cleaning, and Chemistry**. Following the 3 Cs and understanding how they work with your pool's unique anatomy is the key to keep your water balanced and clear:

1. Circulation

Keeping your water properly circulating means your filter system does the heavy cleaning for you. And a pool with good circulation rarely has issues like cloudy water or pool algae.

2. Cleaning

Regularly cleaning your pool surfaces and removing debris will help prevent larger problems down the line, like cloudy water and algae. While regular cleaning requires more physical effort, it's better than trying to clean up green water.

3. Chemistry

No matter how good your water is circulating or how often you clean your pool's surfaces, none of that will matter if your water isn't sanitized. This means knowing what chemicals to have on hand and when and how to add them the right way.

Circulation   Cleaning   Chemistry

In addition to the 3 Cs, here are a few other helpful tips when it comes to pool care:

Know Your Anatomy

You can't take care of your pool without knowing what its parts do. That involves learning about each piece of equipment and labeling it accordingly. It's such an important step that we cover it first in this guide!

Keep It Simple

Pool care can get confusing, messy, and even dangerous if you start to add too many chemicals or try to mix and match methods for sanitizing your water.

The principles we outline in this guide are simple and straightforward. We know that there are lots of ways to do pool care, including more DIY or homemade methods, but we recommend following a straightforward plan when you're just starting out. You can always add, change, or experiment with things later.

Stick to One Source of Information

We hope you use this guide and Swim University in general for all your pool maintenance needs. But regardless of where you decide to go for pool care help, stick to one source. If you're constantly researching or turning to multiple pool stores for answers, it can lead to more problems and confusion down the line.

Enjoy Your Pool!

It can be hard to remember to slow down and appreciate your pool, especially if you're in the middle of a serious problem. But that's what pools are for—to have fun with family, to relax and unwind, and to soak up the joy they add to our lives. Our hope is that by following these simple principles, you'll be able to spend more time enjoying your pool and less time worrying about how to fix it.

How to Use This Handbook

This guide is packed full of useful information on every page, and we think everything included is valuable for every pool owner. But if you have a specific question or problem, you can also use this guide as a quick reference by skipping to different sections.

Here are some key features of this handbook and how to use them:

Table of Contents

This maps out everything we cover in this guide. If you're not sure where to look for help with a specific issue (like clearing up cloudy water or how to backwash a filter), start with the table of contents.

Section Overview

At the beginning of each section, we've outlined what you'll learn and what questions we'll answer. Use this as a snapshot summary for each section.

Action Steps

At the end of each section, we outline some simple action steps to take based on what you've learned.

This can be a one-time action, like labeling your filter pipes or calculating how many gallons your pool holds. Or it can be an ongoing task, like setting up a weekly schedule to brush your pool walls and test your water.

Visual References

We've included diagrams, graphics, and tables throughout the text to help you better understand complex pool concepts.

This includes diagrams of the inner workings of common pool equipment and tables to help you quickly calculate chemical dosing.

Glossary of Terms

If you ever feel confused about any specific pool care terminology, there's a glossary of terms at the end of the guide.

Additional Resources

Wondering what brand to buy or what specific products we recommend? Here's a list of our favorite pool tools, chemicals, and equipment that we regularly update: www.swimuniversity.com/tools.

About Swim University

Matt Giovanisci, the founder of Swim University, started working in the pool care industry at age thirteen. He was a stock boy and water tester for a local pool store on the weekends. Over the years, he continued to work in pool care, moving to bigger pool and spa companies along the way.

Matt was helping thousands of pool and hot tub owners every year, but he wanted to share his knowledge and unique teaching style on a larger scale. So he launched Swim University in 2006.

Since then, Swim University has made pool and hot tub care easy for millions of homeowners. And each year, we continue to help more people with water chemistry, cleaning, and troubleshooting.

Swim University Is Now a Family-Run Small Business

What started as a solo project has grown into a tight-knit family team, committed to producing the best pool care content out there. And we're proud to have our entire team and product line based in the USA.

Contact Us

Finally, if you have any questions about this guide, feel free to reach out to matt@swimuniversity.com. We love hearing customer feedback and success stories. With all that said, let's dive in!

2

~~~

POOL ANATOMY

Understanding Your Pool's
Systems and Equipment

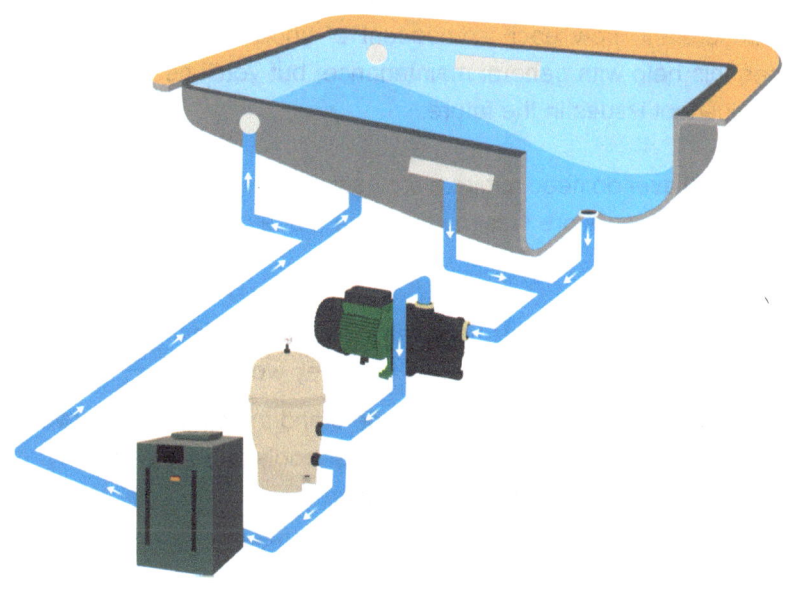

POOL ANATOMY
Understanding Your Pool's Systems and Equipment

One of the most valuable things you can do to care for your pool is to understand how each component of your pool works. Not only does this help with general maintenance, but you'll be able to better troubleshoot issues in the future.

And if you ever do need to hire a professional, this will help you narrow down the issue before wasting time and money. In this section, you'll learn about:

1. **Pool Anatomy 101:** Learn about the three main sections of a pool's plumbing system and how they work.

2. **Inground Pool Anatomy:** Understand the difference between concrete, fiberglass, and vinyl liner pools and the typical plumbing setup for inground pools.

3. **Above Ground Pool Anatomy:** Understand the difference between above ground pool materials and how water flows through a standard above ground pool system.

4. **Pool Size, Shape, and Volume:** Calculate how many gallons your pool holds.

5. **Pump and Filter Systems:** Understand common pool plumbing and equipment, and map out how water flows through your pool's system.

6. **Filling Out Your Pool Profile:** Create a simple profile of your pool, equipment, and water flow to reference for future maintenance or troubleshooting.

Pool Anatomy 101: The 3 Sections of Your Pool's Plumbing

There are three main sections of your pool's plumbing system: the suction side, the filtration system, and the pressure side. Each section is responsible for pulling water out of your pool, filtering, and treating your water, and then sending sanitized water back into your pool.

Your pool may have additional pieces of equipment or a different number of skimmers, drains, or returns. But the flow of water and anatomy of the plumbing is essentially the same.

1. Suction Side (Water Flows Out of Pool)

This is the side that takes in water from the pool and introduces it to the filtration system. Your pool pump sucks in the water from the pool through the skimmer, which is the rectangular port in the pool wall. If you have an inground pool, it also pulls water in through the main drain(s).

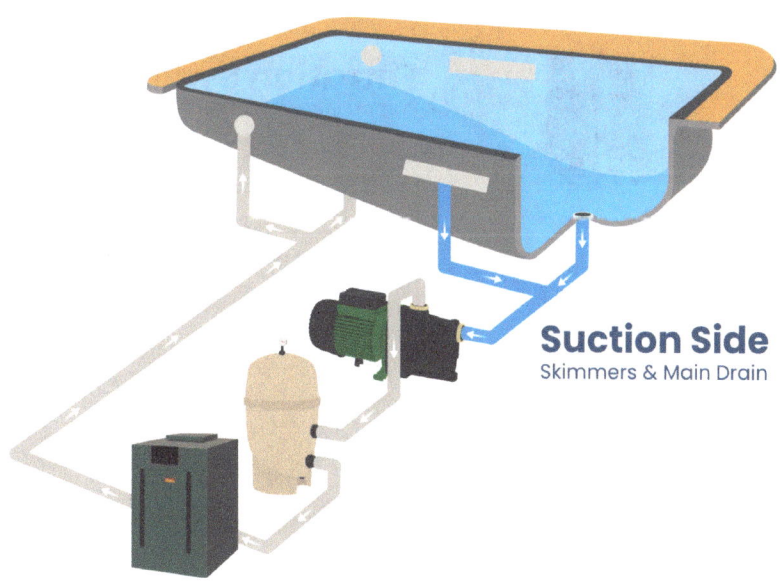

Suction Side
Skimmers & Main Drain

2. Filtration System (Water Flows through Pump, Filter)

Your pool pump and pool filter make up the filtration system.

Once the water is sucked in from the pool, it passes through the pump and into the filter. Then the filter cleans the water by removing debris and contaminants.

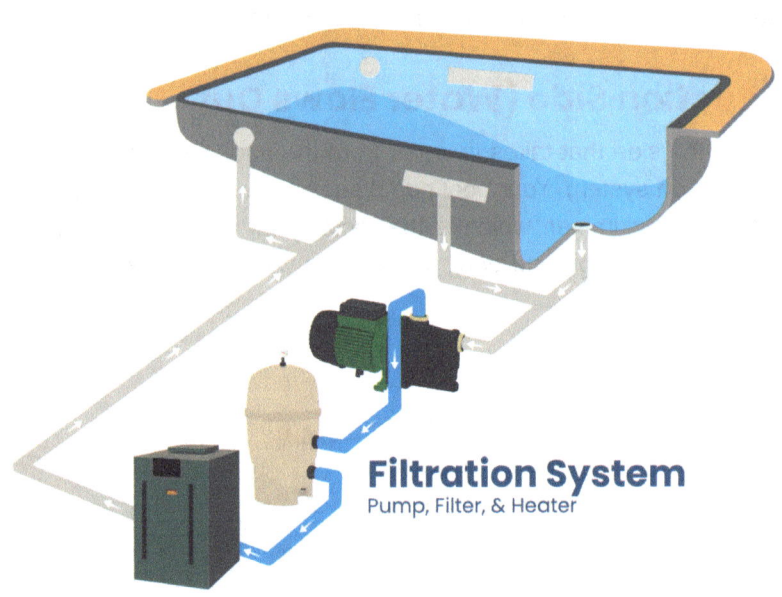

Filtration System
Pump, Filter, & Heater

3. Pressure Side (Water Flows Back to Pool)

This side of the pool pushes water from the filtration system back into the pool, completing the circulation process. After water passes through the filter, it's pushed back out into the pool through the return jet(s).

Some pools have additional equipment after the filter, like a heater or automatic chemical feeder, which treats the water before it returns to the pool.

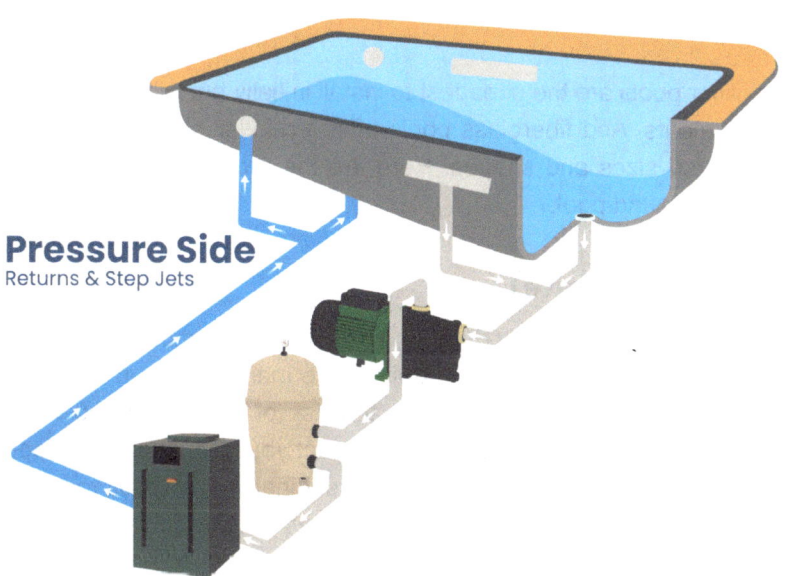

Pressure Side
Returns & Step Jets

Inground Pool Anatomy

Inground pools are made from different materials that impact their care and longevity. They also feature components not found in above ground pools, like main drains. Here are the different types of inground pools and the common anatomy features found across them all.

Types of Inground Pools

Inground pools can be made of concrete (or gunite), vinyl, or fiberglass. In general, concrete pools offer the most variety of size, shape, and design. But they require the most cost and maintenance in the long run.

Vinyl liner pools are the cheapest to install initially but will require liner replacements. And fiberglass pools offer a midtier pricing option but with limited sizes and shapes. Here are the pros and cons of each type of inground pool:

Concrete (Gunite)

These pools are extremely durable, and allow for the most size, shape and design choices. But they require more maintenance in the long-run. The porous surface increases the risk of algae and you'll use more chemicals, since concrete can impact your pH. And you'll need to resurface and retile every 10–15 years. Finally, it's difficult to repair a concrete pool that uses a specific decorative tile or stone.

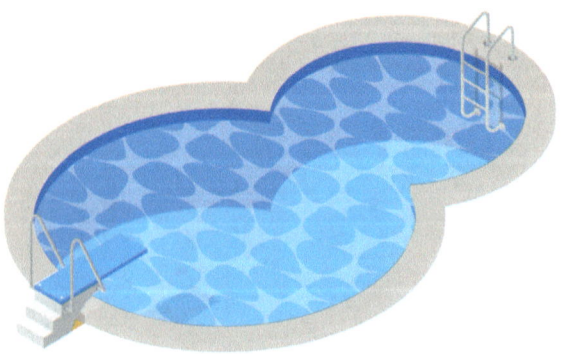

Vinyl Liner

Pools with vinyl liners have the lowest upfront cost and include customizable shapes and sizes. The surface is nonabrasive and nonporous, meaning algae is less likely to cling to the surface. But you need to replace the liner every 8–10 years, and it rips or tears easily if it comes into contact with sharp objects.

Fiberglass

These pools are the lowest maintenance. They're manufactured in a controlled factory setting and installation is quick compared to other pool types. And the nonabrasive surface means no resurfacing or liner replacement. But you're limited to predetermined shapes, designs and sizes. And repairs may not match the original color or finish of your fiberglass. This is also a higher initial cost than other pool types, especially vinyl liner pools.

Components of an Inground Pool

There are several standard components in an inground pool:

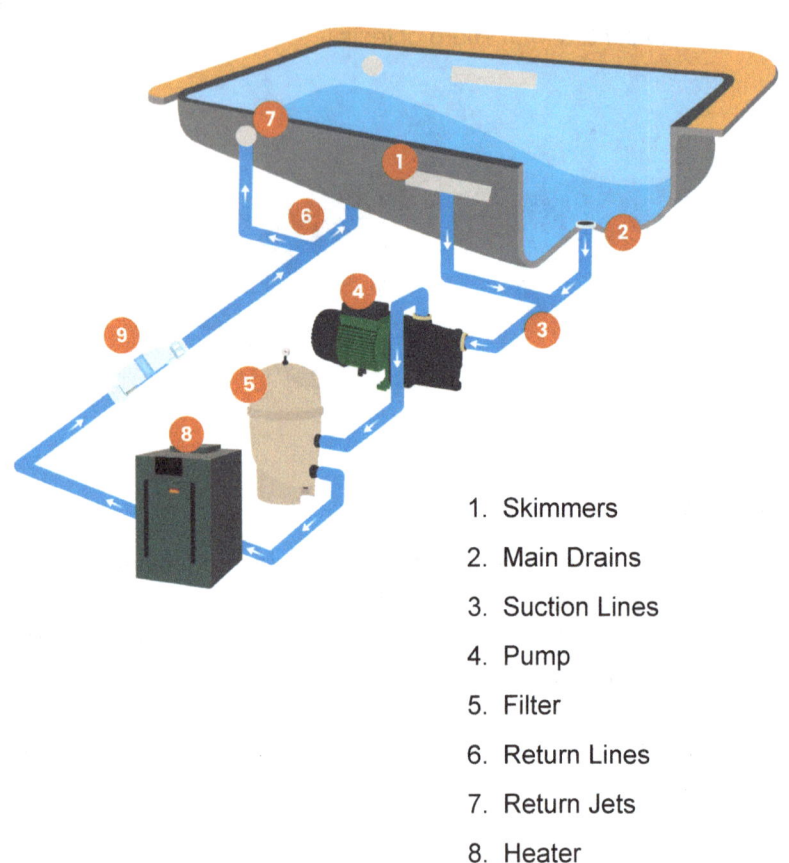

1. Skimmers
2. Main Drains
3. Suction Lines
4. Pump
5. Filter
6. Return Lines
7. Return Jets
8. Heater
9. Sanitation System

1. Skimmers

Pool water enters the skimmer (or skimmers). A skimmer is the rectangular port built into the side of the pool. Some pools contain unique suction-side inlets instead of skimmers. These include overflow perimeters, vanishing edges, or infinity edges, which flow into a tank, then later flows into the pump.

The concrete or plastic skimmer ports contain skimmer baskets. The baskets are there to catch larger debris, such as leaves, twigs, bugs, and anything else that's too large to go through your filter.

Do You Need a Skimmer Weir Door?

Skimmers sometimes have a moving door known as a weir. But they're not entirely necessary. And they tend to break easily. However, it can help keep debris from going back into the pool when the pump's off. It also regulates the amount of water entering the skimmer when the pump is running and helps trap the debris it collects.

If you have a weir already installed, great! But it's not necessary to get one unless you notice lots of debris reentering your pool.

2. Main Drains

Usually located in the floor of the pool's deep end, the main drain's name may be a little misleading. While it can be used to drain the pool, it's seldom used that way.

Normally, it performs the same function as the skimmers, pulling water from the pool and into the pump. This helps improve circulation, as water is pulled both from the top of the pool by the skimmers and from the bottom by the main drain.

> ## Newer Inground Pools Have Two Main Drains
>
> This is a safety measure to reduce the suction force in case something—or someone—blocks one of the drains. Older inground pools may not have two main drains. Use caution when near a single drain.

3. Suction Lines

These pipes, usually made of PVC, carry the pool water from the skimmer and main drain to the pump.

4. Pump

The pool pump contains an impeller, which spins fast enough to create a vacuum. That vacuum pulls the water from the pool, through the skimmers and main drains, and into the filtration system.

The impeller is powered by a motor. As the water passes through the pump, the force changes from pulling to pushing, and the pump pushes the water into the filter.

5. Filter

While sanitizers like chlorine kill viruses and bacteria, the filter cleans water by removing fine debris, tiny particles, and even some bacteria. Pool filters are available in three varieties: sand, diatomaceous earth (D.E.), and cartridge.

6. Return Lines

These pipes are the opposite of the suction lines but are also made of PVC. They carry pool water from the filter to the return jets.

7. Return Jets

Once the filtered water has passed through the return lines, it arrives at the return jets, where it reenters the pool. In addition to sending water back into the pool, return jets also push the water around the pool. This helps direct water—and even debris—toward the skimmers and back to the filter system.

Another area where you might find these jets are on the steps leading into your pool. These help keep the steps clean since they tend to gather debris.

Other Optional Components

8. Heater

Whether a gas, electric or heat pump, or solar heater, this component heats your water after it has passed through the filter.

9. Sanitation System

A chemical feeder or an automatic chlorinator is an easy, automatic way to chlorinate your water. This is the last piece of equipment installed after your pump, filter, and heater and before the water is returned to the pool. This is also the place where you would install a salt water generator.

10. Suction Side Vacuum Line (Pool Cleaner Jet)

If you have a dedicated vacuum line, you'll notice a port located on the side of your pool wall. The valve at your pump will divert water through this line.

11. Pressure Side Booster Pumps

This is an additional pump for boosting water pressure in your system. It can be used to power pressure-side pool cleaners.

12. Water Features and Other Add-ons

Waterfalls, water fountains, and other water features are powered by water returning to your pool after it's been filtered. You may have other fixtures and add-ons like diving boards or slides.

13. Hot Tub and Pool Combinations

Integrated hot tubs are positioned on the end, side or corner of the pool. A dam wall between the spa and pool keeps the water separate. Spillover or overflow spas are connected to your pool through a small fountain or curtain of water. This water moves from the hot tub and into the pool. You may have a dedicated air blower system to activate the jets. But your hot tub likely shares the same plumbing system as your pool.

Draining an Inground Pool

There may be times when you need to partially drain your pool and refill it with fresh water. **But you should never completely drain your inground pool unless you need to make a major repair.**

When an inground pool is drained and the liner or surface is exposed, the liner or surface can blister and crack. Without the weight of the water pressing down on the inside of the pool, it's possible that your entire pool will literally pop out of the ground.

The risk is even higher if you've had heavy rain or live in an area with a high water table. If you do need to drain out some water, consider draining just half the water from the pool and refilling it. And if you need to make a major repair to the floor or interior, call a professional. Do not completely drain the pool when the weather is extremely hot or after heavy rain.

Above Ground Pool Anatomy

The maintenance and care of an above ground pool depends on the pool's material and whether it's a permanent or temporary structure. Here are the different types of above ground pools and the common features found across each one:

Types of Above Ground Pools

Temporary vs. Permanent

Above ground pools are either permanent or temporary fixtures. If you take your pool down every year, you do not need to worry about balancing calcium hardness levels or winterizing your pool equipment or plumbing.

Inflatable vs. Framed Pools

Like other temporary pools, inflatable pools require less long-term maintenance and are taken down for storage in the off-season. But they're less sturdy, and they often require patching when leaks appear. Pool frames require more set up but are sturdier.

Types of Materials

Pool frames are usually made from steel, resin, or aluminum. They are then lined with a vinyl liner. Here are the pros and cons of each frame type:

- **Steel:** Steel frames are the strongest frame available. They're cheaper compared to aluminum frames. And newer steel frames are treated to resist rust. But it's the heaviest frame and hardest to disassemble and move. It may also need extra coating to prevent corrosion and oxidation.

- **Aluminum:** These frames are flexible and easy to disassemble and move. But they require coating to prevent oxidation, and oxidized aluminum can rip a hole in your liner. Finally, they can be more expensive than steel.

- **Resin:** Resin frames have no rust, oxidation and erosion issues. And they won't get hot like aluminum or steel. But it will need a coating to protect it from cracking and flaking in the sun's UV rays. And the cost of the frame depends on how much resin you use.

Components of an Above Ground Pool

There are several standard components in an above ground pool:

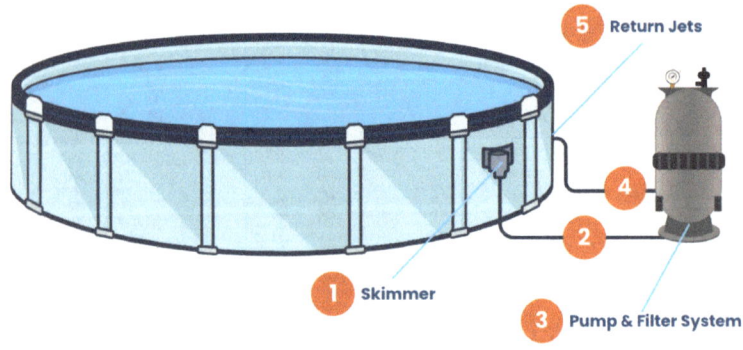

1. Skimmers

Pool water enters the skimmer (or skimmers). A skimmer is the rectangular port built into the side of the pool. It sometimes has a moving door (known as a weir). A weir isn't necessary, but it can prevent debris from floating back into your pool. These plastic ports contain skimmer baskets, which catch larger debris such as leaves, twigs, bugs, and anything else that's too large to go through your filter.

2. Suction Lines

These pipes carry the pool water from the skimmer to the pump.

3. Pump and Filter

The pool pump contains an impeller, which spins fast enough to create a vacuum that then pulls the water from the pool, through the skimmers, and into the filtration system.

Depending on the size of your above ground pool, you may have an all-in-one pump and filter. The filter cleans water by removing fine debris, tiny particles, and even bacteria that may have made it past the sanitizer. Above ground pools usually use sand or cartridge filters.

4. Return Lines

The opposite of the suction lines, they carry pool water from the filter to the return jets.

5. Return Jets

Once the filtered water has passed through the return lines, it arrives at the return jets, where it reenters the pool. In addition to sending water back into the pool, return jets also push the water around the pool.

This helps direct water—and even debris — toward the skimmers and back into the filter system. Depending on the size of your above ground pool, you may only have one return jet.

Other Optional Components

6. Pool Heater

Whether a gas, electric or heat pump, or solar heater, this component heats your water after it has passed through the filter.

7. Sanitation System

A chemical feeder or an automatic chlorinator is an easy, automatic way to chlorinate your water. This is the last piece of equipment installed after your pump, filter, and heater and before the water is returned to the pool. This is also the place where you would install a salt water generator.

8. Water Features and Other Add-ons

Waterfalls, water fountains, and other water features are powered by water returning to your pool after it's been filtered. You may have other add-ons like steps, diving boards, or slides.

Draining an Above Ground Pool

If you have a permanent above ground pool, you should not need to completely drain it as part of your maintenance. Consider partially draining and refilling to make repairs or change the water.

But if you do need to completely change out the water, make sure the weather isn't extremely hot to avoid sun and UV damage. And be sure to refill your pool as soon as possible. Do not keep your pool drained for more than a day or two. This will prevent the liner from stretching, shrinking, or getting damaged by the sun.

Pool Size, Shape, and Volume

Knowing how much water is in your pool is incredibly important for pool maintenance. It will help you determine how long to run your filter system and the amount of chemicals you need to add to your pool.

Round Up Your Pool's Volume

You don't need to calculate your pool's volume to the exact gallon. Just be sure to round up if you're estimating. For example, if you end up calculating your volume at 17,900 gallons, round up to 18,000 gallons.

Pool Water Level

In order to calculate your pool volume, be sure to measure from the depth of your water, not the height of the wall or the depth of the pool. You're calculating how much water is in your pool, and it's probably not filled up to the top. Your water level should hover in the center of the skimmer plate.

Calculating How Much Water Is In Your Pool

You can use the pool volume reference chart below to quickly calculate the volume of common pool shapes and sizes. These are estimates, so you'll always get more accurate results if you measure it yourself.

Always measure the depth of your water, not the height of your wall. Or you can use our online pool volume calculator at: www.swimuniversity.com/pool-calculator/

Above Ground
48" Wall Height

Pool Size	Gallons
15' Round	5,300
18' Round	7,600
20' Round	9,400
24' Round	13,600
27' Round	17,200
28' Round	18,500
11' x 25' Oval	6,500
15' x 25' Oval	7,800
15' x 30' Oval	8,900
18' x 33' Oval	10,600
18' x 38' Oval	14,000

Above Ground
52" Wall Height

Pool Size	Gallons
15' Round	5,800
18' Round	8,300
20' Round	10,200
24' Round	15,300
27' Round	18,600
28' Round	20,000
11' x 25' Oval	7,000
15' x 25' Oval	8,400
15' x 30' Oval	9,600
18' x 33' Oval	11,500
18' x 38' Oval	15,200

Inground
Average Depth

Pool Size	Gallons
12' x 24' Rectangular	10,800
16' x 32' Rectangular	19,200
16' x 36' Rectangular	21,600
18' x 36' Rectangular	24,300
20' x 40' Rectangular	30,000
16' x 32' Oval	17,200
18' x 36' Oval	21,700
20' x 40' Oval	26,800
17' x 33' Grecian	19,700
17' x 37' Grecian	22,200
20' x 36' Grecian	24,300
20' x 44' Grecian	30,300
16' x 30' Kidney	14,900
16' x 34' Kidney	16,500
20' x 38' Kidney	20,200

However, if you want to calculate your pool volume by hand, here's a quick guide.

Manual Pool Volume Calculations

To get your pool's volume, you need to calculate your pool's surface area and average depth. And to do that, you'll need a few basic metrics:

- Length (L)
- Width (W)
- Depth (D) or Height (H)
- Diameter (d), for round pools
- Radius (r), for round pools
- Pi (3.14), for round pools

You'll need another key part for your calculations: **one cubic foot of water contains 7.5 gallons**.

So in order to figure out how many gallons your pool holds, you'll multiply your final cubic foot measurement by 7.5 to find the volume of your pool. Let's see what this looks like with different pool shapes.

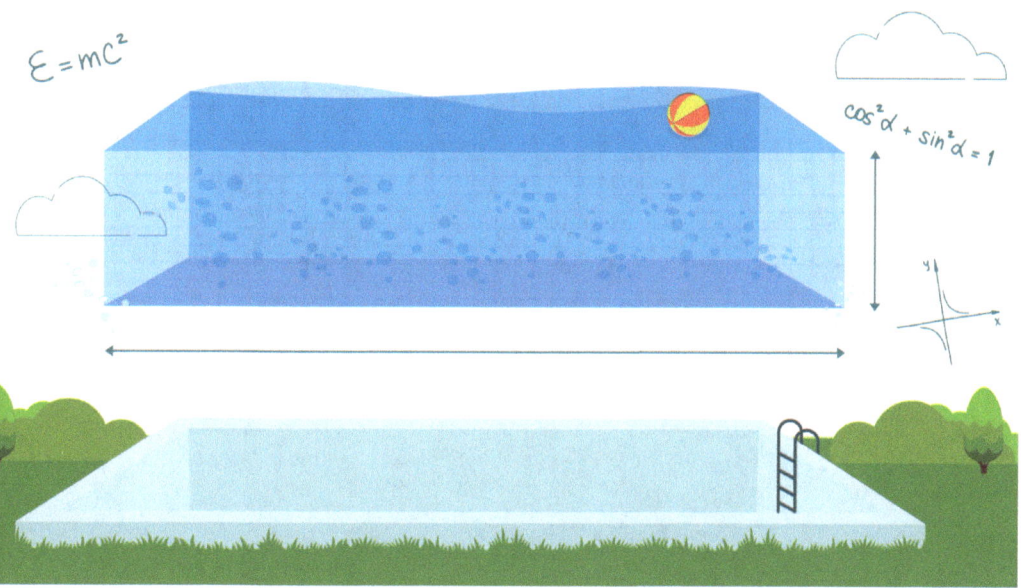

Measure Your Water Depth Correctly

Be sure to measure the depth of your water, not the height of the wall or the depth of the pool. You want to know how much water is in your pool, and it's probably not filled up to the top.

Same Depth Pools: Square or Rectangular

Length x Width x Depth x 7.5 = Pool Volume (Gallons)

To calculate the volume of a rectangular pool with a constant depth throughout, you'll need the length, width, and depth. Remember there are 7.5 gallons in each cubic foot of water. Multiply the cubic feet of the pool by 7.5 to get the total number of gallons.

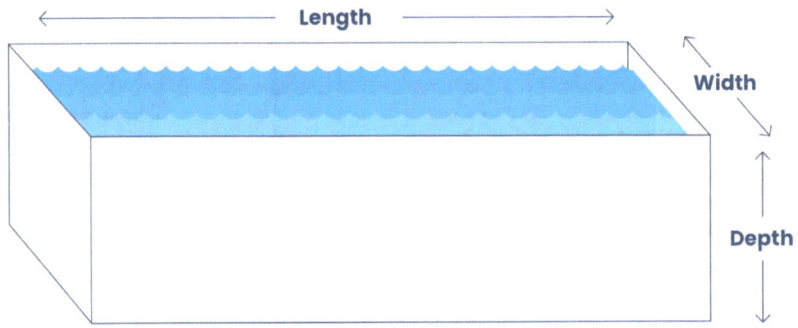

Variable Depth Pools: Square or Rectangular

Length x Width x Average Depth x 7.5 = Pool Volume (Gallons)
Use this formula if you have a shallow end and a deep end. For example, if the shallow end is 3 feet and the deep end is 9 feet, and the slope of the pool bottom is gradual and even, then the average depth is 6 feet.

If most of the pool is 3 feet, then suddenly drops to 10 feet, treat the pool as two parts. Measure the length, width, and average depth of the shallow end, then take the same measurements for the deep end. Calculate them separately, and add the totals together.

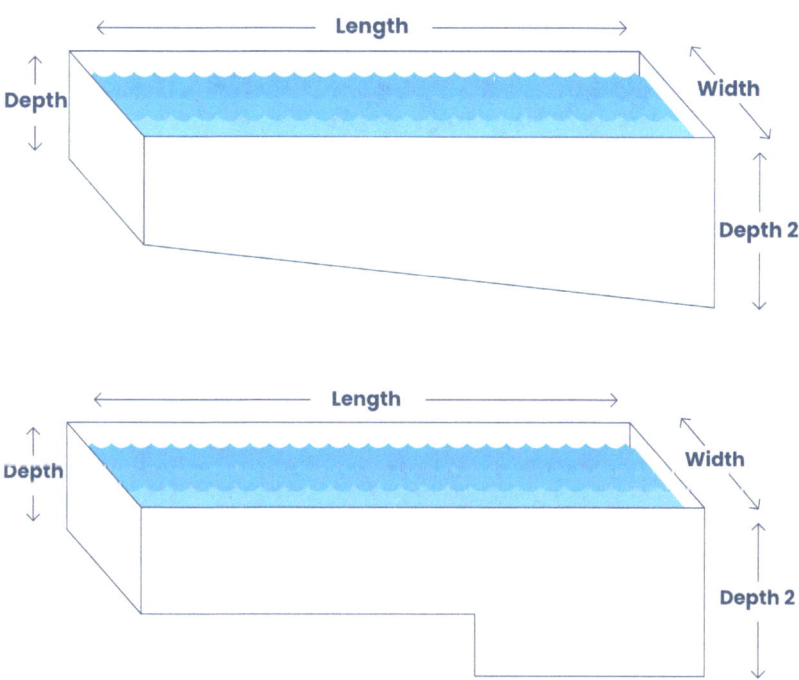

Round Pool or Oval Pools

3.14 (Pi) x Radius Squared x Depth x 7.5 = Pool Volume (Gallons)
To calculate a round pool, you'll need the diameter, which is the distance across the broadest part of the circle. Then divide that in half to get the radius.

For example, if the widest length of your pool is 24 feet across, the radius is half that, so 12. To get the radius squared, multiply the radius times itself: 12 x 12 = 144. Lets say your 24-foot round pool is 4 feet deep. Your formula would be: 3.14 x 144 x 4 x 7.5 = 13,564.8 (which we'll round to 13,600 gallons).

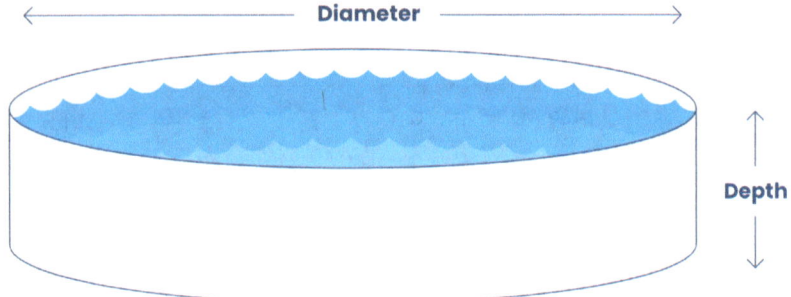

Kidney or Irregularly-Shaped Pools

There are two methods used to calculate the volume of irregular shapes. First, you can imagine the pool as a combination of smaller regular shapes. Measure these various areas and use the calculations described previously for each square or rectangular area and for each circular area. Then add these volumes together to determine the total capacity.

If these calculations don't work properly for you because you have an unusual pool shape, or you just want everything to be more accurate, ask a pool professional to take the measurements and figure out the volume for you.

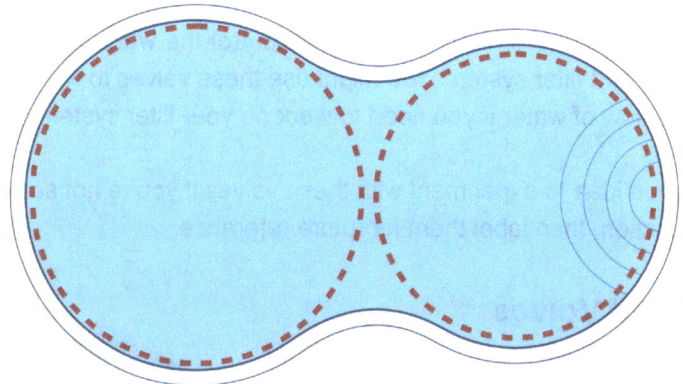

Pump and Filter Systems 101

Now that you understand the general structure of your pool, it's time to talk about the "heart and soul" of your pool system: your pump and filter. Rather, it's the "heart and kidneys," since this system is in charge of pumping water through the plumbing and filtering out contaminants. If your pump or filter isn't working properly, your water isn't being sanitized and circulated.

Once pool water leaves your pool and passes through your skimmer, it enters into your pump and filter system. This consists of valves that control the flow of water, the pump, the filter, and optional water treatments, like heaters and chemical feeders.

1. Valves

Your pool has one or more valves that control the water flowing into the pump and filter system. You might use these valves to temporarily stop the flow of water if you need to work on your filter system.

It's a good idea to experiment with these valves if you're not sure how they function, then label them for future reference.

Shut-Off Valves

Depending on your system, the only valves you might see are called shut-off valves. These valves have only one function, and that's to shut off the water supply to your filter system.

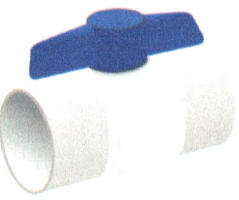

Generally, you'll see these valves at the front of your pump, but they could be located in other areas.

Multidirectional Valves or 3-Way Valves

If you have an inground pool, you might have a multidirectional valve or a three-way valve.

These are also called Jandy valves. They change the flow of water from one pipe to another or split the flow to two pipes.

Generally, you'll see these valves on both the suction side and the pressure side of your filter system.

For Inground Pools: Pull from Both the Skimmer and Main Drain

If you have an inground pool, set up your valves so you're pulling water from both your skimmers and main drains. By pulling water in from both the top of and the bottom of your pool, you'll improve your circulation.

There will be times when you'll only use one skimmer or just the main drains. For instance, if your pool is cloudy or you have a lot of dirt and debris on the floor of the deep end, you'll want to only pull water from the main drains to clear it up. But for regular pool use, pull water from both skimmers and drains.

2. Pump

The pump is responsible for pulling water out of the pool. It then pushes the water into the filter. Your pump consists of two components: the pump housing and the motor.

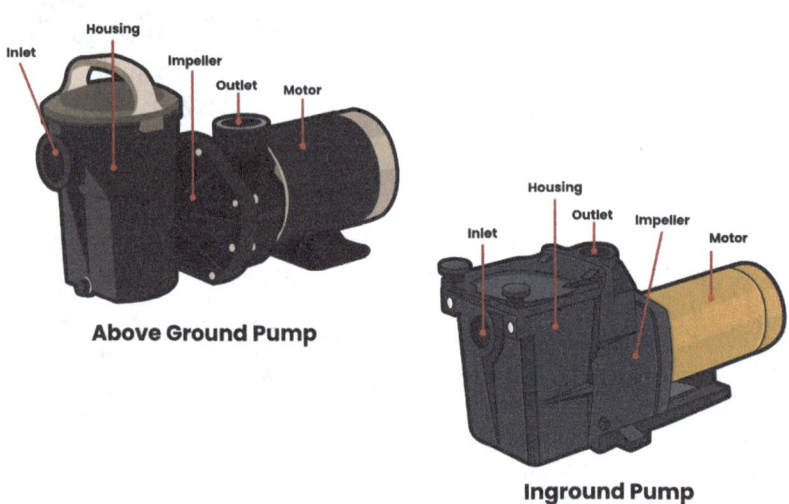

Above Ground Pump

Inground Pump

Pump Housing

This is the main body of the pump, which has a bucket, a lid, and a basket inside. There is also an impeller, which spins fast enough to create a vacuum. That vacuum pulls the water from the pool, through the skimmers and main drains, and into the filtration system.

Motor

This is the heavy cylinder behind the bucket with the lid. Its job is to spin the impeller. Because of this motor, pumps are measured by horsepower. Pumps usually range from ¾ to 3 horsepower. The larger your pool, the more horsepower you'll need.

3. Filter

After water leaves the pump, it enters your filter. There are three types of filters: sand, D.E. (diatomaceous earth), and cartridge filters. While each type helps filter out tiny particles from your pool water, some are more powerful (and more maintenance) than others.

Sand Filters

Water flows into a multiport valve and down through a thick bed of filter sand. This sand filters out tiny contaminants, and then that filtered water is sent back to your pool.

- **Pros:** Sand filters require little maintenance besides backwashing. Backwashing involves reversing the flow of water to dislodge built up contaminants in the filter. You'll also only need to replace the sand about every five years.

- **Cons:** They're the least effective when it comes to filtering smaller contaminants compared to the other two types of filters.

D.E. Filter

This filter uses D.E., which is a fine white powder made of diatomaceous earth, and a set of filter grids or fingers. The outside of the grids is coated with D.E. powder, and as the water passes through, it's filtered and returned to the pool.

- **Pros:** They're very effective and filter out smaller contaminants better than any other filter type.

- **Cons:** They require the most maintenance. The D.E. powder will need to be replaced every time you backwash. And the grids or fingers need to be cleaned at the end or beginning of every pool season.

Cartridge Filters

Cartridge filters are a tank with one or more large round filter cartridges inside. These look like an air filter from a car or like cartridge filters in a hot tub. The water is pushed through the filter mesh and then back to your swimming pool.

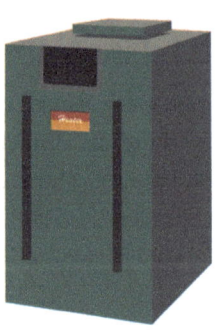

- **Pros:** When properly taken care of, cartridge filters are more effective than sand filters at filtering contaminants.
- **Cons:** They require some manual maintenance and replacement cartridges. You'll need to remove the cartridges and rinse them down with a hose regularly. Also, at the beginning or end of each year, they'll need to be soaked in a filter cleaning solution or completely replaced.

Be sure to check out the Circulation Section for information on how to backwash and clean each type of filter.

4. Heaters

There are several types of pool heaters, including natural gas, electric, heat pumps, and solar.

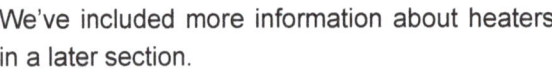

Although it's not a necessary piece of equipment when it comes to circulation and cleaning your pool, it will extend the life of your pool season. This is installed after the filter.

We've included more information about heaters in a later section.

5. Automatic Sanitizers

Sanitizing systems, like chlorinators, chemical feeders, and salt water systems, are the last piece of equipment in your filtration line. These systems automatically sanitize to your water right before it returns to your pool.

Do Not Sanitize Your Water Before Your Heater!

The water coming out of your chemical feeder, automatic chlorinator, or salt water system is treated with chemicals. If that water flows into your heater, it will take a toll on the inside of a heater over time.

Chemical feeders are common for adding chlorine tablets or pucks. But you may have another system installed here, like an in-line mineral system, ozonator, UV system, or salt water generator. Be sure to check out the Chemistry Section for more information on these different types of sanitizer systems.

6. Booster Pumps (Optional)

You might have more than one pump. If you do, chances are you have a pump dedicated to providing more pressure to an automatic pool cleaner, fountain, waterfall, or slide. It's a good idea to know how many pumps you have, what they all do, and what brand and horsepower they are.

Action Steps: Fill Out Your Pool Profile

Having an accurate profile of your pool anatomy and equipment will save you time with repairs, troubleshooting, and general maintenance.

- Gallons of water
- Construction date (if known)
- Material (concrete, vinyl, etc.)
- Number of skimmers, returns, main drain, optional vacuum/ waterfall lines
- Accessories (diving boards, slides, etc.)
- Pump (make, model, age)
- Filter (make, model, age)
- Heater (make, model, age)
- Booster pump (make, model, age)
- Chemical feeder (make, model, age)
- Salt water, mineral, ozonator, or UV system (make, model, age)

Your Pool Profile

Pool Size & Stats

Length: _____ Width: _____ Round: _____

Volume: _____

Construction Date: _____ Material: _____

Skimmers: _____ Returns: _____ Drains: _____

Ladders: _____ Diving Boards: _____ Slides: _____

Equipment

Type of Filter: _____

Brand: _____ Model: _____ Serial #: _____

Type of Pump (HP): _____

Brand: _____ Model: _____ Serial #: _____

Type of Booster Pump: _____

Brand: _____ Model: _____ Serial #: _____

Type of Heater: _____

Brand: _____ Model: _____ Serial #: _____

Type of Chemical Feeder: _____

Brand: _____ Model: _____ Serial #: _____

Type of Automatic Cleaner: _____

Brand: _____ Model: _____ Serial #: _____

3

~~~

CIRCULATION
How to Maintain Good Water Flow

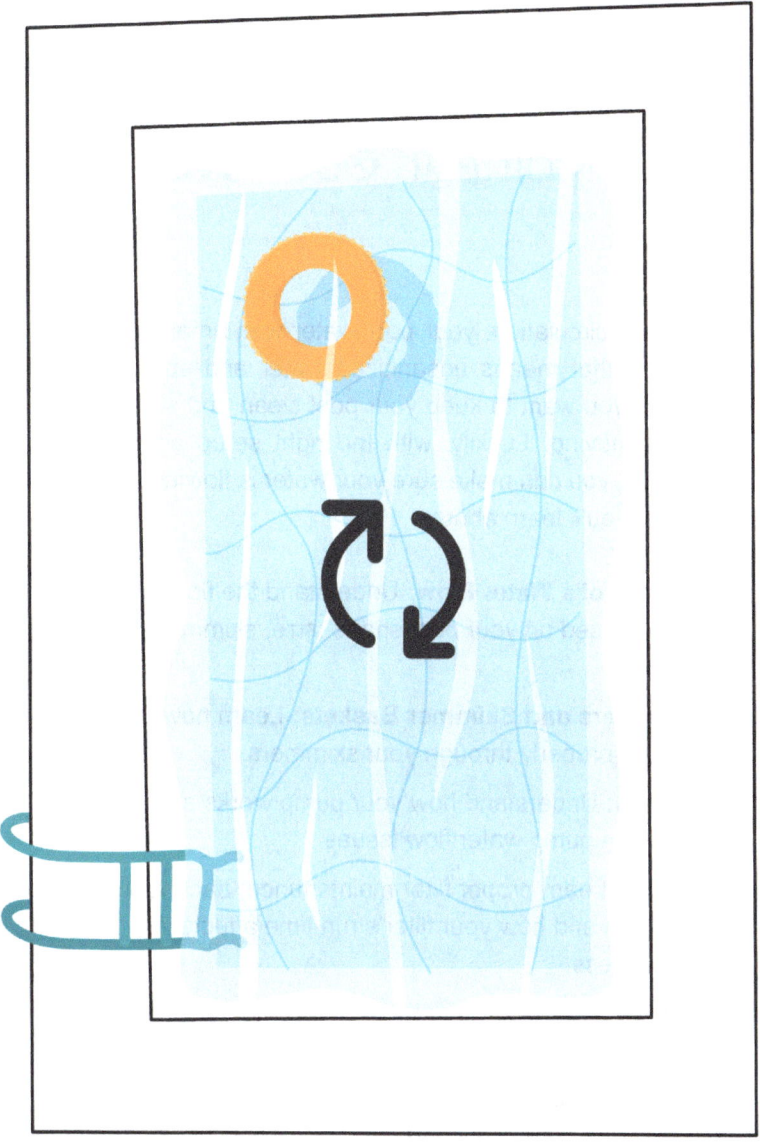

CIRCULATION
How to Maintain Good Water Flow

Without good circulation, your pool water won't make it to your filter system. And that means unsanitized water and spots for algae to bloom. So if you want to keep your pool clean and swimmable, keep your water moving. Luckily, with the right setup and some simple maintenance, you can make sure your water is flowing as it should. In this section, you'll learn about:

1. **Your Pool's Water Flow:** Understand the flow of your pool water based on your pool shape, size, skimmers, and return jets.

2. **Skimmers and Skimmer Baskets:** Learn how to keep water flowing properly through your skimmers.

3. **Pumps:** Understand how your pump works and how to solve common pump water flow issues.

4. **Filters:** Learn proper filter maintenance, backwashing, and cleaning and how your filter's run time affects your pool's cleanliness.

5. **Return Jets:** Understand how to position your return jets for proper water flow.

6. **How to Improve Pool Circulation:** Learn other tricks for increasing water flow and boosting circulation in your pool.

7. **Circulation Action Steps:** Create a simple map of your water flow, label valves and pipes, and adjust your return jets.

Your Pool's Water Flow

Like we discussed in the Pool Anatomy Section, understanding the flow of your pool water is a critical part of pool maintenance. If you know how the water moves in your pool, you can help keep your water properly filtered and troubleshoot issues, like weak return jets. As a reminder, here's how water flows through your pool's system:

- **Water Flows Out of Pool (Suction Side):** Water flows into your skimmers and/or main drain and into your pump and filter system.

- **Water Flows through Pump and Filter:** Water passes through the pump, then the filter. It might also pass through a heater or automatic chemical feeder.

- **Water Flows Back into Pool (Pressure Side):** Water is returned to the pool through return jets and other features like step jets, booster pump lines, waterfalls, and fountains.

You can see the water circulating in your pool by looking at the points where water exits (via skimmers) and reenters your pool (via return jets). Depending on your pool's construction, you may have one or more skimmers, main drains, return jets, or step jets.

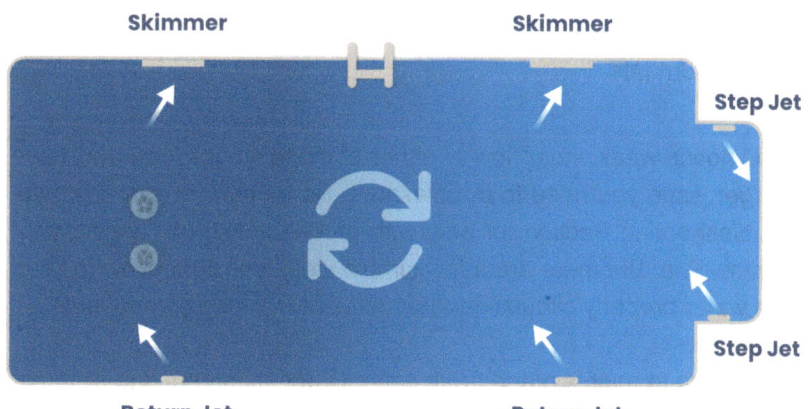

51

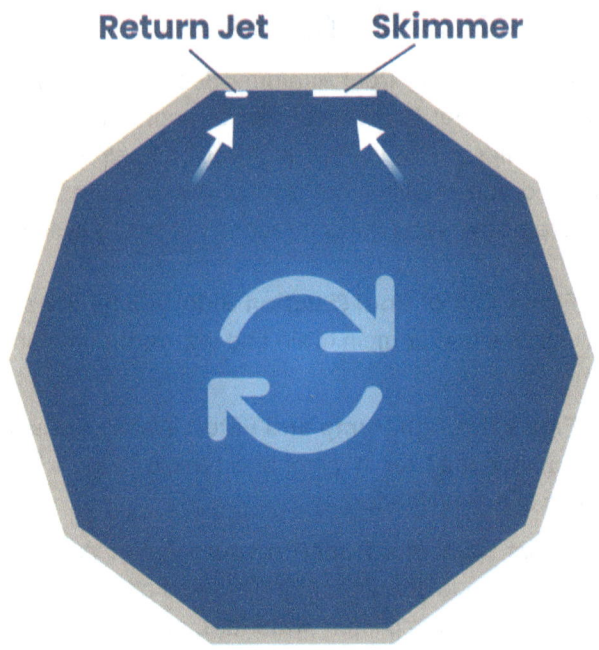

Return Jet   **Skimmer**

Regardless of your pool's size and shape, the water circulates through your system in the same order:

1. Skimmer and skimmer baskets
2. Pump
3. Filter
4. Return jets

If you notice weak water flow at either of these stages, you may have a larger issue you need to troubleshoot. So be sure to check out the Troubleshooting Section for help with problems like unclogging your skimmer line. But there are a few simple steps you can follow to keep your water properly circulating through each of these components.

Here's how to maintain and troubleshoot your skimmers and skimmer baskets, your pump, your filter, and your return jets.

Skimmers and Skimmer Baskets

Your skimmer is your first line of defense when it comes to filtering out debris in your pool. And keeping your skimmer line clear is critical to keeping the rest of your filter system flowing. As the water passes through the skimmer basket, the skimmer collects larger debris. This stops things like leaves and twigs from getting into your filter—and that means your filter can focus on capturing smaller contaminants.

Besides filtering out debris, a skimmer can be used for several other things:

Manual Vacuuming

You can insert your vacuum hose into the skimmer's suction hole (underneath your skimmer basket). Or you can keep the basket in place and use a skimmer vacuum plate. As you vacuum, water will be forced through the pool's filter system, resulting in cleaner, clearer water. For more information on how to vacuum, be sure to check out the Cleaning Section.

Adding Chlorine Tablets

Some people add chlorine tablets directly to their skimmer basket. As the water is pulled through the skimmer, it runs over the tablets and dissolves them. But be careful: you don't want to leave any partially dissolved tablets in the pool skimmer when your pump isn't running. The highly chlorinated water can end up sitting in one place or the tablet's acidity can damage your equipment.

Filtering Smaller Particles

If you want to increase the amount of contaminants picked up by your skimmer, cover your skimmer basket with a skimmer filter sock (or even pantyhose). The finely knit fabric will help catch smaller debris.

Skimmer Components

Here are the main components of your skimmer:

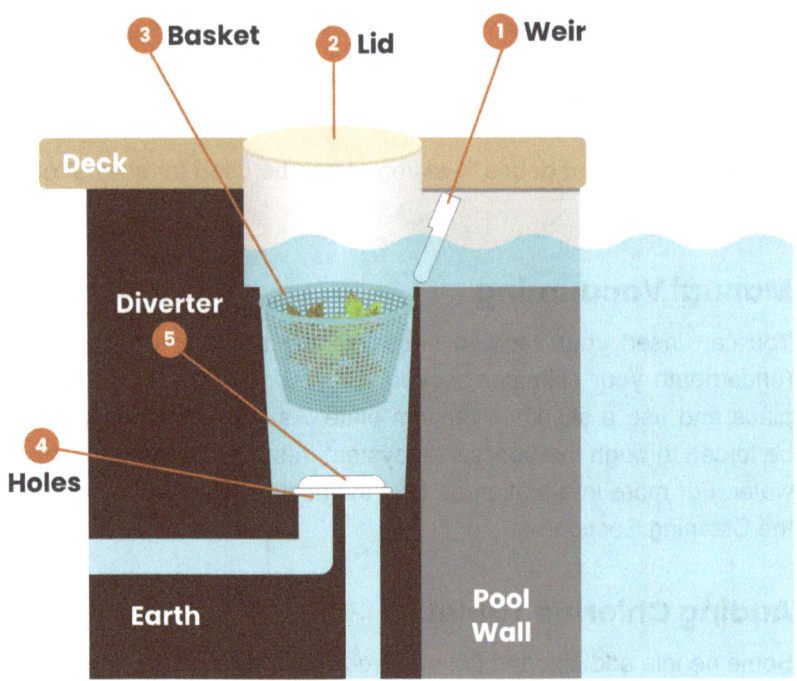

Watch Your Water Level!

For water to pass through your skimmer and into your pool pump, your water level should come about halfway up the skimmer. If the water dips below the skimmer entirely, your pump will run dry and risk overheating and damage.

1. Weir

This is a moving door over the front of the skimmer. It opens and closes and regulates the amount of water entering the skimmer. When you turn the pump off, the weir closes so that debris collected in the skimmer basket doesn't float back into the pool. If you don't have a weir door, that's okay. But you may want to install one if you have issues with debris floating back into your water.

2. Lid

This is what you remove to access your skimmer basket.

3. Skimmer Basket

This is where debris collects before entering your pump. It should be checked and emptied of debris once a week.

4. Holes in Skimmer Well

When you remove your skimmer basket, you should see one or two holes. If you have two holes at the bottom of your skimmer well:

- The hole furthest from the pool wall leads directly to the pump.
- The hole closest to the pool wall pulls water from the main drain or floor drain.

5. Skimmer Diverter, Float Valve, or Equalizer

This helps divert suction away from the skimmer to the main drain if needed. If your water level gets too low or your skimmer is clogged, the diverter will engage and start sucking water from the main drain.

This prevents your pump from running dry or burning up if there's not enough water coming in from the skimmer. The settings on this valve also help you regulate how much suction is normally coming from your main drain.

Skimmer Cleaning

To clean your skimmer, simply take the cover off the skimmer, pull out the basket, and dump it out. Then put the basket back in the skimmer and replace the cover. **Clean out your pool skimmer at least once a week.** And if you have a smaller pool that you use often or you're constantly seeing debris in your basket, clean it more often. The longer debris sits in your skimmer basket, the more likely it will start to break up and decay.

And as we mentioned, if you want to increase the amount of contaminants picked up by your skimmer, cover it with a skimmer filter sock or pantyhose.

Is There a Clog in Your Pool Skimmer Line?

If your pump is pulsing or the water intake into the pump is slow, there could be a clog in your skimmer line. First, make sure your skimmer basket is empty and your pool's water level is high enough. Then find out which pipe is blocked.

With your pool pump running, check each line one at a time using your pool diverter valve (a.k.a. Jandy valve). Switch the valve between the skimmers and main drain. If one line has low pressure, that means it's clogged with debris or there's an air pocket. As you test these lines, be sure to always leave one line open. You never want to run your pump with all the intake valves closed and no water flowing.

For help unclogging something lodged in your skimmer line, check out the Troubleshooting Section of this guide.

Pump

The pump is the heart of your pool's plumbing system. Without it, you won't have any pool circulation, and water won't flow from your pool and through your filtration system.

Water should be moving through your pump whenever it's running. If it runs without water, the pump's motor can overheat and seize up. This can happen when there's air in the line. Luckily, air in the line is relatively easy to correct and prevent with some routine maintenance and understanding of your pump's anatomy.

Pump Components

Here are the main components of your pool pump:

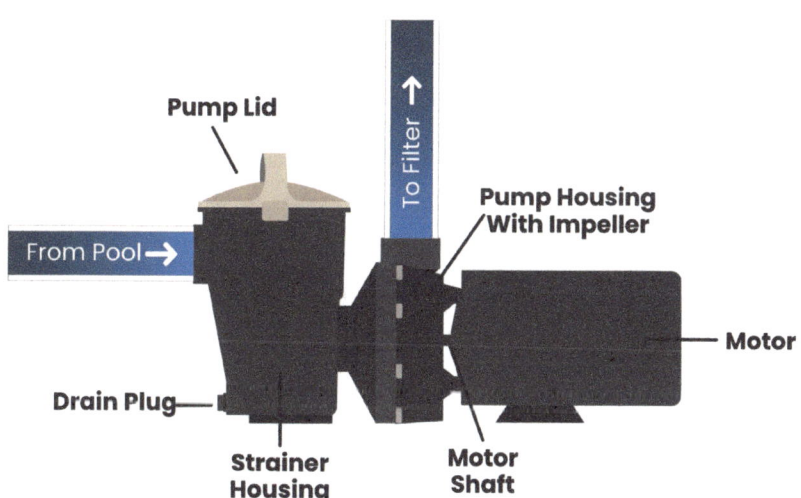

Pump Lid

This is usually transparent, so you can watch the pump function without taking the lid off.

Strainer Housing with Basket

This is where pool water first enters the pump. The basket inside the housing collects debris.

Drain Plug

This is used to drain the pump during winterization. You may have more than one drain plug on your pump.

Pump Housing with Impeller

This is the main control center where the impeller, diffuser, and seals live. The impeller spins on the motor shaft, creating a vacuum that pulls water from your pool and toward your filter.

Pump Motor and Shaft

The motor spins the impeller.

Pump Types, Speed, and Size

There are three types of pumps: single-speed, dual-speed, and variable-speed pumps. We recommend a variable-speed pump for power, efficiency, and energy savings.

Variable-Speed Pumps

These high-efficiency pumps use less friction and consume less power. You can run them at lower speeds when you're just filtering the water and higher speeds when you're adding chemicals or cleaning the water. They also turnover your water more quickly. And because they have lower revolutions per minute (RPM) than single- and dual-speed pumps, they're also quieter.

Single-Speed Pumps

The single-speed refers to the fact that the motor spins the impeller at only one speed according to the horsepower of the motor. These are the least efficient pumps.

Dual-Speed Pumps

These pumps have two speeds: low and high. The higher speed equates to that of a single-speed pump. The lower speed uses less energy but may not be as efficient at water turnover.

The Importance of Variable-Speed Pumps

As of this writing, the United States requires that all new or replacement pumps over 1.0 horsepower (HP) must be variable-speed pumps.

Pump size is measured in horsepower, which corresponds with the pump's flow rate (measured in gallons per minute). Your pump needs to be powerful enough to pull in and filter ALL the water in your pool every day. This is called the **turnover rate**. As a general rule, run your pump for at least 8 hours a day to turnover your water.

But if you want to know the exact time it takes to filter all your water, here's how to calculate your turnover rate: **Turnover Rate (Minutes) = Pool's Volume (Gallons) ÷ Pump Flow Rate (Gallons per Minute)**

For example, if your pool is 15,000 gallons and you have a pump with a flow rate of 40 GPM (gallons per minute), you'll have a turnover rate of 375 minutes. That means it takes a little over 6 hours to filter all the water in your pool.

You can use a similar formula to calculate what size pump you'll need: **Pump Flow Rate (Gallons per Minute) = Your Pool's Volume (Gallons) ÷ (Turnover Rate in Hours * 60)**

For example, if your pool is 15,000 gallons and you want your water to completely turnover in 8 hours:

- 15,000 ÷ (8 * 60) = GPM
- 15,000 ÷ 480 = GPM
- 31.25 = GPM

You'll need a pump with a turnover rate of a little over 31 GPM.

Round Up Your Pump Size

You need a pump that can handle the full capacity of your pool. That's why it's always smarter to get a pump that's a bit bigger than you need. Just don't get one that's overly large, or you'll waste money and energy.

When to Run Your Pool Pump

Just as important as how long to run a pool pump is when to run it. Running it at the optimal time can help save you money.

Option 1: Run Pump During Nonpeak Hours

The rate you pay for electricity changes throughout the day, depending on when more people are using more power and putting more strain on the grid. Peak hours vary from location to location. Try to schedule your pool pump run time around those hours to keep your cost lower. Using a programmable pool timer will help you turn the pump on and off at the right times.

Option 2: Run Pump From Sunset to Sunrise

Usually nonpeak hours occur at night, especially if you live in a warm climate where people are more likely to run their air-conditioning during the day. Also, running your pump is usually necessary after you've added chemicals to your pool. In order to get the chemicals dispersed throughout the water, it has to be moving.

Option 3: Run Pump for Nonconsecutive Hours

While you want to run your pool pump for at least 8 hours, it doesn't have to be 8 hours straight. Working around nonpeak utility hours, you can run your pump for 2 hours here, 7 hours there, then another 3 hours there. As long as it runs for at least 8 hours in every 24-hour period, you're covered.

Keep Your Pump Running When It's Cold!

Water expands when it freezes, so it's important to keep your pump running and your water moving when the temperature drops. And if you're shutting down your pool for the winter, you may want to consider moving your pump inside.

Pump Maintenance

Your pump is one of the most important pieces of pool equipment you own. That's why it's worth performing some regular inspections to make sure it's functioning well. Here's what to check on your pool pump, especially at the beginning and end of the pool season:

Pump Basket

Any debris not caught in your skimmer basket can make its way to your pump basket. Check and empty your pump basket once a week when you check your skimmer basket. And be sure to only remove the pump basket when the pump is off.

Pump Lid Seal

If your pump lid isn't sealed properly, it can introduce air into your system. Check the pump lid seal O-ring for cracks and damage. Use a lubricant specifically made for O-rings (not petroleum jelly) or replace it if it's completely worn out.

Pump Connections

Check the unions and connection points between the pump and the rest of the plumbing. Again, any weak connections can introduce air into the system. You may want to consider adding plumber's tape to looser connection points—or even the pump's drain plugs.

If you notice that your pump won't retain water pressure or there's air in the system, you likely need to prime your pump. This can happen when air gets sucked in through the skimmer after backwashing your filter or even after opening your pool for the first time in the spring.

Be sure to check out the Troubleshooting Section for a step-by-step guide on how to prime a pump and for help with other pump problems.

Filter

One of the quickest ways to improve your pool circulation is to clean your filter. A clean filter means your pump can push more water from the pool and through your filter media. And that's where smaller contaminants are captured (and filtered out) before the water reenters the pool.

We'll cover the common components of most filters and how to clean or backwash each type.

Filter Valves: Multiport and Push-Pull

There are two types of filter system valves. The most common valve is called a multiport valve, and it's located at the top or side of your filter tank. The second is called a push-pull valve.

A Multiport Valve usually has these seven settings:

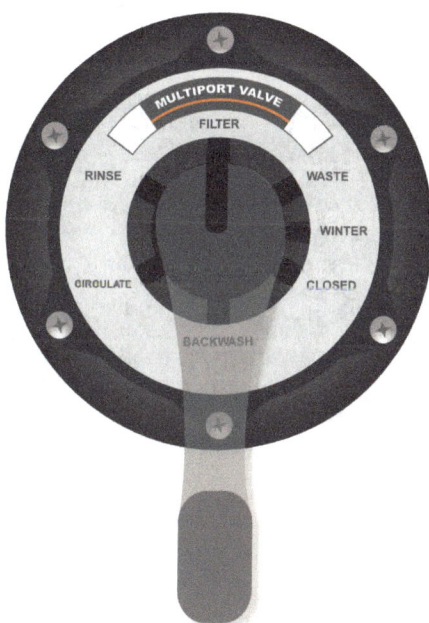

1. Filter Setting

This is the filter's "normal" operating mode. On the filter setting, pool water passes from the pump through the filter media and back into the pool.

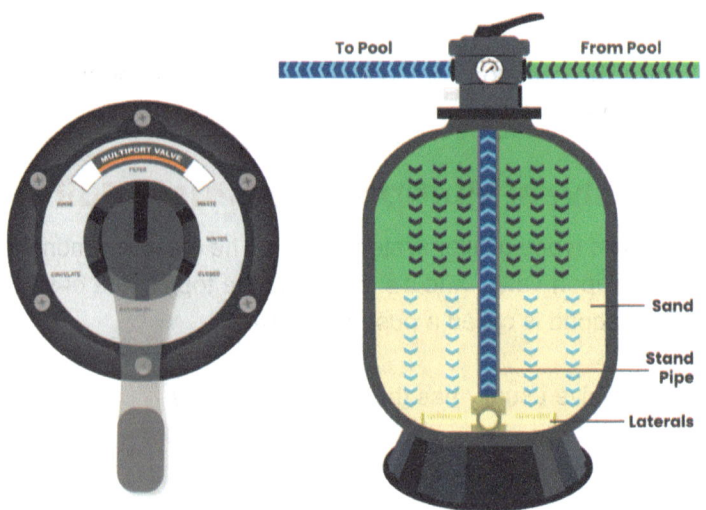

Keep Your System OFF When Turning the Multiport Valve Handle!

Any time you move the handle on your multiport valve to switch positions or settings, you must turn off your pump. Keeping the pump running while moving the handle can cause you to blow the gasket in your valve.

2. Backwash Setting

Use this setting when you need to backwash a sand or D.E. filter. Backwashing reverses the flow of water in your filter, dislodging any smaller debris and contaminants that have built up in your filter media. As water passes from your pump through the filter, it moves inside your filter in a reverse direction and then exits through the waste port.

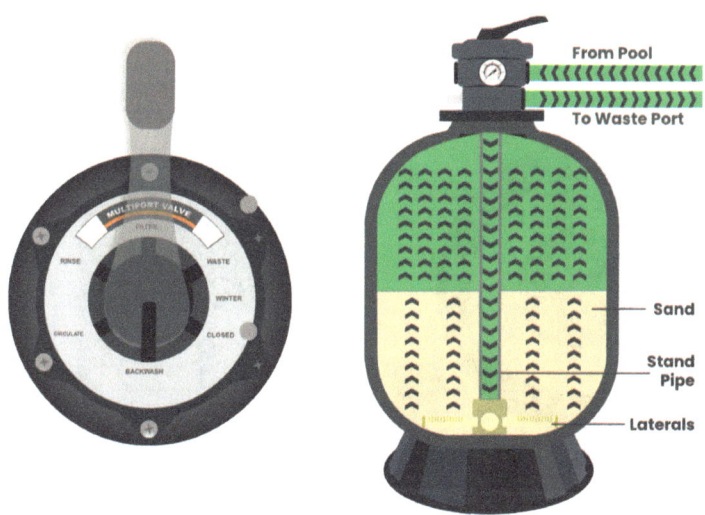

65

3. Rinse Setting

Use this setting to rinse your filter after backwashing to help ensure no dirt gets back into your pool. It helps compact the filter media again after backwashing has dislodged it. Similar to the backwash setting, this setting directs pool water from your pump, through the filter, and out through the waste port.

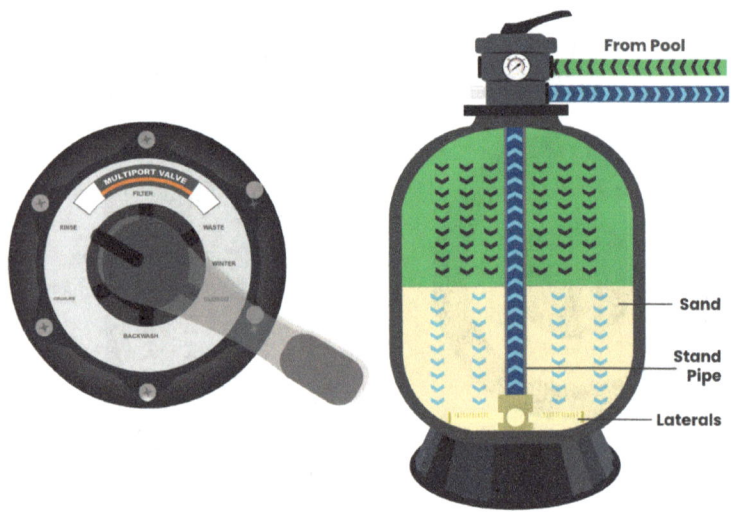

4. Waste Setting

You will use this setting if you are manually vacuuming your pool and you need to remove a lot of contaminants. If you have a lot of dirt, debris, or algae to vacuum, it can be too much for the filter to handle, and it may end up back in your pool. The waste setting bypasses the filter completely and just gets rid of the dirty water through the waste port, never touching the filter media.

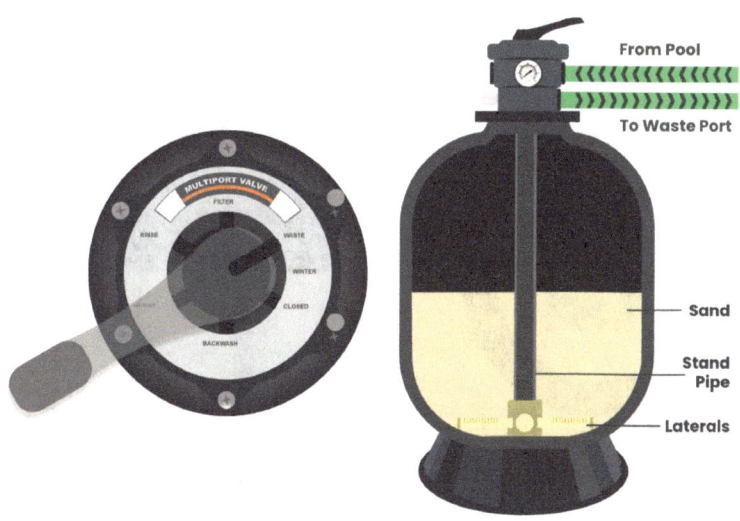

5. Recirculate Setting

This setting directs pool water from your pump into your multiport valve and back into your pool, never touching the filter media. Essentially, the recirculate setting just spins the water around your pool and through your plumbing without cleaning it. Some chemicals, such as flocculant, recommend you do this. But you'll rarely use this setting.

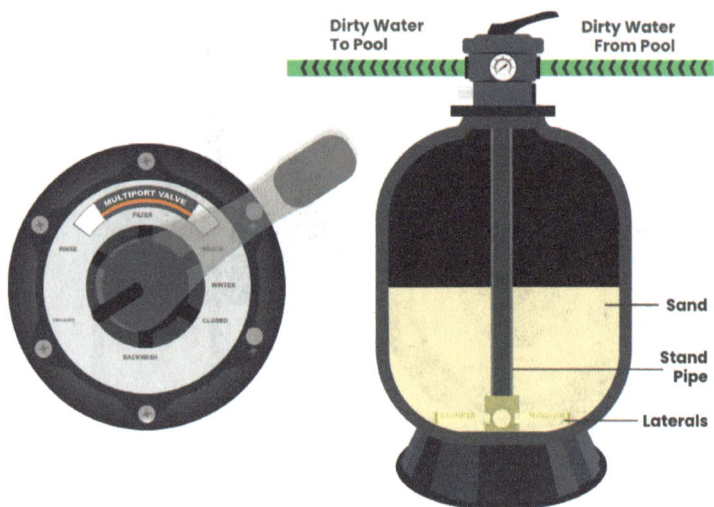

Dirty Water To Pool   Dirty Water From Pool

Sand

Stand Pipe

Laterals

6. Closed Setting

This setting closes all the ports in your multiport valve. It's used for closing your pool or for completely stopping water from going through the multiport valve.

7. Winter Setting

This is usually located between the Waste and Closed setting. You may not have a setting for this or you won't see a groove. This setting opens all the ports in your multiport valve. It's used for closing your pool by letting the water inside the valve expand when it freezes.

Push-Pull Valves

These valves only have two positions: filter and backwash. All it does is direct the flow from input to output. These are commonly found on D.E. filters. The valve starts out in the filter position. This position allows water to flow from the pump, into the filter, and back out to your pool.

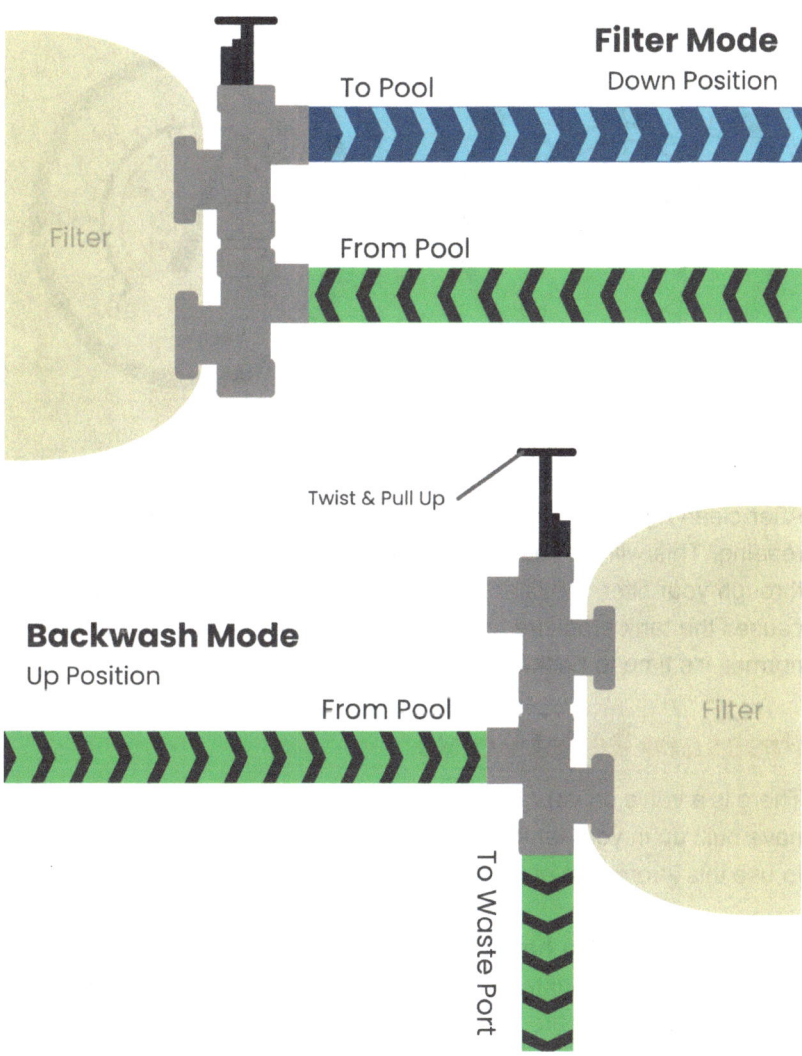

Filter Mode
Down Position

To Pool

From Pool

Twist & Pull Up

Backwash Mode
Up Position

From Pool

Filter

To Waste Port

69

Filter Pressure Gauge

No matter what type of filter you have, you'll want to keep an eye on your pressure gauge. This gauge tells you how much pressure is in your tank, measured in pounds per square inch (PSI). This will indicate when it's time to backwash or clean your filter.

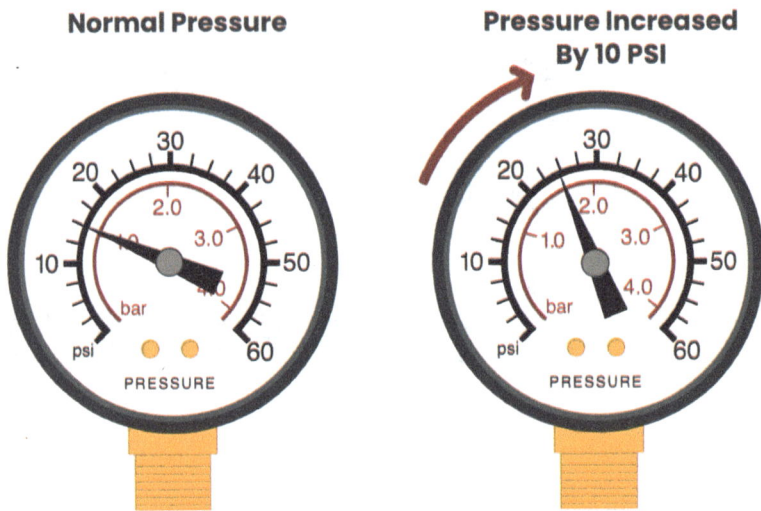

After cleaning or backwashing your filter, take a note of the pressure reading. This will be your normal running pressure. As water passes through your filter, the filter gradually fills up with dirt and debris. This causes the tank pressure to rise. Once it rises to about 10 PSI above normal, it's time to backwash or clean your filter.

Pressure Relief Valve

There is a valve on your filter that you can twist to release air that may have built up in your tank. If you have a push-pull valve, you will need to use this in order to operate the valve.

Multiport valves also have a pressure relief valve that can be used to relieve small amounts of pressure. When you twist the valve, air is released, and when the air has all escaped, water will start squirting out from the valve to indicate you've released all the air.

Connections and O-Rings

Like you do with your pool pump, be sure to check your filter connections, unions, and filter O-rings for wear and tear.

Filter Types and Cleaning

There are three different types of filters: cartridge, sand, and D.E. filters. Each one has specific care requirements that we'll cover later in this section. Because they work in tandem with your pump, make sure your filter is the optimal, corresponding size:

Optimal Filter to Fit Different Pump Sizes				
Pump Size (Horsepower)	Flow Rate (GPM)	Sand Filter (Sq. Ft.)	D.E. Filter (Sq. Ft.)	Cartridge Filter (Sq. Ft.)
3/4 HP	40	2.7	24	100
1 HP	50	3.4	36	150 – 200
1.5 HP	65	4.3	48	300
2 HP	87	5.8	60	400
2.5 HP	105	7.0	72	500
3 HP	120	8.0	84	600

As part of regular pool maintenance, you'll need to clean your filter. And the process depends on the type of filter you have:

- **Cartridge Filter:** Remove your cartridges and spray them down once a week during heavy use. Soak cartridges in a cleaning solution once a month.

- **Sand Filter:** Backwash your sand filter when pressure reads over 10 PSI. Replace the sand every three to five years.

- **D.E. Filter:** Backwash your D.E. filter and replace the D.E. powder regularly. Perform a deep clean once a season or when pressure reads over 10 PSI.

What Is Backwashing?

As water regularly passes through your sand filter or D.E. filter, it leaves behind dirt, debris, and other contaminants in the filter medium or sand. Over time as water flows through, that filter medium will become clogged, which can reduce your filter's effectiveness.

When you backwash, you're sending water backward through your filter and out your filter's waste port or drain port. This forces all the debris caught in the filter medium to dislodge and clear out. You'll need to regularly backwash a sand filter or D.E. filter, but you do not need to backwash if you have a cartridge filter.

How Often to Backwash or Clean Your Filter

As we mentioned, you should clean your cartridge filter or backwash your sand or D.E. filter if the pressure gauge reads above 10 PSI. But filter pressure gauges may not always be reliable, and they tend to fail over time on cheaper filters. So here are a few other ways to tell if your filter is dirty and needs backwashing or cleaning:

- **Low Water Flow from Return Jets:** If you notice low water flow out of your return jets, it's a sign you need to backwash or clean your filter. Generally, when the flow rate drops, you'll see an increase in PSI.

- **Cloudy Pool Water:** If your water clear, or you can see visible debris in the water that the filter should have removed, that can be an indication your filter isn't filtering effectively.

- **After Heavy Rain or Debris Load:** If a large amount of dirt or debris gets into your pool water, like after a big rainstorm, you'll likely need to clean your filter.

Don't Backwash Too Often!

Weirdly enough, a little debris in your filter is a good thing. Extra debris caught in your filter helps trap finer particles. Backwashing too often can stir up the sand and allow small particles to pass through the filter and back into the pool. While some people suggest backwashing your filter once a week during the pool season, that's not totally necessary. Backwashing means you lose a lot of water. So just remember, a little debris in the filter isn't a bad thing.

How to Backwash a Sand Filter

The backwashing process is easy, but following the right steps in the right order will help you avoid filter damage and get your filter system as clean as possible. The only extra supply you'll need is a backwash hose.

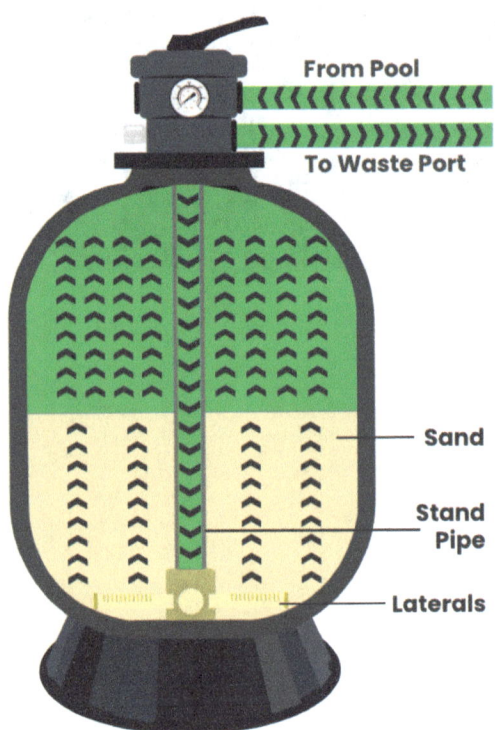

From Pool

To Waste Port

Sand

Stand Pipe

Laterals

1. Turn Filter System Off

Once the system is off, remove the skimmer basket, especially if it's full of debris.

2. Attach Backwash Hose

Connect the hose to your filter's waste port. This is also known as the waste line or backwash port. Your backwash hose will have a lot of water flowing out of it, so be sure the end is placed in an appropriate spot where water can flow out.

3. Turn Valve to Backwash

Turn your multiport valve to the backwash position. Then turn the filter system back on. Water should be flowing out of the backwash port and through the hose.

4. Backwash Until Clear

Let the water run for 1–2 minutes or until the water runs clear. Check the water clarity coming out of the end of your backwash hose or check your filter sight glass.

5. Rinse the Filter

Turn your filter system off and turn the filter valve from backwash to rinse. This will help remove sand from your lines before the water flows back into your pool. If you don't have a rinse setting, use the waste setting. Turn your filter back on and rinse the filter for about 30 seconds.

6. Run Your Filter System Normally

Turn the filter system off and turn the multiport valve back to the Filter setting. You can now turn the system back on and run it regularly. Refill, test, and balance your pool water as necessary. The backwash process removes water from your pool, and you'll need to rebalance your chemicals. If you're still experiencing signs of a dirty sand filter after backwashing, it's time to reevaluate:

- Check all your pool chemical levels to make sure something else isn't causing cloudy water, like your pH or calcium hardness.

- Check for damage to your sand filter. If your sand filter is very old or very cheap, you could have a cracked lateral inside the sand filter tank, or your entire filter may need replacing.

- Check the rest of your pool plumbing system for clogs or leaks. If you have low return jet pressure, you could have a leak or clog in the pressure side of your pool.

How to Clean a Sand Filter

Once a year, you'll want to clean your sand using a sand filter cleaner. Here's how to add sand filter cleaner to your system.

1. Backwash the filter for 3–5 minutes to remove debris.
2. Turn off the pump and turn the valve to filter.
3. Remove the pump's strainer lid.
4. Pour a sand filter cleaner into the strainer basket and replace the lid.
5. Turn the pump on for about 15 seconds, just long enough to transfer the cleaner from the pump to the filter.
6. Turn off the pump. Leave it off for at least 8 hours or overnight.
7. Backwash the filter for 3–5 minutes again to remove dirt and debris dislodged by the filter cleaner and then turn the filter system back on.

How Often Do I Need to Change the Pool Filter Sand?

You'll need to change the pool filter sand **every three to five years**. And you'll know it's time to change the sand in your filter if the water is dirtier than usual and the sand is clumped together or greasy.

When you change your sand, be sure to inspect your laterals. Laterals are the bars of the star-shaped section at the bottom of the sand filter. With time, regular wear and tear and pressure from the sand may cause them to break. And if you have a broken lateral, your filter's efficiency will suffer.

How to Clean a Cartridge Filter

This is a straightforward type of filter to clean. With a cartridge filter, you can usually just pull out the cartridge, rinse it off, and put it back.

But sometimes your filter cartridge will need a deeper clean or will need to be replaced altogether.

Here's what you'll need:

- Garden hose with a spray nozzle
- Filter cleaner
- Five-gallon bucket
- O-ring lubricant
- Clean replacement filter cartridge (to swap in while you clean)

Depending on how dirty your filter cartridge is, this process could be quick and easy or it could take overnight.

1. Turn Off Pump and Depressurize Filter Tank

Turn off the pool pump. If you have a timer, make sure you remove anything that'll trip the timer and turn the pump back on. You don't want the pump to come back on when you're cleaning the filter cartridge.

For your own safety, remove air from the system. Turn the air relief valve (usually located on top of the filter) slowly to remove any excess air from the system.

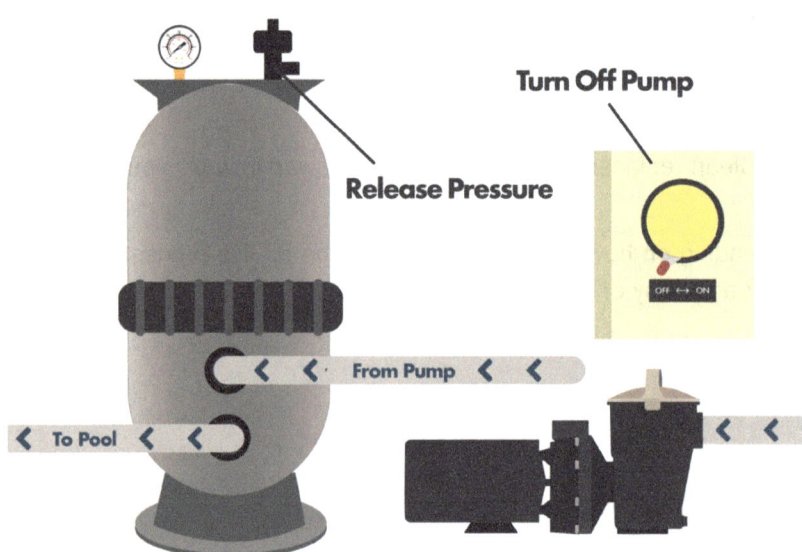

2. Remove Cartridge from Inside Filter Tank

Remove the clamps (or other latching mechanisms) holding the filter together. If you're unsure how to open it, check the owner's manual. Remove the top of the filter.

Then carefully remove the cartridge and set it aside. Inspect it for damage and wear. If you find any cracks or tears or if it's past the point where cleaning will be effective, it's time to get a new filter cartridge to replace it.

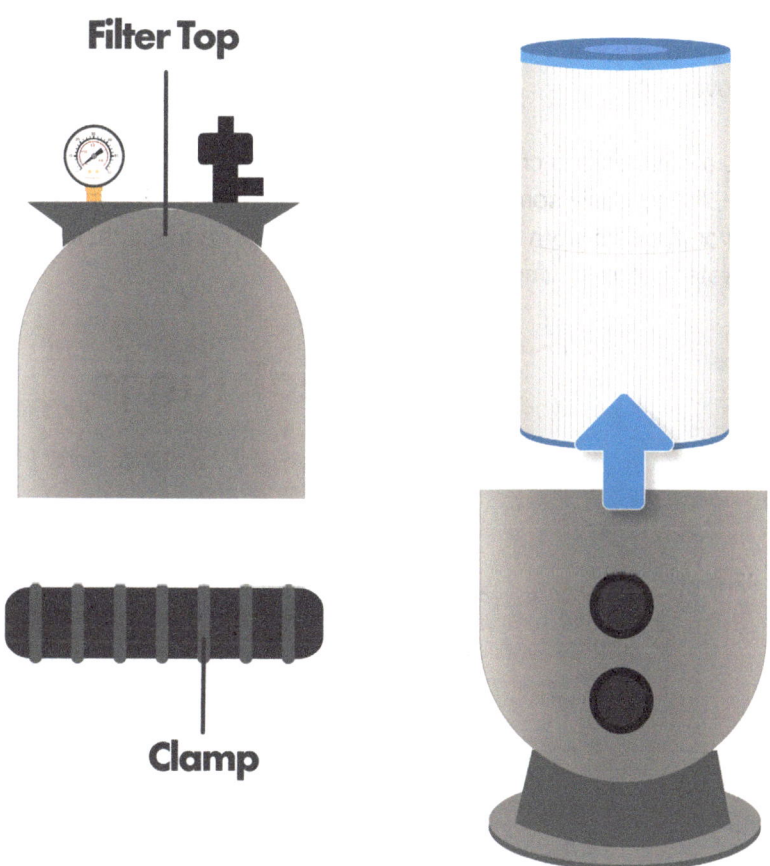

Filter Top

Clamp

3. Clean the Filter Cartridge

Use a spray nozzle on your garden hose to spray down the cartridge, making sure to get between the pleats. If the cartridge is dirty, use a filter cartridge cleaner.

If it's been a while since you've cleaned the cartridge filter, soak the cartridge in a filter cleaning solution overnight. You can use the same filter cartridge cleaner to do this. Use a five-gallon bucket and make sure the cartridge is completely covered with the water and cleaning solution.

Alternatively, you can dilute one-part muriatic acid to 20-parts water in a five-gallon bucket. Place the filters in the bucket and allow them to soak overnight.

Now's a good time to check the O-ring on the filter tank. If it's in good shape, lightly apply some lubricant to keep it that way. But if it's dry-rotted or appears worn out, replace it. Rinse the cartridge thoroughly with water before putting it back in the tank.

The Quick Rinse

Rinse filter(s) with fresh water once a week with a garden hose or in the sink. Spread each pleat to remove debris.

The Cleaner Spray

Spray filter(s) with filter cleaner about once a month. Let them sit for 15 minutes & rinse them with fresh water.

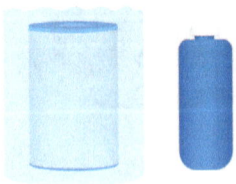

The Deep Soak

Soak filter(s) in diluted filter cleaner for 24 hours. Then, rinse with fresh water.

4. Replace Filter Cartridge and Repressurize

Return the cartridge to the filter and secure it in place. Replace the filter top and close the clamps. Turn the system back on, and open the air relief valve to release any excess air in the system. Keep the valve open until a steady stream of water sprays from it.

Check the pressure gauge to be sure it's in the normal filter pressure range. If the PSI is off, you may have put the filter back together incorrectly or something else may be wrong with the system.

Keep Two Cartridges on Hand to Rotate!

Having two cartridges on hand lets you get your filter system up and running while you're cleaning cartridges or soaking a dirty cartridge overnight.

Remember, you'll want to spray your cartridge filter every week if your pool is in heavy use, and you'll want to soak your cartridge once a month.

Your cartridge will likely need replacing once a year, usually when you open your pool for the season. But you'll also want to replace it when it's worn out or can no longer be cleaned.

How to Backwash a D.E. Filter

Backwashing your D.E. filter involves reversing the flow of water in your filter and replacing D.E. powder. Regardless of your filter gauge or water quality, you'll want to clean your D.E. filter at least once a month.

Before you get started, you'll need a few supplies.

- Backwash hose
- D.E. powder
- One-pound D.E. scooper
- Optional: Five-gallon bucket and muriatic acid

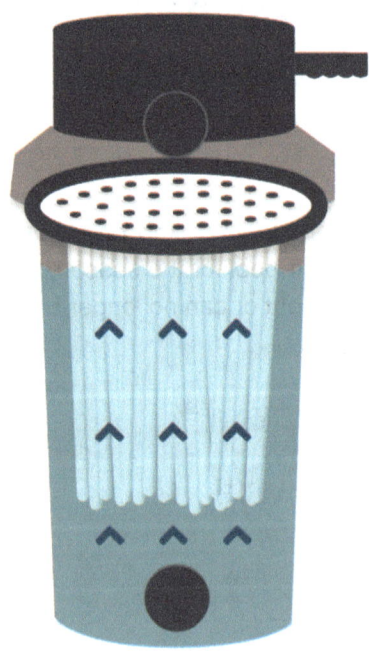

> **How Much D.E. Powder Will You Need?**
>
> This will vary depending on the type and size of filter you have. D.E. powder is measured in pounds, so use a one-pound D.E. scoop to make measuring easy. In a pinch, you can also use an empty one-pound coffee can.

1. Backwash and Drain Your D.E. Filter

Turn off the pump and move the handle on your multiport valve to backwash. If you have a push-pull valve, make sure it's in the backwash position.

Attach your backwash hose to the waste port and turn the pump back on. Backwashing should take one to two minutes or until the water looks clear.

Then turn the pump off and open the air relief valve. Finally, remove the drain plug and let the water drain out of the filter tank.

2. Remove D.E. Filter Manifold

Turn the pump off. Remove the clamps (or other latching mechanisms) holding the filter together. If you're unsure how to open it, check the owner's manual. Open the filter tank and remove the filter manifold, then take out all the grids or fingers.

3. Rinse or Soak Filter Grids or Fingers

Use a spray nozzle on your garden hose to spray down the manifold and grids/fingers, making sure to thoroughly flush all debris, including the D.E. powder. If the manifold is really dirty, use a D.E. filter cleaner.

Either once a year or if the filter manifold is really dirty, you may want to soak it overnight in a muriatic acid solution. You'll only need to do this once a year, usually at the end of the pool season.

Careful with Muriatic Acid!

It's caustic and can cause injury if you're not careful. Remember: muriatic acid is just that—an acid. So protect yourself by using goggles, acid-resistant gloves, and a mask to cover your nose and mouth. We also recommend you wear long sleeves, pants, and closed shoes to protect your skin.

Dilute one-part muriatic acid to 20-parts water in a large plastic trash can with a lid big enough to hold the acid solution and filter manifold. Place the manifold in the trash can, ensuring it's completely covered with the diluted solution. Allow it to soak overnight, then rinse it off with a hose.

4. Put Filter Back Together

Once the complete filter manifold is clean, rinse out the tank with the garden hose, then place the filter back into the tank.

Replace the clamps (or other latching mechanisms) holding the filter together. If you're unsure how to close it, check the owner's manual.

5. Add Fresh D.E. Powder

Mix the appropriate amount of D.E powder with enough water to make a slurry, which is a thin creamy solution. Refer to your filter owner's manual to determine how much D.E. powder you'll need to add.

Make sure the pump is running and pour the slurry directly into the pool skimmer. Then run the pool pump for at least 30 minutes to allow the D.E. to distribute evenly over the filter grids or fingers.

Return Jets

Now that the water has circulated through your skimmer, pump, and filter, it's time for that clean water to return to your pool. Your return jets are the plastic openings in your pool walls that send the water back into the pool after it's gone through the filtration system. Not only do your return jets help move water around, they also help evenly distribute chemicals. You may have either one or multiple return jets.

As the jets return water to the pool, they also keep the water level above the skimmer. This is the only way the water can enter the skimmer and be pushed through the filter. If the pool jets aren't working, your water isn't properly flowing into the filter system and back to the pool.

Positioning Your Return Jets

The first key is making sure your return jets are positioned properly. Your pool jets keep your water moving and return clean water from the filter system back into your pool. They also help distribute chemicals throughout your water so things like chlorine don't just sit in one spot in your pool.

For good pool circulation, you'll need to direct the water flow from your pool return jets. Return jets should be multidirectional, meaning you can adjust them. If your jets aren't adjustable, it's worth purchasing new jet fittings.

For Pools with Only One Return Jet

Point the jet away from the skimmer and downward. This will help push the water from the bottom of the pool toward the surface.

For Pools with Multiple Return Jets

Point the jets in the same direction at a 45-degree angle toward the bottom of the pool.

Try not to aim directly at the skimmers or toward the pool surface.
Your skimmer can only pick up debris if the surface of the water is calm and not moving too fast. That's also why you want to make sure your water level in your pool is reaching halfway up the skimmer.

Also, when your return jets are aimed at circulating the water at the bottom of your pool, you'll help mix that cooler water with warmer water toward the top—giving you a more even temperature in your pool.

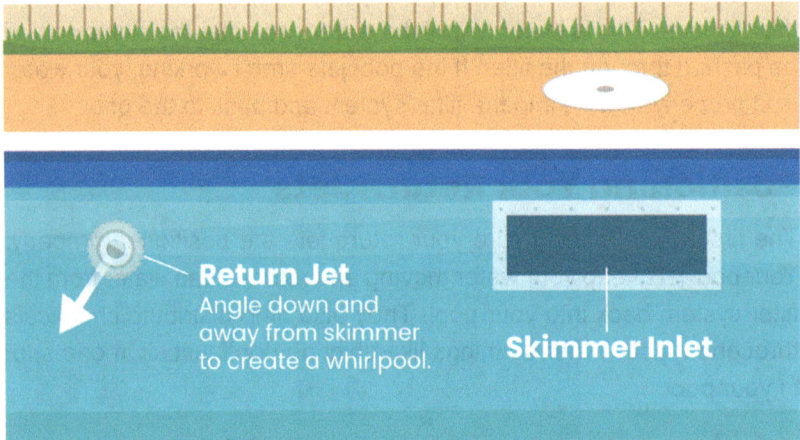

Return Jet
Angle down and
away from skimmer
to create a whirlpool.

Skimmer Inlet

Are Your Return Jets Blowing Bubbles or Experiencing Weak Flow?

If your return jets are blowing lots of bubbles or the water flow is weak, that's a sign of a potential air leak in the filter system. This usually occurs between the skimmer and the pump. And the leak could be at the unions, pump seals, or strainer lid. Another reason your water flow might be weak? A dirty filter system. See the Troubleshooting Section for more help with return jet issues.

Improving Pool Circulation

Here's a quick recap of what we covered to improve circulation and a few other tips to keep your water flowing.

- **Maintain Your Water Level:** If your water dips below the skimmer, your pump could run dry and burn out.

- **Clean Your Skimmer Basket:** Check and remove debris from your skimmer basket once a week to prevent it from clogging.

- **Check Your Pump:** Check your connections and O-rings for damage or wear and tear. And check your pump basket for debris.

- **Backwash or Clean Your Filter:** Backwash your sand or D.E. filter, or clean your cartridge filter as needed. Check to see if your pressure gauge is 10 PSI above normal.

- **Run Your System Enough:** Your pump and filter system should run at least 8 hours each day to completely turnover your pool water at least once.

- **Angle Return Jets:** Aim them at a 45-degree angle toward the bottom of the pool and in the same direction.

- **Watch for Dead Zones:** These are spots in your pool that naturally have poor circulation, like behind ladders, around pool steps, underneath skimmers, and in other crevices. Even if your jets are angled correctly, some dead areas are unavoidable. That means manually taking care of them by brushing your pool.

- **Brush Weekly:** Brushing your pool walls and surfaces helps release any contaminants stuck in crevices or lingering in areas with poor water flow. So brush your pool at least once a week, especially in the dead areas, to help break up debris or algae and get them flowing into the filter.

- **Add Water Features:** Waterfalls, fountains, and other moving water features can help circulate the water.

Action Steps: Map Out and Adjust Circulation

It's helpful to have a map of how the water flows in your pool and through your filter system. This is handy for troubleshooting and basic pool tasks, like backwashing your filter.

- **Map Out the Flow of Water in Your Pool:** If you didn't already map out your water flow in your pool profile, be sure to draw in the flow of water using simple direction lines. How does water leave the return jets? Where are your skimmers? Where are possible dead zones? (Behind ladders, around steps, etc.)

- **Label Valves and Pipes:** Using waterproof markers, write on your valves and pipes to indicate how water flows through your filter system. Be sure to label the direction the water is flowing with an arrow.

- **Adjust Return Jet Angles:** If you haven't already done so, point your return jet(s) down at a 45° angle and away from the skimmer. If you have more than one return jet, be sure they all point in the same direction.

Draw Pool & Circulation Here

4

~~~

CLEANING

How to Keep Your Pool Surfaces
and Water Free of Contaminants

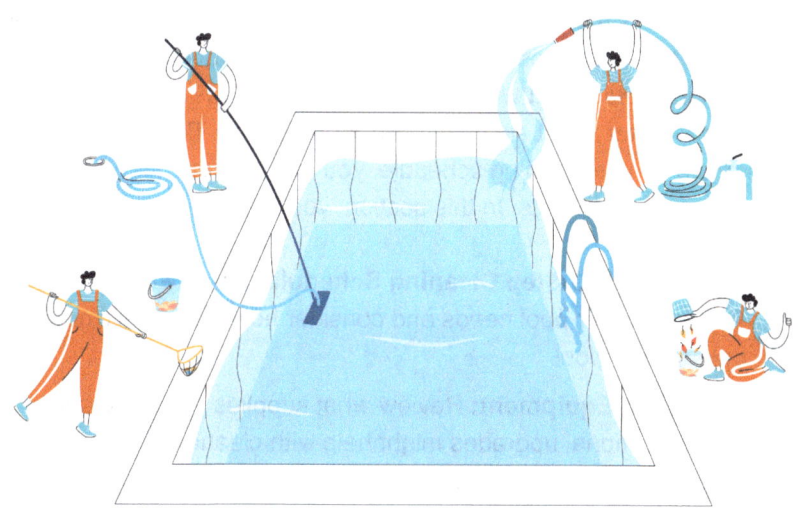

CLEANING

How to Keep Your Pool Surfaces and Water Free of Contaminants

Keeping your pool's surfaces clean and your water free of debris and contaminants is a crucial step to preventing larger issues like cloudy water and algae. Leaves and twigs left floating in your water can clog up your circulation. And with contaminants like algae clinging to your walls, your water won't stay sanitized for very long. But with the right tools and a simple cleaning schedule, you can stay one step ahead of debris and contaminants. In this section, you'll learn about:

1. **The Simple 3-Step Cleaning Schedule:** Learn what type of cleaning your pool needs and consider how often you'll need to clean your pool.

2. **Cleaning Equipment:** Review what supplies you need and which optional upgrades might help with cleaning.

3. **Skimming:** Learn how to remove debris easily and how to prevent them in the first place.

4. **Brushing:** Identify which brush your pool needs and learn the right way to brush your pool's surfaces and crevices.

5. **Vacuuming:** Compare the different types of vacuums, decide which is best for you, and learn how to manually vacuum your pool.

6. **Additional Cleaning:** Learn how to clean other surfaces and special equipment, like heaters and salt cells.

7. **Cleaning Action Steps:** Create a simple cleaning schedule and a list of equipment you want to purchase or upgrade.

The Simple 3-Step Cleaning Schedule

We know that the last thing you want to do is go out to your pool to scoop out leaves or brush your walls. But following a simple weekly cleaning list will help prevent issues like:

- Leaves, debris, bugs, and pollen clogging up your skimmer and filter.
- Microscopic contaminants using up your chlorine and leaving your water unsanitized.
- Algae spores clinging to the sides of your pool and turning into a massive algae bloom.

There are three basic cleaning tasks for a pool:

1. **Skimming:** Removing debris floating in the water.
2. **Brushing:** Removing contaminants clinging to the sides and bottom of the pool.
3. **Vacuuming:** Removing smaller debris, contaminants, and dirt with a manual or automatic vacuum.

Obviously, the more often you clean, the cleaner your pool will be. But constantly cleaning your pool isn't very realistic (or fun). In general, brush and vacuum your pool weekly and skim your water every other

Skimming   **Brushing**   **Vacuuming**

Cleaning Equipment

For cleaning your pool, you'll want to have a few supplies on hand:

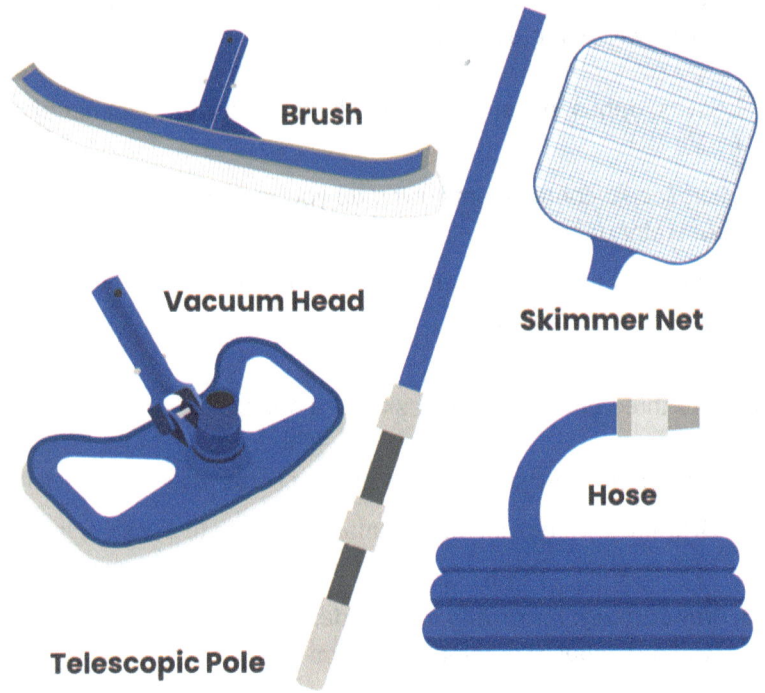

Brush

Vacuum Head

Skimmer Net

Hose

Telescopic Pole

Telescopic Pole

This attaches to your skimmer net, manual vacuum, or pool brush. As its name suggests, a telescopic pole can be extended to different lengths. We recommend buying an 8-foot pole that extends to 16 feet. That should save you from having to lean into your pool to chase debris.

Skimmer Net or Leaf Net

Attached to a telescopic pole, a skimmer net allows you to collect things like debris, leaves, bugs, and twigs that have accumulated on and below the water's surface. You have two options when choosing a skimmer net: a flat skimmer or a leaf net.

Pool Brush

A brush head attaches to your telescopic pole. This helps you scrub your pool's walls and floor, removing dirt and detaching algae spores clinging to your pool walls or floors. You have two options when choosing a brush: nylon or steel bristles.

Vacuum Head and Vacuum Hose

A manual pool vacuum helps you remove smaller microscopic contaminants from your water. This vacuum head attaches to your telescopic pole and uses suction from the suction side of your pool to vacuum up particles and debris.

An automatic or robotic pool cleaner can help with regular weekly vacuuming. But you'll still need a manual vacuum for removing things like algae or flocculant.

In the next few sections, we'll cover the different types of cleaning equipment and how to use each one.

Skimming

Skimmers and skimming are two different pool terms, but they serve a similar purpose. A skimmer (a.k.a. the rectangular port on the side of your pool where water flows in) captures debris in its skimmer basket. But skimmers and skimmer baskets can quickly become clogged if there's too much larger debris like leaves. That's where skimming comes in to help. Skimming is the act of using a skimmer net or leaf net to remove debris.

> ### Cleaning Schedule: Skim Your Pool Every Other Day
> This helps prevent the accumulation of debris in your skimmer line, skimmer basket, pump basket, and filter. And regularly removing larger contaminants will help improve the circulation of your entire system.

Types of Skimmer Nets

There are two types of skimmer nets:

1. **Flat Skimmer Nets:** This flat net is just for quick surface skims.

2. **Leaf Nets:** This is a deeper net to catch and remove lots of debris.

Flat Skimmer Net   **Leaf Net**

A flat skimmer net is handy for fishing out smaller debris and easier to shake off as you go. But a leaf net lets you fish out larger amounts of debris without having to empty it as you clean. We recommend having both on hand and using the leaf net for larger cleanup days.

Just be sure to buy a high-quality, heavy-duty skimmer net. Cheaper ones tend to break often, and you'll just be wasting money by having to buy skimmer nets all season long, year after year.

How to Skim Your Pool

As you skim the water, move the skimmer net in the same continuous direction. This lets you pick up leaves and debris without having to continually empty it.

Automatic Skimmers and Solar Skimmers

In addition to a good net and your built-in skimmer, there are other types of skimmer systems that can help you keep on top of debris:

Automatic Skimmers

These skimmers are usually connected to the return line with a hose. The water pressure from the hose activates the skimmer's propellers so it can pull in debris and particles. This is a great way to consistently and automatically skim away smaller debris and small bugs. But they do require your pump to be on in order to run.

Solar Skimmers

These are propelled around your pool's surface, thanks to built-in solar panels. Solar skimmers are also capable of picking up larger debris and don't require your pump to be on to function. While you won't need to connect them to your return line, these skimmers are more expensive.

Pool Covers

One of the best things you can do to save you time skimming is to purchase the right cover for your pool. If you can prevent debris from happening in the first place, you won't need to remove them with a skimmer net.

Keep your pool covered when it's not in use. And consider purchasing a mesh net to prevent leaves from getting into the water, especially in the fall.

Brushing

Brushing loosens up any algae spores, bacteria, and dirt that are clinging to the bottom or walls of your pool. Without brushing, you'll likely have pockets of contaminants that can fester into larger issues.

> ### Cleaning Schedule: Brush Your Pool Every Week
>
> This helps remove contaminants stuck to your pool. Once removed from surfaces, they'll be able to pass into your filter system where they'll be captured.

Types of Pool Brushes

There are two types of pool brushes: nylon bristles and stainless-steel bristles. A stainless-steel brush will easily break algae's hold on walls, steps, and wherever else it may be hiding. A regular nylon bristle pool brush is a gentler option. The type of pool brush you need depends on your pool's surface:

- **Unpainted Concrete Pools:** Use a brush with both stainless-steel and nylon bristles.
- **Gunite Pools:** Use a brush with stainless-steel bristles.
- **Fiberglass, Vinyl, or Painted Concrete Pools:** Use a brush with nylon bristles only.

Just like skimmer nets, it's wise to purchase a heavy-duty pool brush since you'll be using it frequently, and cheaper brushes tend to break.

How to Brush Your Pool

Once a week, brush the walls, ladders, and corners of your pool. Be sure to get into every nook and cranny possible to brush away any lurking algae formations. Brushing will push any algae spores into the water, making it easier for chlorine or other sanitizers to kill it. So be sure to get into any areas where contaminants might be accumulating or where there's not a lot of flow or circulation (a.k.a. dead zones).

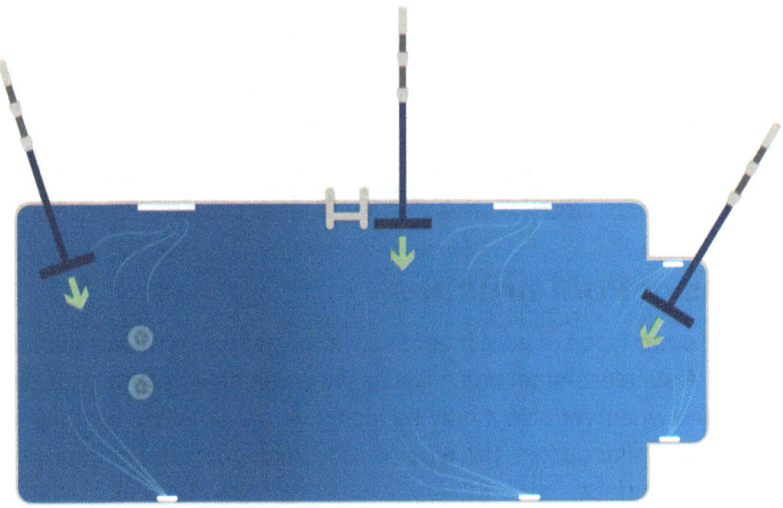

However, if your pool has developed a serious algae problem, brushing isn't going to remedy it. So be sure to check out the Troubleshooting Section for more help with algae removal.

Vacuuming

While skimming helps remove floating debris and brushing helps dislodge buildup on your pool surfaces, vacuuming handles the rest. Pool vacuums help pick up dirt, smaller debris, and contaminants that might sink to the bottom of your pool. And it can help prolong the life of your filter.

Cleaning Schedule: Vacuum Your Pool Every Week

This removes smaller, microscopic contaminants from the water. You can use a manual vacuum or an automatic pool cleaner for this task.

Why You Need a Manual Vacuum

Every pool owner needs to own a manual vacuum. While an automatic pool cleaner is handy for regular weekly maintenance, a manual vacuum is the only thing that will clear up cloudy water or algae. A manual vacuum uses the following pieces of equipment:

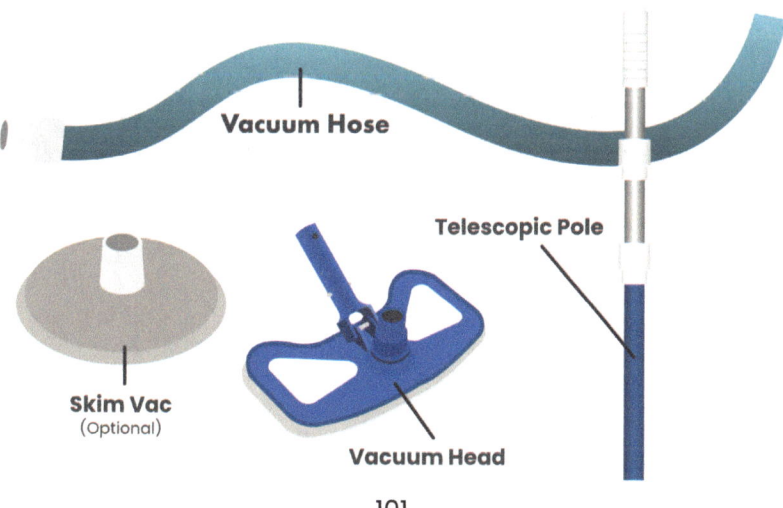

Vacuum Hose

Telescopic Pole

Skim Vac
(Optional)

Vacuum Head

- **Pool vacuum head** (also called a vac head)
- **Telescopic pole** to attach to the vac head
- **Pool vacuum hose** long enough to reach every area of your pool
- **Skim vac or vacuum plate** (if you want to use your skimmer basket)

How to Manually Vacuum a Pool

Before you get started, make sure the pool pump and filter are running. You also want to check that you're running at a good starting pressure. If you have a sand filter or D.E. filter and the pressure is high, backwash it before you vacuum. If you have a cartridge filter, make sure the cartridges inside are cleaned and ready to go.

Set Up Your Filter First!

If you're vacuuming up algae, cloudy water, or flocculant, change your filter valve settings to the WASTE SETTING if you have a multiport valve or push/pull valve. This will bypass your filter and send the dirty water out through the waste port.

If you have a cartridge filter, just remove the drain plug and attach a backwash hose. Your pool water level will drop while you vacuum. Use a garden hose to add fresh water while you're vacuuming.

1. Attach Vacuum Head and Hose to Telescopic Pole

First, ensure the pump and filter are running. Attach the vacuum head to the open end of the telescopic pole. Attach one end of the hose to the vac head. If the hose is slippery, use a hose clamp to keep it in place.

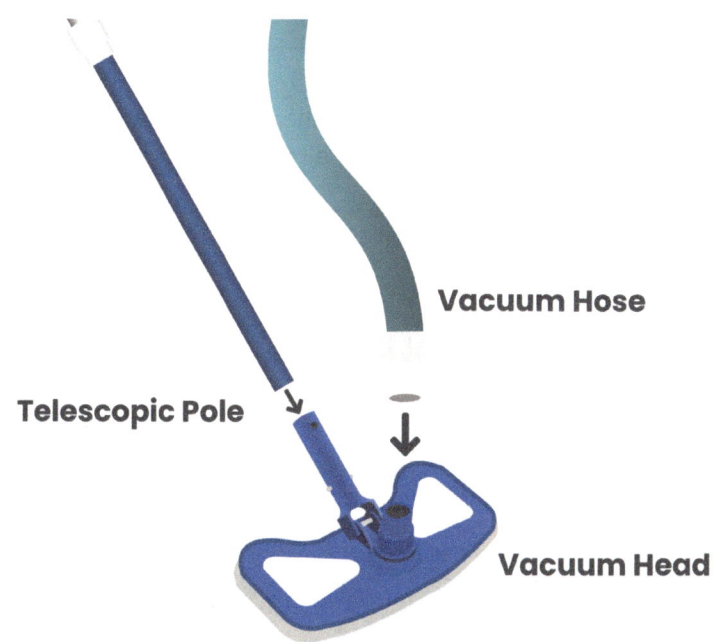

Vacuum Hose

Telescopic Pole

Vacuum Head

2. Fill Vacuum Hose with Water to Remove Air

Place the vacuum head, telescopic pole, and hose in the pool, making sure the head rests on the bottom of the pool. Place the other end of the vacuum hose against a return jet in the pool. This will push water through the hose and drive all the air out.

Triple-check to make sure the vacuum inlet is the only line open to the pump. If not, particles and debris will also be sucked in by the pump and undo all your hard work.

Note: You'll see air bubbles rising from the vacuum head on the floor of the pool. Once the air bubbles stop, all the air is out of the hose.

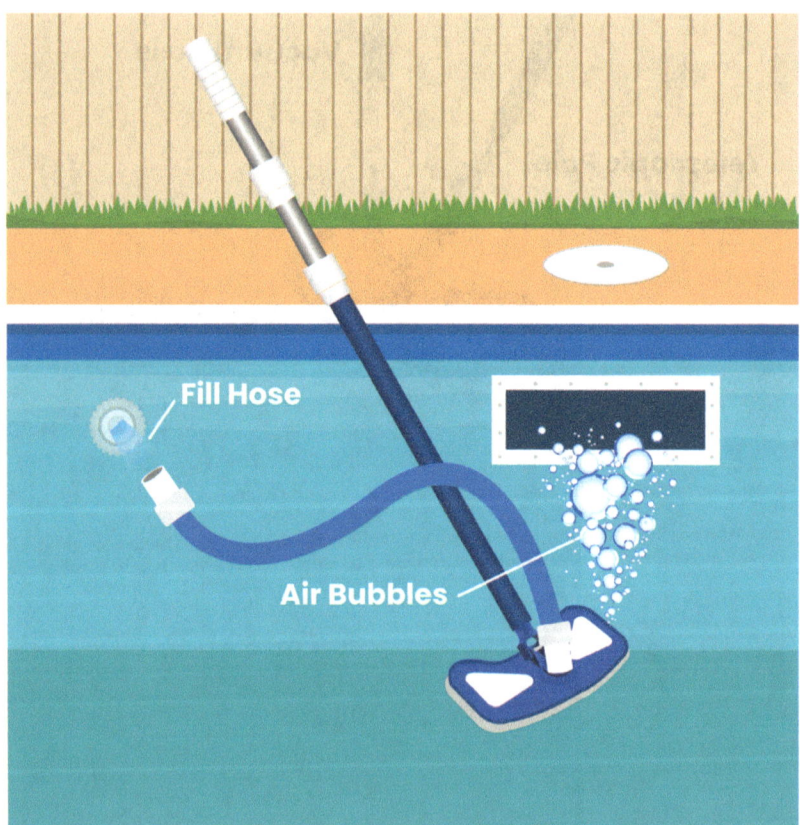

3. Attach Vacuum Hose to Pool Skimmer

Attach the skim vac plate to the end of the hose you'd previously placed against the return jet, block the opening with your hand, and bring it over to the skimmer. Insert it in the skimmer on top of the basket and be sure to create a good seal or suction will be lost.

If you're not using a vacuum plate, remove the skimmer basket inside. Use your hand to block the end of the water-filled hose. Then place the hose into the skimmer inlet, making sure it's firmly inserted into the suction hole at the bottom of the skimmer.

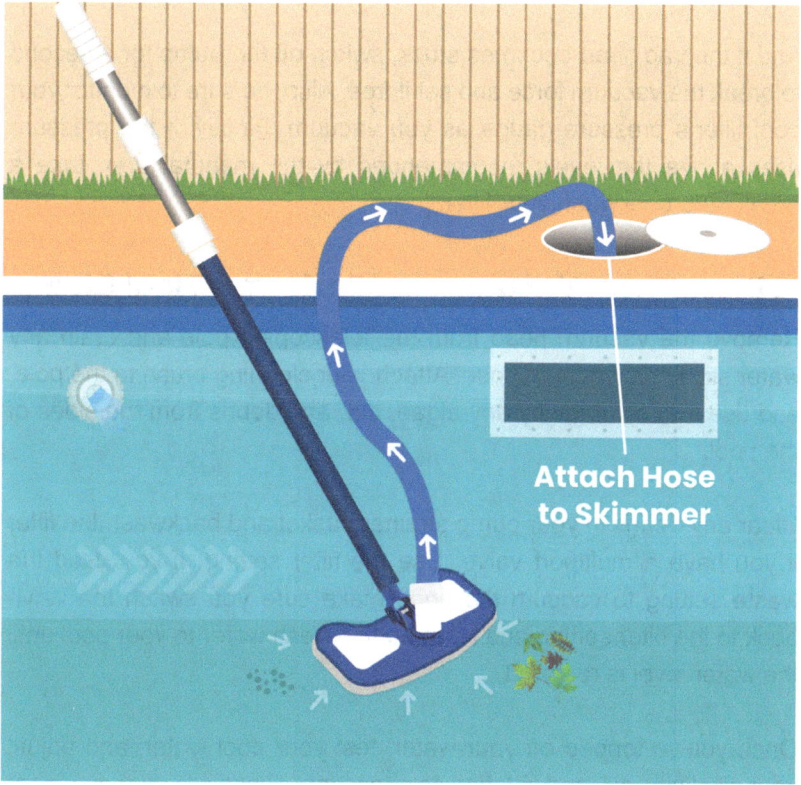

Attach Hose to Skimmer

Note: Whichever method you choose will create the suction that pulls material through the vac head, up through the hose and into the skimmer, and then through the filter system. If your vacuum loses suction, just follow the prep steps again to restore it.

4. Start Vacuuming

Now that you've built a powerful siphon using your filter system, you can vacuum the floor of your pool. Start at the shallow end (if you have one) and move toward the deep end of the pool. If you have a round pool, just start at one side and move left or right across the floor.

Use long, slow sweeping strokes to clean. Make sure your strokes overlap slightly to avoid leaving any debris behind. Rushing will just kick up debris, which will reduce visibility and take hours to settle down again. If the water does become cloudy, give it a couple of hours to resettle, then come back and vacuum again, repeating as necessary.

And if the vac head becomes stuck, switch off the pump for a second to break the vacuum force and set it free. Also, be sure to monitor your pool filter's pressure gauge as you vacuum. Finally, if the pressure rises above the levels recommended by the manufacturer, take a break, and backwash your filter.

5. Disconnect Vacuum and Perform a Final Clean

Remove the vacuum head from the telescoping pole and drain any water still in the vacuum hose. Attach your cleaning brush to the pole, and use it to scrub away any algae, dirt, and debris from the sides of the pool.

Clear any debris in your pump strainer basket and backwash the filter if you have a multiport valve. Use the filter setting. If you used the waste setting to vacuum the pool, make sure you switch the valve back to the filter setting and keep adding fresh water to your pool until the water level is restored.

Once you've topped off your water, test your pool water, and adjust your alkalinity, pH, and chlorine as necessary. Rinse all your equipment with fresh water, dry it, and return it to storage. This will help keep it in top working condition and avoid unnecessary wear and corrosion.

Automatic Pool Cleaners

Automatic pool cleaners are devices that drive around your pool sucking up debris. These are great for weekly, routine vacuuming. But you will still need to have a manual vacuum on hand for removing algae, cloudy water, and flocculant. There are three types of automatic pool cleaners: robotic pool cleaners, pressure-side pool cleaners, and suction-side pool cleaners.

1. Robotic Pool Cleaners

These independent cleaners vacuum your pool without connecting to your filter system. Simply plug them into an electrical source, drop them in your pool, and let them do all the hard work on their own. All you have to do is empty the built-in filter bag when they get full of debris. These are by far the best automatic pool cleaners on the market. But they're more expensive than suction-side or pressure-side cleaners. And they cost more to repair should anything go wrong. So be sure to buy a high-quality robotic pool vacuum with a good warranty.

2. Pressure-Side Pool Cleaners

Pressure-side cleaners hook up to your return line and use the water pressure from your filter system as power. These self-contained automatic cleaners move around the bottom of your pool, picking up debris that are captured in its filter bag.

While they use water pressure to run, they do not hook up to your filter system. That means you simply empty the cleaner's filter bag once it's done and full of debris.

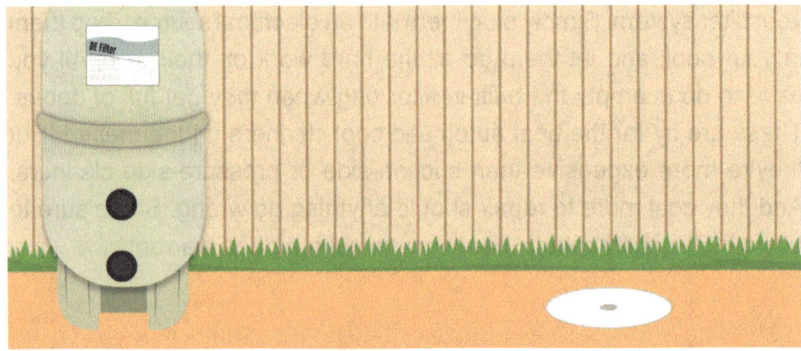

Water Vortex

3. Suction-Side Pool Cleaners

These cleaners hook up the same way you do when you vacuum your pool manually. A suction-side pool cleaner attaches to your pool skimmer. As the skimmer draws in water, it creates a siphon to your filter system. But unlike manual vacuuming, this cleaner moves around the bottom of your pool by itself.

Keep in mind that you'll still be using your filter, and there is a risk of these cleaners picking up something dangerous, like a rock. That's why we recommend the self-contained pressure-side or robotic cleaner since they vacuum up debris without straining your filter system.

Additional Cleaning

Regularly cleaning the pool itself is the most important task. But every so often, you'll want to clean other pieces of pool equipment and the areas that surround your pool.

1. Pool Deck

Sweeping your pool deck and spraying it with a high-powered hose nozzle is usually enough. But sometimes you'll need to disinfect it. Once pool water is out of your pool and onto your deck, the sanitizing chemicals will dissipate and evaporate, meaning your deck can become a breeding ground for bacteria and even algae. And that can become both a dirty and slippery issue.

For cleaning and disinfecting, you can purchase a special pool deck cleaner, which usually comes in a liquid concentrate. Or you can use trisodium phosphate, which is a water-soluble powder. Whichever one you use, once the solution is mixed, you can usually just scrub the deck with a long-handled, stiff-bristled brush.

2. Pool Accessories

Be sure to wipe down railings, ladders, diving boards, slides, and other pool accessories. These can accumulate oils, dirt, and contaminants, especially if they're used often. You can purchase a special pool surface cleaning spray or use diluted vinegar with a soft towel.

3. Pool Filter

No matter how much you skim, brush, or vacuum, if your pool filter is dirty, your water is dirty. Keeping your filter clean involves either backwashing your sand or D.E. filter or cleaning your cartridge filter. Be sure to check out the Circulation Section for how to clean your filter.

4. Pool Heaters and Salt Water Systems

If you have other equipment, like heaters or salt water generators, be sure to inspect them once a month for buildup. Heaters should be inspected every month for corrosion or damage and should be cleaned at the beginning and end of the pool season. This involves cleaning out the heater cabinet and checking the pipes for leaks.

Your salt cell in your salt water system should be cleaned every three months and at the beginning and end of the pool season. That involves checking for and removing scale buildup and deposits. Be sure to check out the Salt Water Pool Maintenance Section for more information on cleaning a salt cell.

Action Steps: Create a Cleaning Plan

Cleaning doesn't have to be hard. Just make sure that you stick to a regular schedule and that you consider upgrading to better supplies that will make your life easier.

- **Create a Simple Cleaning Schedule:** Skim your water every other day and brush and vacuum your pool once a week.

- **Purchase the Correct Cleaning Supplies:** You'll want to have a flat skimmer brush, a leaf net, a pool brush (nylon or stainless-steel) and a manual vacuum.

- **Upgrade to an Automatic or Solar Skimmer:** These can save you from having to manually skim constantly, as they pull in debris, bugs, and leaves.

- **Upgrade to an Automatic Pool Cleaner:** These can be extremely helpful for weekly maintenance. Though they're more expensive, a robotic pool cleaner is a great investment and doesn't connect to your filter system.

- **Upgrade Your Cover:** If debris and contaminants are out of control in your pool, consider installing a mesh cover or an automatic pool cover.

5

CHEMISTRY

How to Keep Your Water Balanced
and Sanitized

CHEMISTRY
How to Keep Your Water Balanced and Sanitized

Your water's chemical levels, like pH and chlorine, help keep your pool free of things like bacteria and algae. They also help protect your pool equipment from damage and erosion. So without properly balanced water, your pool and everyone who uses it can be exposed to harmful chemistry levels and contaminants. While pool water chemistry can seem complicated at first, it becomes easier and more intuitive over time. All it takes is a little basic chemical knowledge, the right equipment and supplies, and a simple water balancing routine. In this section, you'll learn about:

1. **Why You Need Chemicals in Your Pool:** Understand the consequences of not adding chemicals to your pool.

2. **Water Testing:** Learn how to test and read your results and determine which levels need adjusting.

3. **Pool Chemistry 101:** Learn about the essential chemical levels you need to test and how to balance in your water.

4. **Types of Sanitizers and Sanitizer Systems:** Compare sanitizers, including different ways of adding it to your water.

5. **Shocking Your Water:** Understand how pool shock works and how regular shocking helps prevent algae.

6. **How to Add Chemicals:** Learn what chemicals you need, how to add them to your pool, and in which order.

7. **Additional Chemicals:** Learn about optional chemicals you can add to improve your water.

8. **Chemical Safety and Storage:** Understand proper chemical handling.

9. **Chemistry Action Steps:** Create a simple water testing and balancing plan to keep your levels in check.

Why You Need Chemicals in Your Pool

Every time someone swims in your pool, they affect your water chemistry by leaving behind body oil, hair, dead skin, shampoo, and soap. So without chemicals to help remove and neutralize contaminants, your pool will quickly turn into a giant, stagnant bathtub.

But why can't pools be kept in a more "natural" state, like a lake or a pond? Unlike a natural body of water, your pool doesn't have an ecosystem of animals, plants, and beneficial bacteria to keep the water naturally balanced. Your pool will end up more like a swamp over time. Sanitizing your water with chlorine or bromine is critical to keeping algae and bacteria at bay. And other chemicals, like pH, alkalinity, and calcium hardness, help keep your sanitizer working.

So while you can't have an entirely chemical-free pool, there are several methods to help you use less chemicals in your water. Ozone, UV, and mineral systems can help reduce your need for higher chlorine levels. And salt water systems can help you avoid handling chlorine altogether. We'll cover sanitizer options later in this section.

Regardless of what sanitizer systems you have in place, you'll need some amount of chemicals in your water. Be prepared to test and balance the chemical levels in your pool water regularly.

Water Testing

The goal of keeping your water balanced is to keep your pool sanitized and your water clear. In order to keep your water balanced, you'll need to know your chemistry levels.

Plan on testing and balancing your pool water chemistry once a week when your pool is open. But you may need to test more often if you're dealing with cloudy water, algae, or any water clarity issues. It's also a good idea to test in unusually warm weather or after a storm.

Know Your Water Source

Your water source can drastically affect your chemistry levels. Well water contains more minerals, like copper and iron. And hard water can increase your calcium hardness levels. These contaminants can make it more difficult to keep your chemistry balanced, and they can stain and damage pool surfaces. Use a hose filter when you fill your pool to remove some of these minerals.

How to Test Your Water

When it comes to testing, you have a few options:

- **Test Strips:** These are the most cost-effective and easiest way to test your pool water. But they're limited in what they measure, and they can be easily contaminated if they're left unsealed or exposed to moisture.

- **Liquid Test Kits:** If you need a broader range of testing options or more accuracy, liquid test kits are a better choice. But they require precision when adding liquid reagents; otherwise, you could get inaccurate results.

- **Digital Readers:** These are fast, accurate, and great for anyone who has trouble reading color. However, they're more expensive than other types of pool test kits.

- **Pool Store Testing:** If your readings are "off the chart" or you need to test for things like total dissolved solids and metals, you can take a water sample to your local pool store. These tests are more thorough.

One of the most important factors in testing is how you collect your water sample.

Take the sample from as close to the middle of your pool as possible. Do not take the sample near the skimmer or return jets.

Using a clean cup (or bottle with a cap if you're taking it to the store), hold it upside down so the opening faces the pool floor. Then insert the cup into the water elbow deep. Turn it right side up to collect the sample.

Now you have your water sample. The process is the same for a liquid test kit, except you're using the kit's plastic tester instead of a glass.

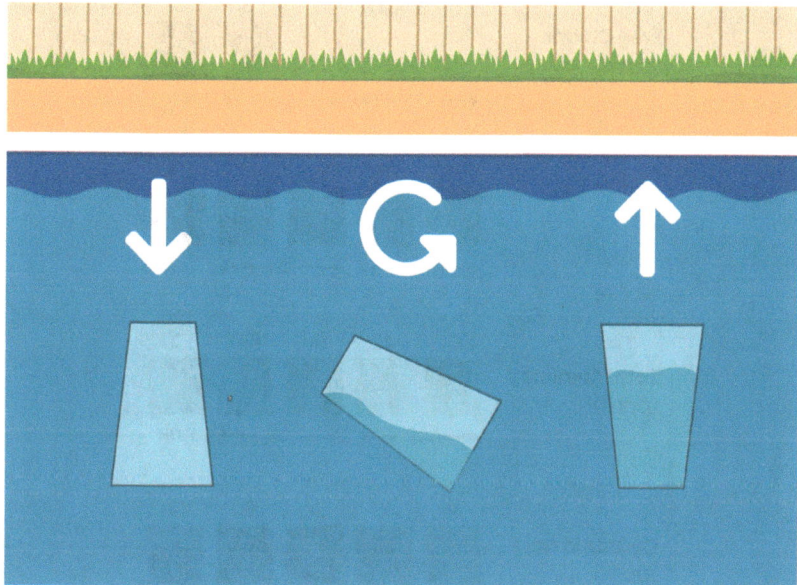

now ready to dip your test strips in the water sample. Wait 15 seconds after dipping. Do not touch or shake the test strips. Here's what a typical pool water test strip chart looks like:

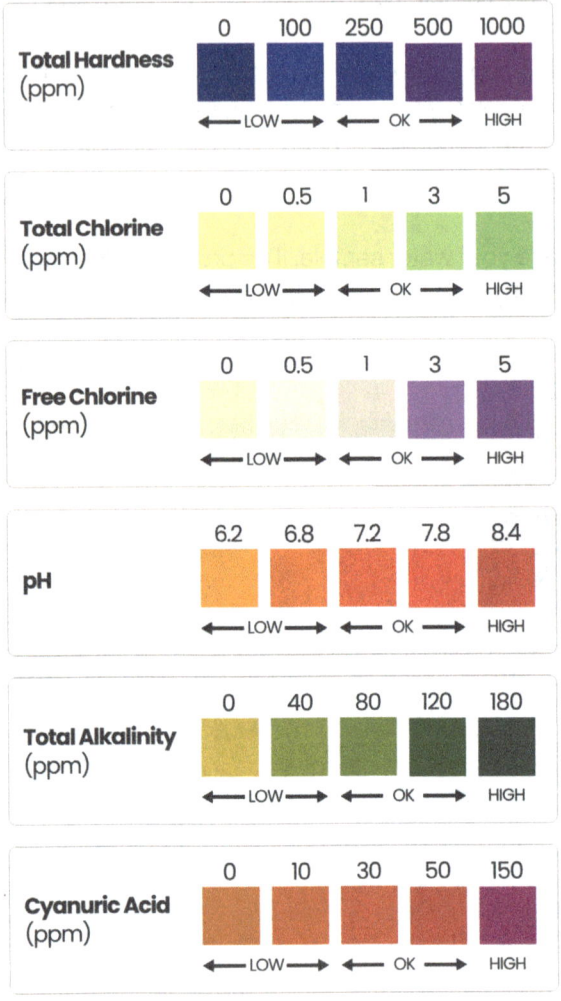

Regardless of which type of testing kit you use, your pool water chemistry levels should be within the ideal range or the OK range. But not every chemical needs to have regular, weekly testing. We'll review which chemical levels are the most important to test regularly (and why) in the next section.

Pool Chemistry 101

The three most important levels to test and adjust every week are total alkalinity, pH, and chlorine (or bromine). Unless you're having water issues, your other levels, like calcium hardness and cyanuric acid, can be tested and adjusted less frequently.

Here are all the chemical levels you need to measure and the roles each chemical plays in your overall water balance.

Total Alkalinity

- Ideal Range: 100–150 PPM
- Testing Frequency: Weekly

Your total alkalinity (TA) helps other chemicals work properly, so it's usually the first chemical you'll adjust. Alkalinity acts as a buffer to protect your pH from fluctuating drastically. So when your alkalinity is unbalanced, your pH can become unbalanced too. And pH is extremely important to protect your pool equipment and keep your sanitizer working properly.

Total alkalinity should be between 100 and 150 parts per million (PPM). While most test strips suggest an alkalinity range between 80 and 120 PPM, we find that keeping your alkalinity levels a bit higher helps keep your pH more stable. But if your pH tends to be high, you don't need to keep your alkalinity high

High Alkalinity Problems

The most common chemical that raises alkalinity is cyanuric acid (a.k.a. CYA or chlorine stabilizer). This is found in stabilized chlorine products, like trichlor tablets. Certain types of pool shock, like cal-hypo shock, can raise your alkalinity and pH levels as well.

And if you have low chlorine levels and lots of swimmers in the water, that can disrupt your total alkalinity and pH levels as well. If your alkalinity is too high, it can bring up your pH levels with it and your chlorine won't sanitize the water as effectively.

High alkalinity can also lead to calcium buildup, cloudy water, and irritated eyes and skin.

Low Alkalinity Problems

Alkalinity decreases when rainwater or fresh water is added to your pool. Acid rain, in particular, can cause alkalinity levels and pH levels to decrease. The lower your alkalinity, the lower your pH level. And that causes acidic water, which can cause long-term damage to all your equipment and pool surfaces.

How to Raise Your Alkalinity

The easiest way to raise your levels is by adding sodium bicarbonate, a.k.a. baking soda. You can purchase an alkalinity increaser product, but the active ingredient is usually sodium bicarbonate. Adding this to your water will also raise your pH, so be sure to retest both levels after adjusting.

How to Lower Your Alkalinity

To lower your alkalinity, use either muriatic acid or sodium bisulfate (a.k.a. dry acid or pH reducer). You can also dilute your pool with fresh water, but that will reduce all your other chemical levels.

Raise Alkalinity with Baking Soda

Increase By Parts Per Million	5,000 Gallons (18,927 Liters)	10,000 Gallons (37,854 Liters)	15,000 Gallons (56,781 Liters)	20,000 Gallons (75,708 Liters)
	Pool Volume			
10 ppm	0.75 lbs / 340 g	1.5 lbs / 680 g	2.25 lbs / 1.02 kg	3.0 lbs / 1.36 kg
20 ppm	1.5 lbs / 680 g	3.0 lbs / 1.36 kg	4.5 lbs / 2.04 kg	6.0 lbs / 2.72 kg
30 ppm	2.25 lbs / 1.02 kg	4.5 lbs / 2.04 kg	6.75 lbs / 3.06 kg	9.0 lbs / 4.08 kg
40 ppm	3.0 lbs / 1.36 kg	6.0 lbs / 2.72 kg	9.0 lbs / 4.08 kg	12.0 lbs / 5.44 kg
50 ppm	3.75 lbs / 1.70 kg	7.5 lbs / 3.40 kg	11.25 lbs / 5.10 kg	15.0 lbs / 6.80 kg
60 ppm	4.5 lbs / 2.04 kg	9.0 lbs / 4.08 kg	13.0 lbs / 5.89 kg	18.0 lbs / 8.16 kg
70 ppm	5.25 lbs / 2.38 kg	10.5 lbs / 4.76 kg	15.75 lbs / 7.14 kg	21.0 lbs / 9.52 kg
80 ppm	6.0 lbs / 2.72 kg	12.0 lbs / 5.44 kg	18.0 lbs / 8.16 kg	24.0 lbs / 10.88 kg
90 ppm	6.75 lbs / 3.06 kg	13.5 lbs / 6.12 kg	20.25 lbs / 9.18 kg	27.0 lbs / 12.24 kg
100 ppm	7.5 lbs / 3.40 kg	15.0 lbs / 6.80 kg	22.5 lbs / 10.20 kg	30.0 lbs / 13.60 kg

pH

- Ideal Range: 7.4–7.6
- Testing Frequency: Weekly

pH is naturally unstable in water, but it's one of the most important levels to keep in range. Rainwater, swimmers, and just about anything that enters the water can affect your pH level. When the pH is too low, it means your water is acidic. When it's too high, your water is basic. Human tears, for example, are pH neutral (7). If tears had a low pH, our eyes would burn when we cried. And if tears had a high pH, crying would dry out our eyes. Here's what the pH scale looks like:

124

Your pH level not only affects swimmers, but it can impact your chlorine's effectiveness, pool equipment, and surfaces when it's imbalanced. High pH inhibits your sanitizer, causes cloudy water, stains surfaces, and damages vinyl liners and covers. And low pH causes skin and eye irritation and corrodes pool surfaces and equipment.

High pH Problems

Certain types of chlorine (like trichlor tablets) and shock (like cal-hypo shock) will raise pH. Your water source could also have naturally high pH. And new plaster finishes in a pool can also raise your levels. Even water features, like fountains, can raise your pH by aerating the water. If your pH levels stay high (above 7.8), you might notice itchy eyes and skin, cloudy water, algae growth, and even damaged pool parts.

Low pH Problems

Heavy rain can lower your pH levels since rainwater has a pH of around 5. Acid rain in particular will bring down your levels even more. Low pH can also happen after having lots of people in your pool in a short period. Over time, low pH levels will erode pool parts made of metal or concrete and reduce your sanitizer's ability to kill contaminants. In the short term, low pH can cause itchy, irritated eyes and skin.

How to Raise Your pH

There are two different chemicals you can use to raise the pH in your pool: baking soda (a.k.a. sodium bicarbonate) or soda ash (a.k.a. sodium carbonate). The active ingredients in most pH Increaser products are the same.

How to Lower Your pH

You can lower pH in a pool with either pH decreaser (sodium bisulfate) or muriatic acid. And if you're adding something to your pool that's causing high pH (like cal-hypo shock), consider stopping until your pH levels drop down. If you have a salt water pool, your salt water generator produces naturally high pH levels. So adjust your run times to help prevent your pH from rising too high.

Raise pH with Soda Ash

Your Starting pH Levels	Pool Volume				
	1,000 Gallons (4,500 Liters)	5,000 Gallons (19,000 Liters)	10,000 Gallons (37,500 Liters)	15,000 Gallons (60,000 Liters)	20,000 Gallons (75,000 Liters)
7.2 – 7.4	0.6 oz (17 g)	3 oz (85 g)	6 oz (170 g)	9 oz (255 g)	12 oz (340 g)
7.0 – 7.2	0.75 oz (21 g)	4 oz (113 g)	8 oz (227 g)	12 oz (340 g)	1 lb (454 g)
6.6 – 7.0	1.25 oz (35 g)	6 oz (170 g)	12 oz (340 g)	1 lb (454 g)	1.5 lb (680 g)
Under 6.6	1.5 oz (43 g)	8 oz (227 g)	1 lb (454 g)	1.5 lbs (680 g)	2 lbs (907 g)

Lower pH with Muriatic Acid

Your Starting pH Levels	Pool Volume				
	1,000 Gallons (4,500 Liters)	5,000 Gallons (19,000 Liters)	10,000 Gallons (37,500 Liters)	15,000 Gallons (60,000 Liters)	20,000 Gallons (75,000 Liters)
7.6 – 7.8	1.25 oz (35 mL)	6 oz (170 mL)	12 oz (340 mL)	18 oz (510 mL)	24 oz (680 mL)
7.8 – 8.0	1.5 oz (43 mL)	8 oz (227 mL)	16 oz (454 mL)	24 oz (680 mL)	1 qt (907 mL)
8.0 – 8.4	2.5 oz (71 mL)	12 oz (340 mL)	24 oz (680 mL)	1.25 qt (1.18 L)	1.5 qt (1.42 L)
Above 8.4	3.0 oz (85 mL)	16 oz (454 mL)	1 qt (907 mL)	1.5 qt (1.42 L)	2 qt (1.89 L)

What Happens If Your pH and Alkalinity Won't Balance?

Remember that your alkalinity levels help keep your pH levels in check. So balance your alkalinity first, then your pH. But it's not uncommon for one of these levels to remain unbalanced as you start to adjust your chemistry. Maybe you added enough muriatic acid to bring the pH into range, but your alkalinity is still too high. Or you've added enough dry acid to bring down your total alkalinity, but now you have low pH.

If both your pH and alkalinity levels are too low, add soda ash to help bring them up. However, if only your pH is too low, aerate your water. Using a water fountain or pool aerator will create bubbles that help outgas carbon dioxide in the water. As carbon dioxide leaves the water, the pH will rise without impacting your alkalinity.

Finally, if you need to bring down your alkalinity but not your pH, you can add more muriatic acid while aerating your water to keep your pH levels up.

Chlorine

- Ideal Range: 1–3 PPM (free chlorine)
- Testing Frequency: Weekly

Chlorine keeps your pool sanitized by killing contaminants, bacteria, and algae. If your chlorine levels are too low, your pool water is vulnerable to algae blooms and unsafe swimming conditions. But if they're too high, that can also be dangerous for swimmers. As active chlorine gets used up in your pool, it produces chloramines (a.k.a. combined chlorine). When you notice a chlorine-like smell in your pool or irritated eyes or skin, that's actually the chloramines in your water, not your chlorine. So it likely means your chlorine levels are too low.

How can you tell how much of your chlorine is "used up" (a.k.a. combined chlorine) and how much is still active and sanitizing your water? When you test your water, you'll notice there are two different chlorine measurements: free chlorine and total chlorine.

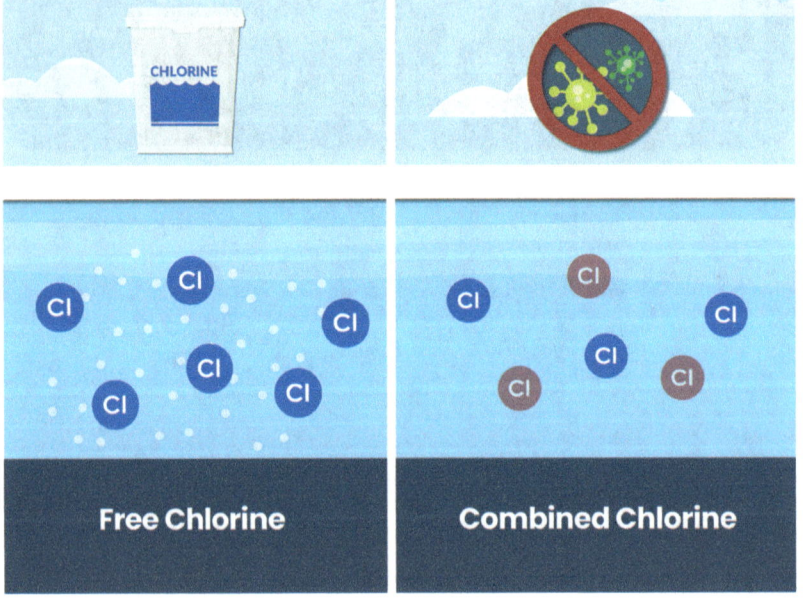

Free Chlorine vs. Combined Chlorine vs. Total Chlorine

Free chlorine is the amount of chlorine that's free or available to sanitize your pool. When you add chlorine to your water, you're increasing the amount of free chlorine in your pool. Aim for between 1 and 3 PPM, with 3 PPM being ideal.

Combined chlorine happens when free chlorine begins to react (or "combine") with contaminants in the water. It's essentially "used up" chlorine that can't sanitize as well as free chlorine. This is how chloramines are formed. Your combined chlorine should be no more than half of your free chlorine levels. Ideally, your combined chlorine levels should be 0 PPM, but anything under 0.5 PPM is okay.

Total chlorine is the sum of the combined chlorine and free chlorine in your pool water. If your total and free chlorine levels are the same, that means there's no combined chlorine in your water. But if your total chlorine is higher than your free chlorine, the difference of the two is your combined chlorine level.

High Chlorine Problems

Too much chlorine in your pool usually means you've simply added too much to your water. This can happen if you've added too many chlorine tablets or you've just shocked your pool. It can also happen if you've added too much chlorine after adding a chlorine stabilizer.

Chlorine stabilizer, a.k.a. cyanuric acid or CYA, slows the process of the sun burning away your chlorine. High chlorine levels can be harmful to swimmers, especially their lungs, skin, and eyes. And it also damages pool surfaces, like vinyl liners.

Low Chlorine Problems

Chlorine levels at or below 1 PPM mean your pool water isn't sanitized, which can lead to algae growth and bacteria buildup. And if your free chlorine is too low and your combined chlorine (a.k.a. chloramines) are too high, you'll notice a chlorine-like smell in your water and skin and eye irritation.

How to Raise Your Chlorine

Start by making sure you're regularly adding enough chlorine to your pool. This includes checking your chlorinator, salt water generator, and other chlorine-distributing methods. Then test and adjust your cyanuric acid levels.

If your CYA is too low or too high, that can hinder your chlorine's effectiveness. But if your chlorine levels are still too low, even after adding your regular chlorine, shock your pool water with a chlorine-based shock. This will raise your free chlorine levels and break up combined chlorine.

Finally, if your chlorine levels continue to remain low, even after shocking, you may have a high chlorine demand issue. Be sure to check out the Troubleshooting Section for more help.

How to Lower Your Chlorine

First, make sure you stop adding any additional chlorine to your water as you try to lower your levels. Then let the sun burn off some of the chlorine or dilute your pool with fresh water.

Remember that proper pH levels help make sure your chlorine works effectively, so be sure to adjust that level before adjusting your chlorine.

For a quicker solution, consider using a chlorine neutralizer. This is one of the quickest and easiest ways to lower your chlorine levels. But it's easy to overdo it, which will significantly lower your pH. So start with small amounts.

What If Combined Chlorine Is Still High?

If your free chlorine levels are normal (around 3 PPM) but you still need to bring down your combined chlorine or chloramines, use a non-chlorine shock (oxidizer). This will break up the chloramines and reduce your combined chlorine without increasing your free chlorine levels.

Bromine

- Ideal Range: 3–5 PPM (total bromine)
- Testing Frequency: Weekly

If you have a bromine pool, you'll notice a "total bromine" reading on most standard test strips. Your bromine levels need to stay in range to keep your water sanitized. Without it, you'll run into problems like cloudy water and algae growth.

Low Bromine Problems

Without enough bromine in your water, your pool is susceptible to algae and bacteria growth. Since it's a slow-dissolving chemical, low bromine readings are common. But lots of contaminants in the water can also use up the bromine quickly, causing the levels to be low.

High Bromine Problems

High bromine levels can cause skin and eye irritation and affect your pool surfaces and equipment. Higher bromine is usually caused by adding too much to your water.

How to Lower Bromine

Bromine doesn't break down quite as quickly as chlorine. As bromine gets used up in the water, it creates waste products, called bromamines. While not as nasty and smelly as chloramines, they still reduce bromine's effectiveness. Adding a weekly oxidizer (a.k.a. non-chlorine shock) will help remove bromamines.

How to Raise Bromine

Because bromine is a slow-dissolving chemical, it's more difficult to quickly raise your levels. A bromine booster product can help, especially if you've added lots of fresh water. Then make sure your bromine-dispensing methods, like your chemical feeder, are working properly and that your other levels, like pH, are balanced.

Calcium Hardness

- Ideal Range: 175–225 PPM (vinyl and fiberglass pools); 200–275 PPM (concrete and plaster pools)
- Testing Frequency: Monthly and at beginning of pool season

Calcium hardness is a measurement of the hardness or softness of your pool water—and it can vary wildly depending on your water source.

Well water, for example, is often higher in minerals, including calcium. So filling your pool with a hose filter is an important step to keeping these levels in check.

Low Calcium Hardness Problems

If the calcium hardness in your water is too low, it can lead to scaling and erode pool walls, plaster, concrete, and grout. It can also cause foamy water.

These levels are usually low if you haven't added any calcium hardness increaser product to the water.

High Calcium Hardness Problems

High calcium hardness levels can lead to scale buildup and cloudy water. These levels can be high if your water source has naturally high calcium levels.

They can also raise over time as pool water evaporates and leaves behind minerals. And high pH levels can also lead to calcium scaling.

How to Raise Calcium Hardness

To raise your levels, simply add calcium hardness increaser to your pool. Usually this is done at the beginning of the pool season. This chemical has more long-term effects, so you don't need to worry about testing or adjusting this level weekly.

CHEMISTRY

How to Lower Calcium Hardness

If you need to lower your calcium levels, you'll have to partially drain and refill your pool with fresh water. Be sure to use a hose filter whenever you fill your pool, especially if you have well water.

High pH can also lead to high calcium hardness. So try adjusting your pH before draining out any water.

Do Temporary Pools Need to Worry About Calcium Hardness?

If you take down your pool at the end of the season every year, you don't have to worry about testing or adjusting your calcium hardness!

Cyanuric Acid (CYA)

- Ideal Range: 30–50 PPM
- Testing Frequency: Monthly or when chlorine issues are present

Cyanuric acid (CYA), also known as chlorine stabilizer or pool conditioner, is a critical chemical that stabilizes the chlorine in your pool. Without cyanuric acid, your chlorine will quickly break down under the sun's ultraviolet rays. It only takes 17 minutes of UV exposure to destroy half of your chlorine!

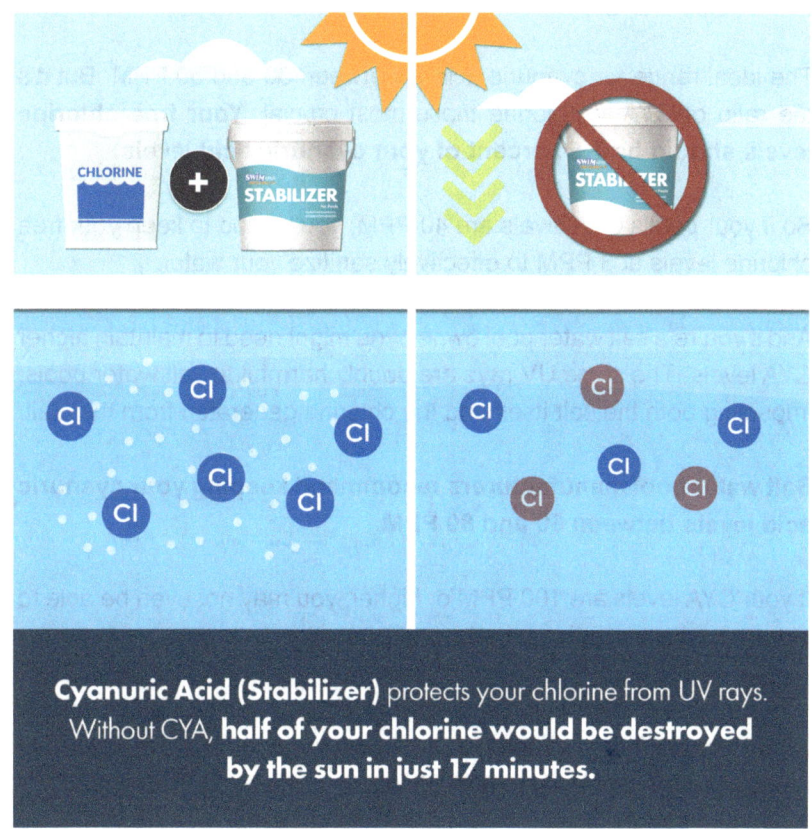

Cyanuric Acid (Stabilizer) protects your chlorine from UV rays. Without CYA, **half of your chlorine would be destroyed by the sun in just 17 minutes.**

Not every pool owner needs to worry about CYA levels. Because cyanuric acid protects chlorine from the sun, it's really only required for outdoor pools (or indoor pools with some ultraviolet light exposure).

Cyanuric acid also stays in a swimming pool for a long time, even after the water evaporates. And more cyanuric acid does not mean more protection from the sun. So always check your cyanuric acid levels before adding more chlorine stabilizer to your water.

Keep in mind that you might already be regularly adding CYA or stabilizer to your water. Chlorine products, like trichlor chlorine tablets, contain cyanuric acid. So every time you add chlorine to your water, you're also adding a stabilizer.

The ideal range for cyanuric acid is between 30 and 50 PPM. But it's the ratio of CYA to chlorine that's most crucial. **Your free chlorine levels should be 7.5 percent of your cyanuric acid levels.**

So if your pool's CYA levels are 40 PPM, you'll need to keep your free chlorine levels at 3 PPM to effectively sanitize your water.

And if you're a salt water pool owner, you might need to maintain higher CYA levels. The sun's UV rays are doubly harmful to salt water pools, impacting both the salt itself and the chlorine generated from that salt.

Salt water pool manufacturers recommend keeping your cyanuric acid levels between 60 and 80 PPM.

If your CYA levels are 100 PPM or higher, you may not even be able to get an accurate reading on a test strip.

When cyanuric acid levels are off the charts, you'll need to take a water sample into your local pool supply store or use a test kit that measures CYA levels up to 300 PPM.

High Cyanuric Acid Problems

If you're adding chlorine to your water, you're likely adding cyanuric acid along with it. Many chlorine products, like trichlor tablets or dichlor granules, are known as stabilized chlorine. This means they already come with CYA.

So every time you add chlorine to your pool, you're adding cyanuric acid. If your CYA levels are high, you may experience algae growth or cloudy pool water. That's because high CYA levels can reduce your chlorine's effectiveness, and that can also disrupt your pool's pH balance.

Low Cyanuric Acid Problems

If you have low CYA levels, you likely aren't using stabilized chlorine to sanitize your water. Rain, splash out, and water dilution can also decrease your cyanuric levels.

So if you've had to partially drain and refill your water recently, you will also have low CYA levels. Pools with very low or no cyanuric acid can experience "high chlorine demand," or the inability to maintain chlorine levels. No matter how much chlorine you add, the levels drop quickly— and low chlorine means algae growth and chloramine buildup.

How to Raise Your Cyanuric Acid

In order to raise your cyanuric acid levels, you'll need to add a pool stabilizer to your water. You can also start using stabilized chlorine, like trichlor tablets, to sanitize your pool. The good news is you'll likely only need to add CYA to your water once or twice per year (usually at the beginning of the season).

But be careful about adding too much. Remember that cyanuric acid does not break down in the water and can stay in your pool for a long time. And stabilized chlorine (like dichlor or trichlor) already comes with CYA, so you'll likely be adding it to your pool water throughout the season.

How to Lower Your Cyanuric Acid

The only effective way to lower your CYA is to partially drain your pool and refill it with fresh water. But if you think your cyanuric acid is too high, the first step is to stop adding more cyanuric acid or stabilized chlorine to your pool before diluting your water.

What about Cyanuric Acid Reducers?

Cyanuric acid reducers have mixed results. These biologically based products work slowly. It can take a week or more to reduce your CYA levels, and many customers have reported seeing no results. And CYA reducers are not cheap. You could partially drain and refill your pool for roughly the same price, depending on the water utility costs in your area. But if you can't dilute your pool water (say because of drought conditions or municipality restrictions), it might be worth trying a cyanuric acid reducer.

Raise Cyanuric Acid with Chlorine Stabilizer

Increase By	Pool Volume			
	5,000 Gallons (18,927 Liters)	10,000 Gallons (37,854 Liters)	15,000 Gallons (56,781 Liters)	20,000 Gallons (75,708 Liters)
10 ppm	6.5 oz 184 g	13 oz 368.5 g	19.5 oz 552.8 g	26 oz 737 g
20 ppm	13 oz 368.5 g	26 oz 737 g	39 oz 1.1 kg	52 oz 1.47 kg
30 ppm	19.5 oz 552.8 g	39 oz 1.1 kg	58.5 oz 1.65 kg	78 oz 2.21 kg
40 ppm	26 oz 737 g	52 oz 1.47 g	78 oz 2.21 kg	104 oz 2.94 kg
50 ppm	32.5 oz 921.3 g	65 oz 1.84 g	97 oz 2.74 kg	130 oz 3.68 kg

Other Chemical Levels

Most pool owners don't need to test for the following levels regularly, but they're helpful to test once a year.

Metals

Metals in your pool can cause staining or discoloration, especially when other chemistry levels are imbalanced. Shocking your pool can also oxidize any metals in the water and lead to pool stains. If you suspect that you have high metal content in your water (like well water), you'll want to test for metals a few times a year. Test at the beginning of the pool season, whenever you fill your pool with fresh water, or if you experience staining issues. Be sure to check out the Troubleshooting Section for more information about metals and staining.

Total Dissolved Solids (TDS)

This reading measures all the solids that are dissolved in your water, including salts, metals, minerals, and other organic matter. The more dissolved solids in your water, the harder it is to keep your water clean and clear. The ideal TDS level for regular pools is 500 to 2,000 PPM. For salt water pools, the ideal level is 5,000 to 6,000 PPM. If you have chronically cloudy water and a salt water pool, you may want to measure your TDS. Lowering this level requires a partial drain and refill.

Salinity Levels (for Salt Water Pools)

Your salt water generator won't produce chlorine if your salt levels are too low. Luckily, salt is usually something you only need to add at the beginning of the pool season since it doesn't evaporate from the water. The ideal salt level is between 2,700 to 3,400 PPM, with 3,200 PPM being ideal. Be sure to check out the Salt Water Pool Maintenance Section for more information.

What About Phosphates?

You've probably seen a product called "phosphate remover," or you've been told to measure your phosphate levels. While algae does feed off phosphates, focusing on eliminating phosphates doesn't solve the overall issue. Your best bet is to maintain proper chlorine levels, regularly use an algaecide to prevent algae from blooming in your pool, and occasionally shock your pool to kill off contaminants.

Types of Sanitizers and Sanitizer Systems

Regardless of the type you use, a sanitizer's job is to keep the water free of bacteria, viruses, algae, and other contaminants that can grow in untreated pool water. There are several different ways to sanitize a pool. Some methods are more hands-off than others, while some sanitizer systems help you reduce the amount of chemicals overall. Here are the different methods for keeping your water sanitized:

Chlorine vs. Bromine vs. Biguanide

Chlorine is the most popular chemical for sanitizing a pool, but some pool owners opt for bromine or biguanide. While each of these sanitizing chemicals help keep your water clean, they work in very different ways:

Chlorine

Chlorine is very effective at killing viruses, bacteria, and algae and helps prevent algae from growing in the first place. Because of its sanitizing power and low cost, chlorine is the most popular option. However, it does produce a waste product called chloramines. This can cause irritated eyes, dry skin, and that distinctive "chlorine smell."

Bromine

The most popular alternative to chlorine, bromine is a gentler but effective sanitizer. It also doesn't break down as quickly as chlorine and remains active longer. And while it still creates waste products called bromamines, they're not as smelly as chloramines. Keep in mind that bromine tablets still contain a small percentage of chlorine. And bromine can cost twice as much as chlorine.

Biguanide

Also known as PHMB (preservative-free polyhexamethylene biguanide), biguanide is a chlorine-free sanitizer. It doesn't produce chloramines, is gentler on your skin, hair, and eyes and doesn't degrade in sunlight. But it's more expensive and not as effective as other sanitizers. It can also cloud your pool water.

Finally, it does require specific chemicals and maintenance that's especially suited to that brand of chemical. Be sure to fully research biguanide before you convert your pool.

What's the Difference Between Stabilized vs. Unstabilized Chlorine?

Stabilized chlorine contains cyanuric acid, also known as CYA or stabilizer. The cyanuric acid protects the chlorine from being destroyed by the sun's UV rays. Unstabilized chlorine doesn't contain cyanuric acid. So it breaks down more quickly in the sun, and you'll have to add chlorine more often.

Pool-grade liquid chlorine, bleach, and some chlorine shocks, like cal-hypo shock, are unstabilized chlorine. Most of the chlorine that's sold as a sanitizer, like chlorine tablets, is stabilized chlorine.

Granules vs. Tablets vs. Liquid

Chlorine comes in three forms: granules, tablets, and liquid chlorine. It also comes in sticks, which work similarly to tablets. Bromine, on the other hand, only comes in granules and tablets.

Granules (Chlorine or Bromine)

Granules dissolve quickly in water, helping fight algae and contaminants fast. It's added directly to your pool water which gives you complete control of the dosage. But since you have to measure and add it yourself, it's more dangerous and cumbersome to handle. And granules won't work in automatic feeders since they dissolve too quickly. Finally, granules made of dichlor chlorine have a lower percentage of chlorine than tablets (around 60 percent).

Tablets (Chlorine or Bromine)

Tablets, or pucks, are placed in floating dispensers, pool skimmers, automatic chlorinators. They usually come in one-inch or three-inch pucks, with smaller pucks better for sanitizing smaller pools. Because these pucks are slower dissolving and provide sustained chlorination, they're more convenient compared to adding granules. But if you want a quick boost of chlorine or you want more control over your chlorine amounts, granules will dissolve more quickly. Finally, trichlor chlorine tablets contain up to 90 percent chlorine (compared to granules). But trichlor will affect your pool's pH.

Liquid Chlorine

Liquid chlorine has the same active chemical as other pool chlorine. It's cheaper than tablets and granules, but it's unstabilized. That means you'll need to add cyanuric acid to protect the chlorine from breaking down in the sun. It also has an extremely high pH and is highly corrosive. It does not have a long shelf life, and you'll need to add a lot of it since it only contains 10–12% chlorine.

Can I Use Bleach as a Sanitizer?

Household bleach is really affordable, easy to find, and contains the same main ingredient as other pool chlorine (sodium hypochlorite). But it has the smallest concentration of chlorine (3–6%) and is also unstabilized. That means you'll not only need to frequently add large quantities to your pool to keep it sanitized, but you'll also need to add a stabilizer to keep it from burning away in the sun.

Adding Tablets to Your Pool

There are three common ways to use pool tablets: floating dispensers, inside the skimmer basket, and in an automatic chlorinator. Keep in mind that your pool water temperature and water pressure can impact the amount of time it takes your tablet to dissolve. And a larger, three-inch tablet will break down more slowly than a one-inch tablet.

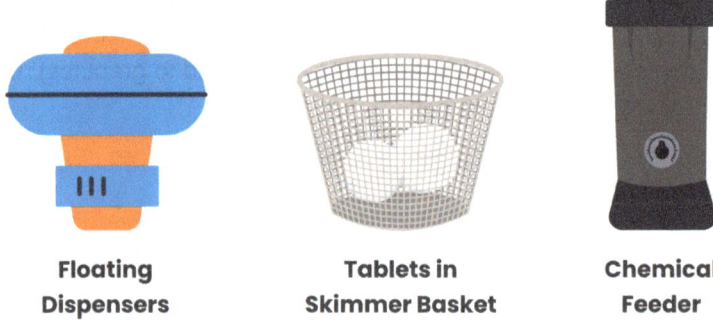

**Floating
Dispensers**

**Tablets in
Skimmer Basket**

**Chemical
Feeder**

Floating Dispensers

These plastic pool gadgets travel around your pool, dispersing sanitizer as the tablets inside dissolve. They're convenient and low maintenance. But they dispense chlorine or bromine unevenly, which means your levels may fluctuate.

They can also get stuck in one spot in your pool, like behind ladders, causing them to dispense too much sanitizer in one spot. And that can discolor and even damage your pool liner.

Tablets Inside the Skimmer Basket

With a continuous water flow through the filter, placing tablets in your skimmer provides a steadier rate of dissolving. As water flows through, it will evenly break down the tablet and send sanitized water through your filter system and back into your pool.

But the tablets will continue to dissolve even when the filter isn't running. Sanitizer can collect in and near the skimmer basket, causing stains, erosion and even equipment damage.

Chemical Feeder or Chlorinators

An automatic chlorine dispenser is the most reliable option. Simply add several tablets into the chlorinator and set the rate you want the tablets to dissolve.

Chemical Feeders or Chlorinators

Also known as an automatic chlorine feeder or chemical feeder, a chlorinator automatically dispenses sanitizer into your water. Installed directly into your pump and filter system, a chlorinator disperses a steady, measured amount of chlorine or bromine into the water right before it returns to your pool.

Pool chlorinators work best with slow-dissolve bromine or trichlor chlorine tablets or pucks. These tablets last longer than granules, giving you more time between chemical additions. And chlorinators use water pressure to dissolve pucks at a steady rate. Granules will dissolve too quickly.

Keep in mind that these pucks or tablets will only dissolve in your chlorinator when your pool pump is running. If your pump is on a timer and turns off, your tablet will not dissolve, and it won't disperse into your pool.

With a little upfront cost and installation, a chlorinator eliminates the need to constantly measure and add chlorine to your water and the need to refill your floating chlorine dispenser. And they can be retrofitted to most pools. But when you're first using your pool chlorinator, be sure to regularly test your chlorine levels until you get a feel for the setting that works best based on your pool.

Can I Use Bromine in a Chlorinator?

You can use bromine in most chlorinators or automatic chlorine feeders. But never use the feeder for bromine if it's been used for chlorine tablets! In general, never mix chemicals, chemical containers, and buckets!

There are two types of pool chlorinators: inline and off-line chlorinators. They both function the same and cost the same (usually under $100). But they are installed differently, and they won't work with every type of pool setup.

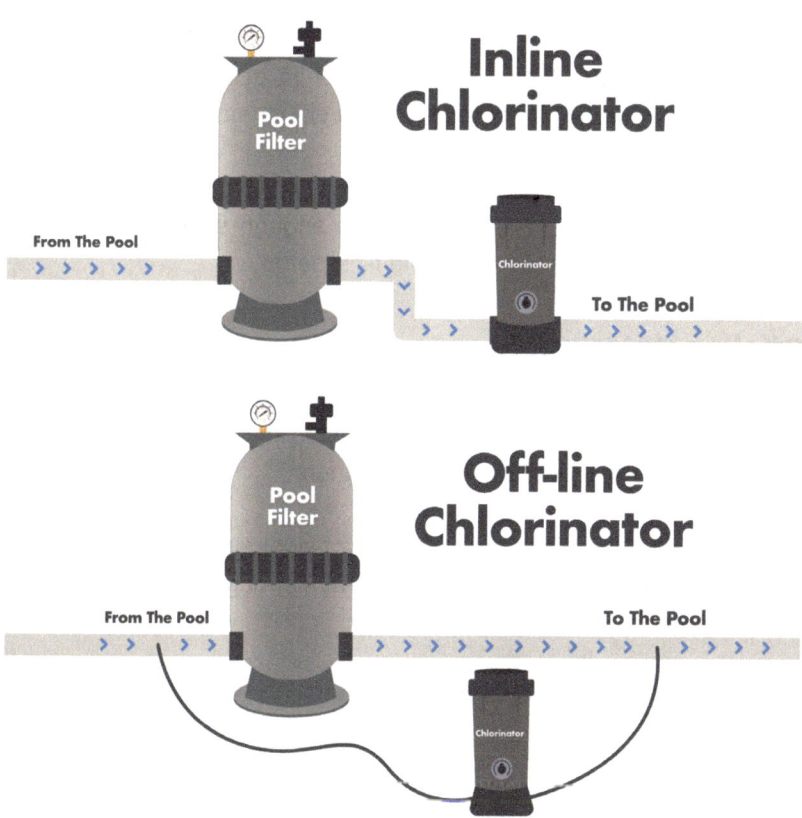

Inline Chlorinator

Installed directly into the plumbing, an inline chlorinator is added after the filter or heater and before the filtered water is returned to the pool. Since it's chlorinating the water after it's passed through the rest of the system, it helps protect pool equipment from corrosion.

Inline chlorinators are plumbed into PVC piping. It's easiest to hard plumb a chlorinator during pool construction or renovation, but it's possible to cut the PVC pipe and install a chlorinator after the fact.

An inline chlorinator is a sturdier option with fewer parts than an off-line chlorinator. But you might not have enough space to install an inline chlorinator into your pump and filter setup.

Off-line Chlorinator

An off-line pool chlorinator is connected with a tube installed on the side of the filter system. It's then connected through a separate line that bypasses the rest of the filter equipment.

Off-line chlorinators are a good option for pool owners that still want an automatic pool chlorinator but don't have enough room to install an inline model.

While you won't need to cut any piping to install, you will still need to cut small holes into your PVC plumbing. And you can only use an off-line chlorinator if you have "hard" PVC piping.

Mineral Systems

Installing a mineral system can help sanitize your water without needing to add a ton of chemicals. These systems use minerals like silver and copper to kill bacteria. And if your chlorine levels ever drop too low, a mineral system ensures that there's always something fighting contaminants.

It's important to know that mineral systems aren't complete sanitizer systems. They're meant to supplement chlorine or other sanitizing pool chemicals, thereby reducing the need for as much of the other sanitizers.
But you will need less chlorine if you use a mineral system.

You'll find three forms of mineral systems available:

In-Skimmer Mineral Systems

One of the easier options, all you have to do is lower the dispenser right into the skimmer basket. Minerals are released into the water as it flows into the skimmer and over the dispenser. Some in-skimmer devices last about six months and can sanitize pools that hold up to 30,000 gallons.

Floating Dispensers

Another easy option is a little dispenser that just floats around your pool. Simply connect a cartridge that holds both minerals and either chlorine or bromine, and let it float in your water.

Inline Mineral System

This connects to your pool's plumbing and can be installed into existing plumbing systems. The dispenser needs to remain accessible so you can change the cartridge when necessary. It releases minerals and chlorine into the water right before they enter your pool.

Ozonators or Ultraviolet Light Systems

This device generates and inserts ozone gas into your pool water. Ozone can kill bacteria and other contaminants. It's installed into your pool plumbing after your filter or any heater.

There are two types of ozonators:

Ultraviolet Light

These ozonators use ultraviolet light to split oxygen molecules into free oxygen atoms to create ozone—and that ozone then sanitizes the water.

Corona Discharge

In these devices, a conductor is ionized by electricity. This converts the oxygen in the chamber into ozone, which sanitizes the water.

While ozonators are clever sanitizer alternatives, they function best in dry climates. So if you live in a humid area, an ozonator's performance will be reduced. Also be aware that if you use an ozonator, you'll need special test strips to test the water for ozone.

You Still Need to Add Some Sanitizer

Mineral, UV and Ozonator systems will not eliminate the need for sanitizer. You'll still have to add chlorine or bromine to your water. But it's far less than you would need normally.

Salt Water Systems

Like other automatic sanitizer systems, salt water systems are installed after the filter (and heater, if you have one) and right before the water reenters the pool. Also known as salt water generators or salt water chlorinators, these systems use the salt that's added to the pool to produce chlorine.

That's right: a salt water pool is a chlorine pool! But instead of adding chlorine directly to your water, you'll add salt. If you want to learn more about salt water pools, there's an entire section on Salt Water Pool Maintenance.

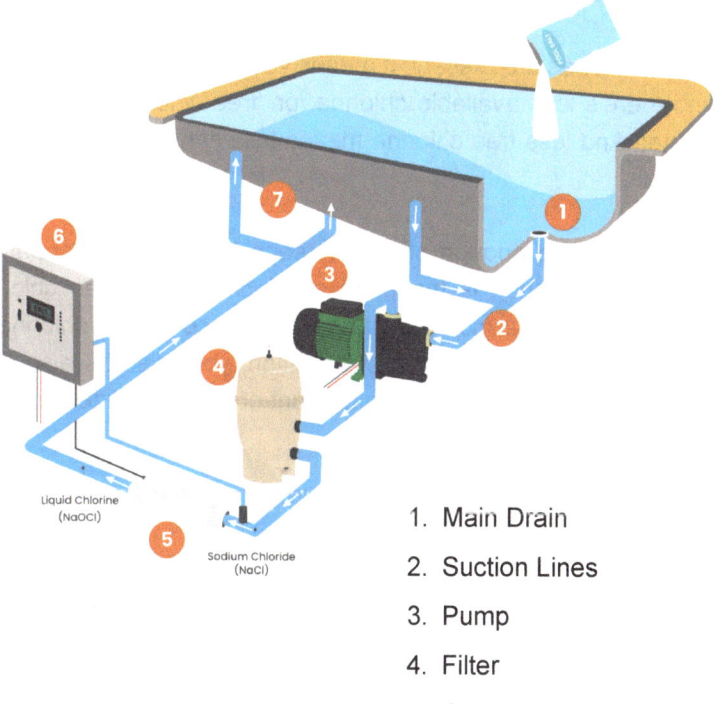

Liquid Chlorine
(NaOCl)

Sodium Chloride
(NaCl)

1. Main Drain
2. Suction Lines
3. Pump
4. Filter
5. Conversion Salt Cell to Chlorine
6. Salt Control Panel
7. Return Lines

Shocking Your Water

"Shocking" is the process of adding a powerful, concentrated dose of chemicals (usually chlorine) to your pool water. This helps get rid of contaminants like algae, and it helps revitalize your pool's regular sanitizer.

Shocking is really useful at the beginning of the pool season or after your pool's been heavily used. And it can also be helpful to shock your pool once a week as part of your regular pool maintenance routine.

Adding shock means you're adding enough chlorine or oxidizer to refresh your sanitizer and destroy the buildup of chloramines. Chloramines are the byproduct of your chlorine that's done its jobs.

When chloramines are present, it means your chlorine has been used up, and there's less available chlorine, or "free chlorine," to sanitize your water. And less free chlorine means less sanitizer keeping your water clean.

The goal is to add enough shock to reach breakpoint chlorination. Breakpoint chlorination is the point at which enough free chlorine is added to break the molecular bonds of the combined chlorine in your water. To reach breakpoint chlorination, you need to raise your free chlorine levels to 10 times the amount of your combined chlorine levels.

Types of Shock

Pool shock comes as either a super concentrated dose of chlorine, a.k.a. chlorine shock, or as an oxidizer, a.k.a. non-chlorine shock.

Chlorine-based pool shock is best for treating algae and cloudy water, but it can affect your other water chemistry levels, like CYA and calcium hardness. On the other hand, non-chlorine pool shock isn't as harsh, and it's a great weekly treatment for refreshing your free chlorine levels. But it's not strong enough to tackle big algae issues.

Not all pool shocks are right for every type of pool or for every pool situation. Some will impact your other levels. So before shocking your pool, test and balance your pool water. And keep an eye on your pH, calcium hardness, and CYA levels before and after adding your shock. Here are three common pool shocks and when to use them:

Cal-Hypo Shock

Calcium hypochlorite shock, or cal-hypo shock, is the most powerful form of chlorine shock out there, with the highest percentage of available chlorine. Use cal-hypo shock if you have algae issues or as a powerful weekly treatment if you have problematic pool water. Because it's such a highly concentrated dose of chlorine, you'll need to wait at least 8 hours before swimming. And it's best to use cal-hypo shock at night. This shock doesn't contain cyanuric acid, which means it's unstabilized and can be destroyed by the sun's UV rays.

Finally, be careful using cal-hypo shock in salt water pools, since it contains calcium and can cause scale buildup in the salt water generator. And cal-hypo might also be too powerful for smaller pools, like Intex pools.

Dichlor Shock

Sodium dichlor, a.k.a. dichlor shock, is another chlorine shock, but it's a little less potent than cal-hypo shock. It's still an effective treatment for algae issues, contaminant buildup, and weekly pool maintenance. And because it contains sodium, it dissolves quickly and can also be used in all types of pools, including vinyl, plaster, painted, and salt water pools.

However, dichlor shock is a stabilized shock, which means it contains cyanuric acid. So it will raise your CYA levels. That means you can add it to your pool during the day since it's stabilized and protected from the sun's UV rays. But it can drastically increase your CYA levels.

Non-Chlorine Shock (Oxidizer)

Non-chlorine shock works as an oxidizer, which means it helps revitalize your existing sanitizer. However, it does not super sanitize your water and kill contaminants on its own. So non-chlorine shock isn't effective at tackling larger issues like algae.

On the other hand, since it doesn't contain harsh levels of chlorine, this is a great shock for weekly treatments or if you want to swim shortly after shocking your pool. And it won't affect your calcium or CYA levels.

Can I Shock My Pool with Bleach?

While bleach does contain the active ingredient chlorine, it's less concentrated than other shock products. So depending on the size of your pool, you'll need to use a lot of it. The goal of shocking is to reach breakpoint chlorination, which means quickly raising your free chlorine levels to 10 PPM or above. And it'll take a lot of bleach to get there.

Depending on your pool's current condition or the type of sanitizer you use, here's what type of shock we recommend using:

Best Shock for Algae

Cal-Hypo Shock. If you've got algae or green water, we recommend using cal-hypo shock. This is the strongest version of chlorine shock and can quickly kill contaminants that have built up in the water. A non-chlorine shock can help revitalize your existing sanitizer enough that it will do the job of killing algae spores. But it won't be enough to kill a larger algae issue.

Best Shock for Salt Water Pools

Dichlor or Liquid Chlorine. While cal-hypo shock is the most effective shock for treating algae, it does contain calcium. And that can build up in your water over time, causing scale buildup in your salt water generator. So if you have a salt water pool, use dichlor shock or liquid chlorine instead. You may also have a "superchlorinate" setting on your salt water generator. While this will add more chlorine to your water, it only raises the free chlorine levels gradually over a longer period. So it won't achieve breakpoint chlorination levels needed to treat things like algae.

Best Shock for Smaller Pools (Under 10,000 Gallons)

Liquid Chlorine or Bleach. If you have a smaller pool, traditional chlorine-based shocks, like cal-hypo shock, might be too strong. Because this shock is sold in doses for 10,000 gallons, it may contain too much chlorine for smaller pools and take too long to dissipate. Consider using liquid chlorine, like bleach, to shock a smaller pool. Household bleach can be powerful enough to kill algae, but it's easy to overdo it, so be sure to take things slowly. One gallon of 5.25% bleach can raise the free chlorine levels in a 10,000-gallon pool by over 5 PPM.

When to Add Shock

We recommend shocking your pool once a week, or at least once every other week to help kill contaminants in your water. The more often you use the pool, the more often you should refresh your sanitizer with pool shock. If you're worried about your chlorine levels increasing drastically, use a non-chlorine shock for maintenance and use a chlorine-based shock when you start to notice issues.

Be sure to add any unstabilized shock (like cal-hypo shock) to your water at night. Otherwise it'll get burned off from the sun. And balance your other levels, like pH and alkalinity, before shocking your water.

How to Add Chemicals

Adding chemicals in the right order will help you avoid wasting time and money. Before you add any pool chemicals, be sure to test your water so you know what you'll need to adjust.

Chemical List

You'll want to have the following chemicals on hand for regular pool maintenance:

- Alkalinity increaser (or baking soda)
- pH increaser (or soda ash)
- pH decreaser (or muriatic acid)
- Chlorine or bromine
- Cyanuric acid (also known as CYA or chlorine stabilizer)
- Pool shock
- Calcium hardness increaser

And be sure you have protective gear like gloves and goggles.

Order of Adding Chemicals

Be sure to wait at least 30 minutes after adding each chemical to let it circulate and dissipate. Some chemicals take even longer, like shock, so be sure to follow the manufacturer's directions.

Then retest the water before adding the next chemical. Your pool pump and filter should be running while you're adding chemicals.

Here's the order we recommend to adjust your water chemistry: **total alkalinity, pH, chlorine (or bromine), cyanuric acid, and calcium hardness.**

1. Adjust Total Alkalinity

Alkalinity helps prevent fluctuations with pH. So adjusting your alkalinity first can help bring your pH into range. If you need to raise your alkalinity, you can use an alkalinity increaser or baking soda. If you need to lower your alkalinity, you'll actually use pH decreaser or muriatic acid.

2. Adjust pH

You can lower your pH with a pH decreaser or muriatic acid. Or if you need to raise the pH, you can use a pH increaser or soda ash.

3. Adjust Chlorine (or Bromine)

The pH helps your sanitizer work more effectively, which is why it's important to adjust your pH first. Add your chlorine or other sanitizer at this point. If you're using chlorine pucks or tablets, keep in mind that it may take several hours for your levels to come into range.

4. Adjust Cyanuric Acid or CYA Levels (if needed)

CYA helps stabilize your sanitizer. Remember that if you've added stabilized chlorine to your pool water, like dichlor or trichlor tablets or granules, you've already added cyanuric acid. Your CYA levels may be fine at this point. You do not need to add CYA in a bromine pool.

5. Adjust Calcium Hardness Levels

These levels do more damage in the long run, like eroding parts in your pool. So you don't need to adjust your calcium hardness right away before swimming. And if you drain and refill your pool each year, you don't need to worry about these levels as much.

At this point, let your pool circulate all the chemicals in the water for an hour or two. Then retest your water one final time.

When Do I Add Shock?

If you need to add shock to your pool at any point, be sure to balance your other levels before shocking your water. Bringing your levels into range, especially your pH, will help your shock work more effectively.

Additional Chemicals

If you only used chemicals to balance your sanitizer, pH, alkalinity, and calcium hardness, you could theoretically keep your pool clean and clear all season long. But there will be times when you need to help your pool fight things like algae, cloudiness, and staining. So in addition to your regular rotation of pool chemicals, here are a few additional products that can be helpful to have on hand:

Clarifier

Water clarifier is a simple and quick solution to help clear up a cloudy pool. Just know that it's only temporary, and once the clarifier dissipates, the cloudiness will return. But it's a handy helper, especially if you have people coming over. And using it once a week will keep your pool looking sparkly and clear.

Pool clarifier clears cloudy water by clumping together small particles and contaminants. When you add a clarifier to cloudy water, those smaller particles coagulate into bigger particles that can be captured by your filter. There's no need to vacuum out or remove the clarifier once you use it. All you have to do is add the clarifier to the water and wait for it to do its job.

Depending on your pool's level of cloudiness, it can take 2 to 3 days to clear up your water using a water clarifier. You'll need to balance your water and run your filter 24-7 while the clarifier is at work. And if you have an algae problem, you'll have to address that first before adding a clarifier. Be sure to check out the Troubleshooting Section for more help on how to use a clarifier.

Flocculant

Pool flocculant, also known as pool floc, clumps together tiny particles in your pool that cause cloudy water. Once those particles have coagulated, the larger clumps sink to the bottom of your swimming pool where they can then be vacuumed out. Unlike clarifier, you won't have to wait days for flocculant to do its job. The particles quickly coagulate together and sink to your pool floor in a matter of hours. And it's extremely effective.

But it does take some effort. Once the clumps form on the bottom of the pool, you'll need to remove them with a manual pool vacuum. An automatic pool vacuum will not work; you'll also lose pool water in the process since you'll need to vacuum on the "waste" setting and bypass the filter. Finally, you can't use pool flocculant with a cartridge filter. Though it works faster than pool clarifiers, it will need 8 to 16 hours to clump together the particles before you can vacuum. So it will be one or two days before your pool is clear. Be sure to check out the Troubleshooting Section for more help on how to use flocculant.

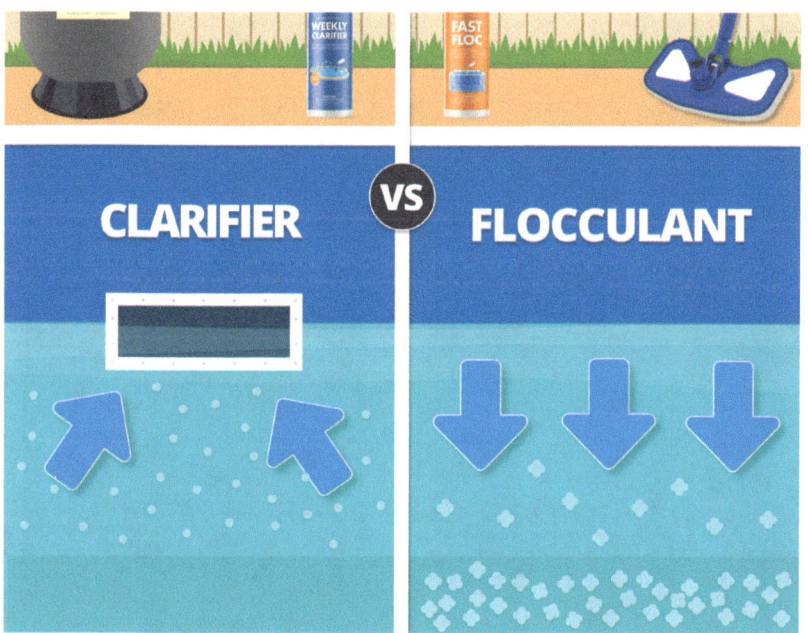

Algaecide

Your best defense against algae is keeping your chlorine or bromine levels in range. And if you notice you already have an algae problem, we recommend shocking the pool. However, algaecide is a great product to have on hand to prevent algae or to contain an early forming algae bloom. It's also smart to add to your water when closing your pool for the off-season.

Despite its name, algaecide won't completely kill the algae, but it can at least keep the algae from continuing to grow and spread. Just be sure to use a copper-free algaecide if you have water with high levels of minerals. This will help avoid staining your pool's walls and floor.

Metal Sequestrant

If your water contains iron or copper, you may notice rust-colored or green pool stains. You can prevent them from reoccurring by using a metal sequestrant. This pool chemical attaches itself to metal particles in the water so they can't settle on surfaces and stain them. If you have hard water or well water, you may want to keep some sequestrant handy.

Chemical Safety and Storage

As necessary as pool chemicals are to have around, they're unfortunately extremely dangerous. Here are several best practices for handling pool chemicals. Always follow the manufacturer's directions and use extra precaution and common sense.

- Wear protective gear, like goggles, gloves, masks, longer clothing, and close-toed shoes.
- Don't add chemicals when it's extremely windy outside.
- Never mix different chemicals in the same bucket. Even residuals are dangerous and can explode or create toxic gas, so use separate buckets for different chemicals.
- Never mix different brands of chemicals, as they could have slightly different active chemicals.
- Never add pool shock to your skimmer. Combining shock and your regular chlorine creates a deadly gas. This is especially dangerous if you have an automatic chlorinator attached to your filter system. If you pour the shock into the skimmer, the chlorine and shock will combine in a very small space and possibly explode.
- Store chemicals away from each other. Even chemical vapors can combust and cause an explosion.
- Store chemicals in a cool, dry, and secure space.

Action Steps: Create a Chemistry Plan

Weekly testing and balancing will help keep most pool problems away. By following a simple pool routine, you'll be able to prevent algae, cloudy water, and contaminant buildup.

- **Create a Simple Testing and Balancing Schedule:** Test your pool once a week using test strips or a liquid test kit. You'll want to monitor fluctuations with pH, alkalinity, and chlorine (or bromine) and adjust those weekly. Test and balance your pool during other tasks, like brushing. Other levels, like calcium hardness and salt, usually don't need to be adjusted as often.

- **Shock Regularly:** Shocking your pool once a week with a non-chlorine shock can help keep your sanitizer refreshed and active. Use a chlorine-based shock if you're experiencing issues like algae.

- **Consider Sanitizer System Upgrades:** While it can be an expensive investment upfront, upgrading your sanitizer system can have tremendous benefits. Installing an automatic chlorinator or adding in a mineral system can help keep your water consistently sanitized and prevent ongoing issues.

- **Stock Up on Supplemental Chemicals:** You'll be able to find most of the chemicals you need at your local pool supply store. But if you're looking to save money, consider stocking up on alternative chemicals, like baking soda (to raise alkalinity) or muriatic acid (to lower pH and clean stains on concrete). Just be sure to read the labels of any products you buy to make sure there's no weird additives. For example, you should only use pool-grade salt with a salt water system.

- **Adjust Your Circulation:** Make sure your filter is clean, your skimmer basket and skimmer line are clear, and your return jets are angled properly to help disperse chemicals more evenly. Read the Circulation Section for more tips.

6

~~~

WATER TEMPERATURE
Heating and Cooling Your Pool

WATER TEMPERATURE
Heating and Cooling Your Pool

Whether you want to extend the length of your pool season or you're in a hot climate and need to cool your water, you've got lots of heating and cooling options. In this section, you'll learn about:

1. **Pool Heaters:** Compare the different types of pool heaters and learn about which ones will work best for your climate.
2. **Solar Covers:** Learn how solar covers trap in heat from the sun and how they work best in a pool.
3. **Aeration:** Learn how to cool down your water with aeration.

Pool Heaters

Your pool's heating time depends on a few things: what type of pool you have, how much water it holds, whether it's insulated or not, and how much sun you get. There are three main options for a pool heater:

1. Gas pool heaters (propane or natural gas)
2. Pool heat pumps
3. Solar pool heaters

The key to choosing the right one is knowing how they work, finding the right size for your pool, and calculating the costs and benefits.

Gas Heaters

Gas heaters use natural gas or propane to heat your water. The pool water passes through your heater while a combustion chamber burns and warms the water before returning it to the pool.

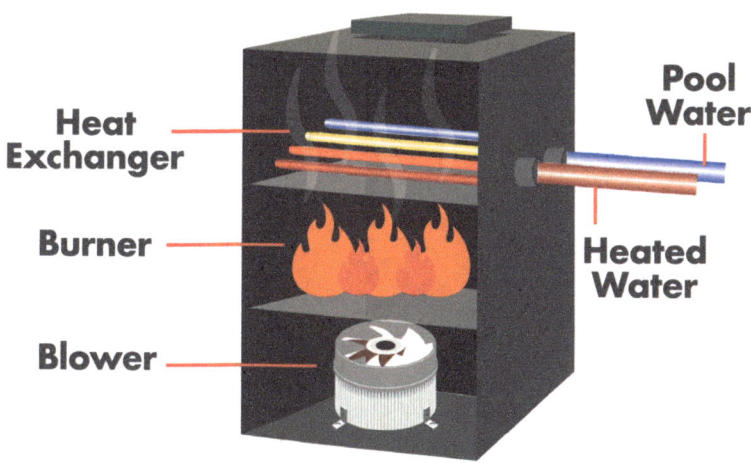

These are the most powerful heaters. They're very efficient and will heat your pool quickly, especially if you live where temperatures are cooler. However, it's expensive to install. And you do have to pay for the gas to keep it running, which can be costly as well.

Natural gas pool heaters require a gas line. So if lines aren't available on your property, you'll either need to pay to have them installed, or opt for a propane pool heater. And keep in mind that propane heaters tend to be more expensive to run than natural gas.

Heat Pumps

Heat pumps draw in warm air from the atmosphere and use that air to heat the pool. It's like a reverse air conditioner. This is a low-energy process that relies entirely on your outside temperature. So as long as the weather is warm enough (around 60°F degrees or higher), heat pumps can be a good option.

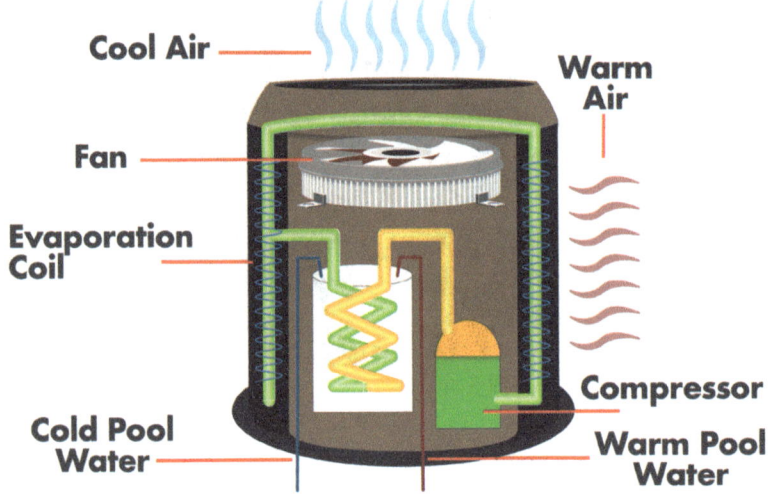

These are extremely more energy efficient and cheaper to operate than gas heaters. But they won't work in colder temperatures and take longer to heat the water.

Solar Heaters

Solar pool heaters work by diverting water from your swimming pool through solar collectors. These collectors then warm the water before it goes back into the pool.

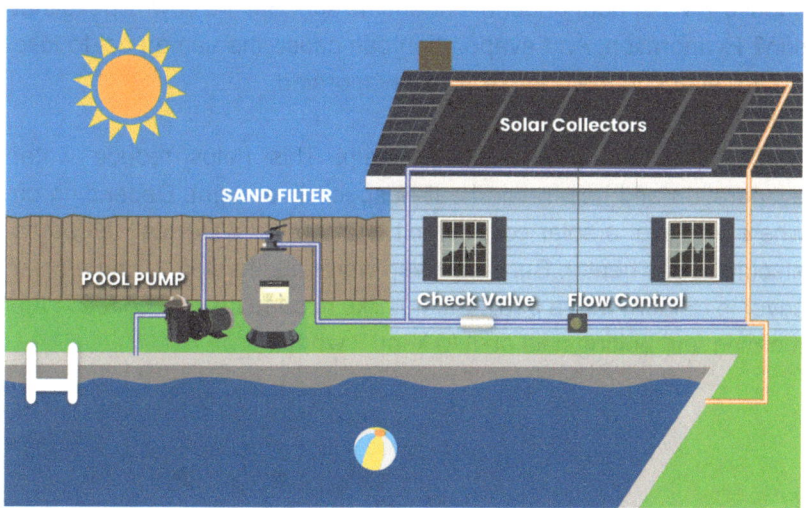

If you're considering installing high-quality glazed solar panels, your initial investment might be higher than other heaters. They average between $3,000 and $4,000 to buy and install but will pay you back over time with energy savings. With an average lifespan of 15–20 years, they're more durable than gas or heat pump models, too. Alternatively, you may also want to consider DIY solar options. Solar domes or rubber or plastic collectors are usually smaller and allow you to install them yourself. And they still operate the same way by collecting the sun's rays and warming the pool water as it passes through. DIY solar options are great for smaller pools. A solar dome, for example, can raise the temperature of your pool water by up to 10°F, especially over several sunny days. But they can be a bit challenging to install and require some extra connectors if you're trying to position it where there's more sun. Finally, if you really want to save money or you're feeling handy, you can try making your own solar heater with black irrigation hose and a sump pump.

Solar Covers

Regardless of how you heat your pool, we recommend getting some type of surface protection—like a solar cover—so you don't lose water and heat from evaporation. Your pool water absorbs sunlight and warmth just by sitting out in the sun. And an average pool will heat up about 0.7°F per hour under the noontime sun. But the downside to that sun? Evaporation. And evaporation can cause the same pool to lose 5°F for every quarter inch of water evaporated.

Here's where solar pool covers help. This helps reduce water evaporation and help retain heat—especially at night. Depending on where you live, a solar cover won't heat up the water as well as an electric or gas heater. But it will keep water and heat in. Using a solar cover in tandem with a pool heater is like heating up your coffee in the morning and putting a lid on it to keep it warm.

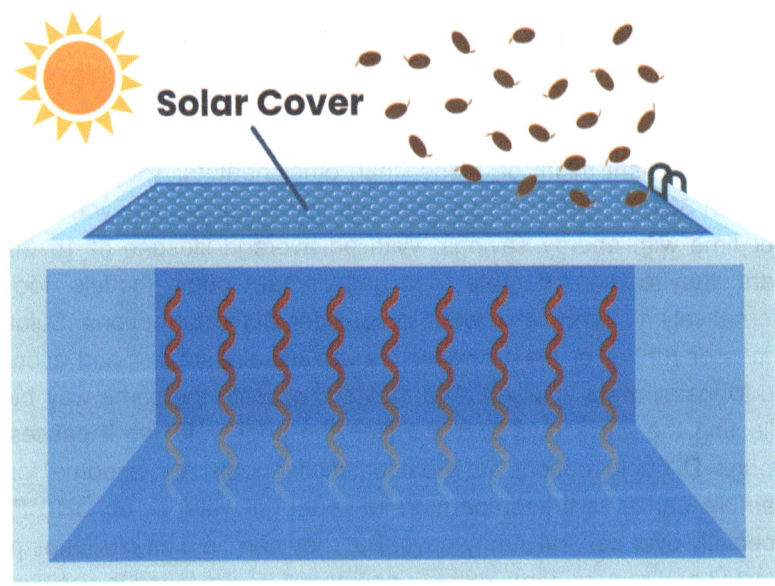

Solar Cover Types

There are three types of solar covers: blankets, rings, and liquid. Solar blankets are large sheets of insulating plastic that look like bubble wrap and lie on top of your pool water. They not only capture the energy of the sun, but they also keep heat in by reducing water evaporation. A solar blanket can prevent 35 to 60 percent of your pool water chemicals from disappearing.

Solar blankets come in three colors:

Clear Solar Covers

These allow more of the sun's heat to penetrate the water and can increase the water temperature by about 15ºF degrees and prevent up to 95% of pool water and chemical evaporation.

Dark Blue Solar Covers

Dark blue solar covers, on the other hand, are great for heat retention. So if you have a gas heater or pool heat pump, your heater won't need to run as long with a dark blue cover.

Classic Blue Solar Covers

These are the midrange option, giving you both the benefits and downsides of a clear and dark blue cover.

Use Solar Blankets Bubble Side Down!

Place your solar blanket bubble side facing down to better heat your pool. As the sun heats the blanket and the bubbles, the bubbles will transfer heat to your pool water.

If you have a large pool or if you swim often, removing the solar blanket can be a little bit annoying. Consider investing in a solar reel. Or you can cut the solar blanket into smaller panels and remove the pieces one at a time.

Another option is to use solar rings instead of a full blanket. Just toss these round discs on your pool when you're not using it to help gain and retain heat.

Liquid Solar Covers: Do They Work?

Liquid solar covers are made from a fatty alcohol that forms a thin layer on top of water and helps prevent evaporation. You can't see it, you can't feel it, and it's safe to swim in. But while liquid solar covers are easier to use, solar blankets are about 25 percent more effective at keeping heat and water in the pool.

Aeration

Pool aerators are a great way to help keep your water cooler and improve your pool's circulation. Aeration happens when a water feature (an aerator, fountain, mister, etc.) pulls air into the water to increase oxygen levels. Dedicated aerators are usually attached to the side of your pool (like your coping or deck) and connected to your return line.

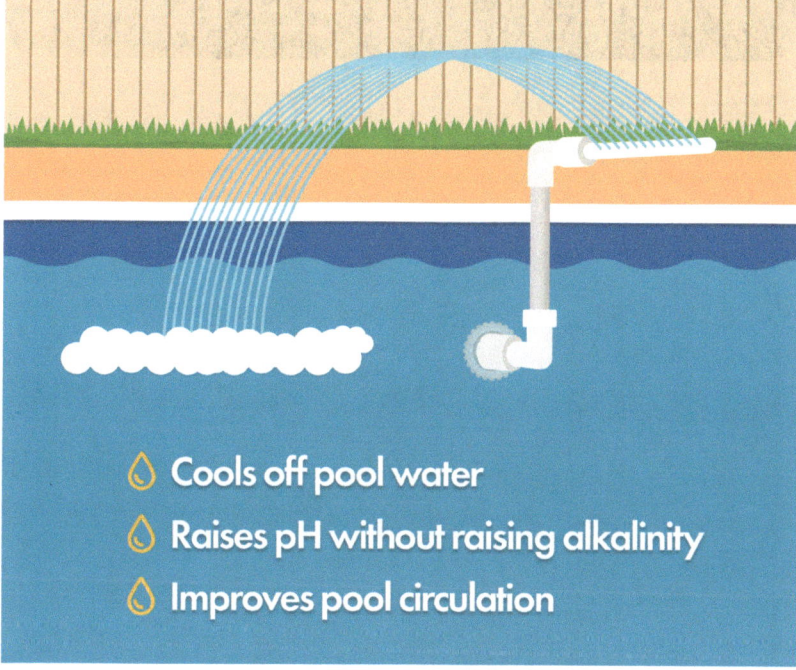

◊ Cools off pool water
◊ Raises pH without raising alkalinity
◊ Improves pool circulation

Exposing water to air will help cool down your pool water, which is especially helpful with hot climates or shallow pools. The additional oxygen created by aeration can reduce your pool water temperature by up to 4°F. And aerating the water is a natural way of raising your pH without affecting your other chemistry levels. For the quickest way to cool your water, run the aerator at night. Cooler air temperatures will bring down the water's temperature faster than running it during the day.

175

Don't Over Aerate Your Pool!

Over aeration can raise your pH levels beyond the recommended range. And high pH levels can damage your pool equipment. To test the effects of aeration on your water, run your aerator or natural aeration features, like fountains and hot tub jets. Then take a reading one or two days later. If your pH has risen dramatically with all other levels equal, you might be over aerating your water.

7

~~~

SALT WATER POOL MAINTENANCE

179

SALT WATER POOL MAINTENANCE

Salt water pool maintenance involves the same core principles as other pools: good circulation, cleanliness, and chemistry. And the pool anatomy looks the same, with the addition of a salt water system installed right before the water returns to your pool:

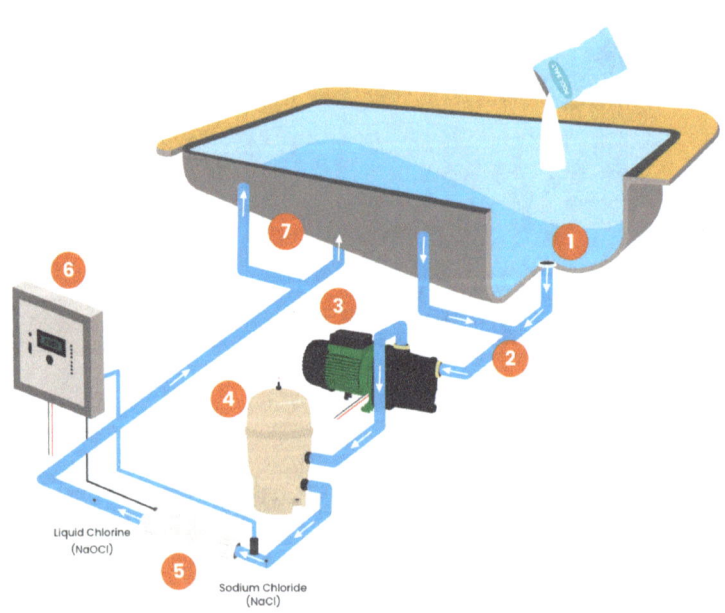

Liquid Chlorine
(NaOCl)

Sodium Chloride
(NaCl)

Salt Water Vs. Traditional Chlorine Pools

Both a salt water pool and a chlorine pool use chlorine to sanitize the water. Regular chlorine pools need chlorine to be added directly to the water.

On the other hand, salt water pool systems use salt that's added to the water to turn it into chlorine. That's right: a salt water pool is still a chlorine pool!

The salt water passes through a system known as a salt chlorine generator or salt water generator. It uses electricity to break the salt down into sodium and chlorine.

Salt water pools have other benefits, like a smoother water feel, less irritation for swimmers, and less fluctuation in chlorine levels:

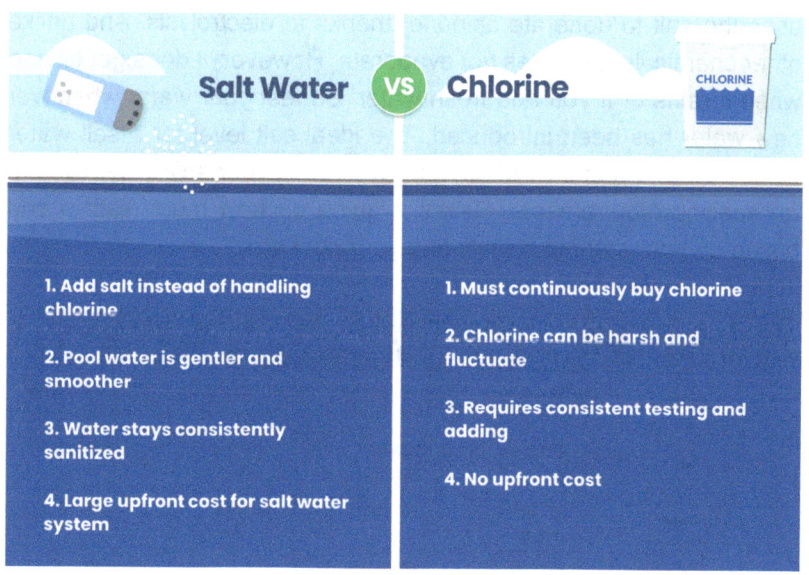

Salt Water VS **Chlorine**

Salt Water	Chlorine
1. Add salt instead of handling chlorine	1. Must continuously buy chlorine
2. Pool water is gentler and smoother	2. Chlorine can be harsh and fluctuate
3. Water stays consistently sanitized	3. Requires consistent testing and adding
4. Large upfront cost for salt water system	4. No upfront cost

When it comes to salt water pool care, there are a few key differences, including watching for high pH and cleaning your salt water cell. Here are the key components to salt water pool maintenance:

1. Add the Right Amount of Salt
2. Maintain Proper Water Circulation
3. Prevent Erosion and Calcium Buildup
4. Check Your Salt Cell Every 3 Months
5. Keep Your Water Balanced, Especially pH and Chlorine
6. Shock Your Pool Every Week
7. Skim, Brush, and Vacuum Every Week

1. Add the Right Amount of Salt

Once you add the initial amount of salt to your water (either when you fill your pool or at the start of the season), you likely won't need any additional salt. That's because your salt water generator continuously uses the salt to generate chlorine, thanks to electrolysis. And unlike other chemicals, salt does not evaporate. However, it does get diluted when it rains or if you add fresh water. So test your water whenever new water has been introduced. The ideal salt level for a salt water pool is around 3,200 PPM. But always check your salt water system for specific requirements. Here's a guide on how much salt to add based on your starting salinity and your pool size:

How Much Pool Salt to Add				
Current Salt Level	10,000 Gallons (37,500 Liters)	20,000 Gallons (75,000 Liters)	30,000 Gallons (112,500 Liters)	40,000 Gallons (150,000 Liters)
0 PPM	267 lbs (121 kg)	533 lbs (242 kg)	800 lbs (364 kg)	1,067 lbs (484 kg)
1,000 PPM	183 lbs (83 kg)	367 lbs (167 kg)	550 lbs (250 kg)	733 lbs (333 kg)
2,000 PPM	100 lbs (45 kg)	200 lbs (91 kg)	300 lbs (136 kg)	400 lbs (181 kg)
3,000 PPM	17 lbs (8 kg)	33 lbs (15 kg)	50 lbs (23 kg)	67 lbs (30 kg)

For example, if you're starting with no salt (0 PPM) and you have a 10,000-gallon pool, you'll need to add 267 pounds of salt. That's about seven 40-pound bags of pool-grade salt.

Remember you can always add more salt if you need to. Start slowly and let the salt circulate and dissolve. Then retest your salinity.

> **Test Your Salt Water Levels Manually Once per Month**
>
> Sometimes a salt water generator can give you an inaccurate salt reading. It's smart to verify how much salt is in your water once a month with a digital salinity reader or salt water test strips.

2. Maintain Proper Water Circulation

If your pool water isn't circulating well, your salt concentration may get too high in some areas. Double-check your salt levels in multiple areas around your pool to make sure the numbers are consistent.

If there's a drastic difference between numbers, angle your return jets toward the pockets of salinity to help circulate dead zones. And keep your water circulating by running your pump and filter at least 8 hours a day.

3. Prevent Erosion and Calcium Buildup

Splash out can cause high concentrations of salt outside of your pool. That can erode parts of your pool, especially limestone or other soft stone coping. So be sure to hose down the area around your pool.

Splash out can also lead to high concentrations of salt on the outside of your pool liner, so rinse this off as well. Finally, if you have an automatic pool cover, rinse off its metal tracks and hardware with a hose every few weeks.

If you see white flakes in your pool, that's usually not salt — it's a buildup of calcium carbonate. Calcium flakes are caused by the high pH byproduct and scale formation in your salt cell. This can happen when you first turn on your salt water generator at the beginning of the season, and it usually resolves after it runs for a bit. But salt water generators are prone to calcium buildup, so avoid using chlorine shocks with calcium, like cal-hypo shock, and be sure to regularly clean your salt cell.

Finally, very high pH levels can also cause corrosion of your pool equipment, so be sure to test and balance your pool's pH regularly.

4. Check Your Salt Cell Every 3 Months

Calcium can build up on your salt cell over time. Even if you don't see calcium flakes in your water, you could have buildup on your salt cell. And if your pH levels or pool water temperature is too high, calcium will build up faster.

Inspect the cell at least every three months, and clean it by hand or with a hose to remove buildup. You can also use a diluted solution of muriatic acid to remove deposits. But be sure to follow any cleaning directions that came with your salt water generator.

Start by turning off the salt water generator and other connected pool equipment. Then unplug the generator and unscrew and remove the salt cell. Inspect the metal plates, looking for white and flakey spots on the metal inside.

If there are no deposits, reassemble the system and check it again in another few months. But if you do see visible deposits, remove any large deposits by hand without forcing your hands into the cell. Rinse the cell with a hose to remove the remnants.

If you still can't remove the deposits, you can use a solution of 5:1 water to muriatic acid. Wear protective gear like a face mask and gloves, and pour the acid into the water to mix it. Cap the cell and pour the acid solution into the salt cell. Allow it to foam for 10 minutes.

When it's done, pour the solution back into the bucket. Use a hose to wash the inside of the cell and put the system back together. Limit chemically cleaning your salt cell as much as you can since using chemicals will damage the cell over time. And do not pour the leftover acid solution on the ground or into your pipes.

5. Keep Your Water Balanced, Especially pH and Chlorine

Your chemistry levels are important whether or not you have a salt water pool, but there are some nuances and challenges you'll face with your pH and free chlorine levels.

While your salt water generator should display the correct chlorine levels in your water, there are times when the system might not be working correctly. And as we mentioned before, salt water systems produce naturally high pH levels. So testing and balancing your water regularly, especially your pH and chlorine, is crucial.

1. Test Free Chlorine Levels Every Week

Keeping your free chlorine levels around 3 PPM ensures that your water is properly sanitized. And while your salt water generator should tell you how much chlorine is in the water, it's worth running a quick 15-second test each week to make sure it's measuring things properly.

Every week, use a liquid test kit or test strips to check the amount of free chlorine in your water. Then adjust your generator accordingly if you find your chlorine levels aren't what they should be.

It's fine to keep the amount of chlorine in your pool a bit higher than 3 PPM. That's because your salt water generator produces and disperses chlorine more evenly throughout the water.

2. Balance Your pH Levels Weekly

Your pH levels can run a bit high in a salt water pool since your salt water generator naturally produces high pH. However, high pH levels (pH above 7.8) can lead to eye and skin irritation as well as scaling on your pool equipment.

That's why you need to test and balance your pH every week. And if you do need to lower your pH levels, you can use pH decreaser or muriatic acid.

Finally, double-check the run times on your salt water generator, since running the salt water pool system is what causes high pH levels. Try not to run your salt system for more than 10 hours every day.

3. Manually Test Salinity Levels Each Month

The majority of salt water generators will display your water's salinity level. But it's always a good idea to test your salt levels manually to make sure your system is working correctly and not displaying a false reading.

Check your salinity levels once a month. Also, check your salt levels after heavy rain or if you had to drain out a significant amount of water.

You can use salt water test strips, but we recommend using a digital salinity reader.

4. Test and Balance Alkalinity, Stabilizer, and Calcium Monthly

In addition to monthly salinity testing, you need to test your alkalinity, stabilizer (or cyanuric acid), and calcium levels every month.

- **Alkalinity:** Total alkalinity acts as a buffer to protect your pH level from fluctuation. But because running your salt water generator naturally increases your pH level, your total alkalinity has less of an impact on your pH. Ideally, your alkalinity level should be between 100 and 150 PPM. But it's all right if your alkalinity levels are slightly below 100 PPM since your pH runs high.

- **Cyanuric Acid:** Also known as CYA or stabilizer, your cyanuric acid levels usually need to be between 30 and 50 PPM. But some salt water pool owners find that it helps to maintain higher CYA levels of up to 80 PPM, particularly for those who find it difficult to maintain an adequate chlorine level.

- **Calcium Hardness:** Your calcium hardness level should be between 200 and 400 PPM. If you have high calcium hardness levels, the mineral can calcify and damage your salt cell or cause scale buildup. If your calcium hardness is too high, you'll need to drain some of your pool water and dilute it with fresh water.

6. Shock Your Pool Every Week

Adding a super concentrated dose of chlorine to your water helps kill algae and bacteria and refreshes your active free chlorine. If your salt water generator is equipped with a "boost" setting, that'll add extra chlorine from your salt water system. This is a great setting to use weekly to help kill contaminants.

You can also add a non-chlorine shock to help keep your chlorine working and active in the water. But if you're experiencing issues like algae, you'll want to add a more powerful dose of chlorine by using granular dichlor shock or liquid chlorine.

When using a stabilized shock like dichlor, keep an eye on your CYA levels afterward. And avoid using cal-hypo shock because it can cause calcium buildup in your salt cell.

We recommend using the boost mode on your generator or shocking your pool once a week, after heavy use, or after a heavy storm. Be sure to retest your water the following day and rebalance any chemicals as needed.

7. Skim, Brush, and Vacuum Every Week

Like any pool, you'll want to make sure your water is free from debris and your pool surfaces are clean. So once a week, use a skimmer net, pool brush, and pool vacuum to clean your water.

This will not only help keep the surfaces clean, but it will keep the salt in your water circulating properly.

8

~~~

INTEX OR SMALLER POOL MAINTENANCE

INTEX OR SMALLER POOL MAINTENANCE

Intex pools have a lot of the same needs as larger-sized pools. But because they hold less water, they have some specific equipment and chemical requirements. So like any pool, be sure you know how many gallons of water your pool holds.

Besides maintaining good water circulation, cleanliness, and chemistry, here are a few specific maintenance tips to keep in mind for Intex pools or any type of smaller above ground pool with a pump and filter system.

1. Water Testing and Balancing is Extra Important

Smaller pools are more susceptible to chemical fluctuations. That's why it's so important to test and balance your water often during the pool season, especially if your pool is getting a lot of use or there's lots of debris or rain getting into your pool.

Ideally, you'll want to test and adjust your water twice a week. But definitely at least once a week.

2. Use the Right Amount of Sanitizer

Use granular chlorine or smaller one-inch chlorine pucks instead of larger three-inch tablets. Granular chlorine works well for small pools because you can broadcast the chlorine evenly around the water and add just enough based on your pool size.

While chlorine tablets are very convenient, they can get stuck in one spot in your pool if you're using a chlorine floater. Be sure to use the smaller one-inch tablets and pay attention to the dial on your floater.

And regardless of how you sanitize your pool, be sure to keep your pool filter system on and circulating when you use them.

Finally, some Intex pool owners use bleach to sanitize their water. Since it's such a low concentration of chlorine, you might need to add a lot of it. And keep in mind that it will burn up in the sun, so be sure to test your water regularly, even twice a week, if you choose to use bleach. Also keep your chlorine levels in the appropriate range.

How Long Do You Need to Wait After You Add Chemicals in a Smaller Pool?

Wait 20 minutes to an hour after you adjust your alkalinity and pH. It needs to fully mix into the water with your system running before testing again. Then retest your water and add chlorine and your CYA (if needed). Wait another 20 minutes to an hour, keeping the filter system running.

3. Use the Right Shock

For Intex pools, we recommend shocking your pool once a week, using a non-chlorine shock. Adding weekly non-chlorine shock speeds up the process of oxidizing chloramines, keeps your water sanitized, and helps fight algae.

If you use chlorine shock, you run the risk of your chlorine levels getting too high with a smaller amount of water. Just make sure your pH, alkalinity, and chlorine levels are always in the right ranges before you shock your pool.

Shock is usually sold in one-pound bags (for 10,000 gallons of water). If your pool only holds 5,000 gallons, you'll only need half of that. So look for non-chlorine shock sold in a plastic container with a sealable lid. That way, you're not opening loose bags of shock and leaving chemicals exposed to the air. Non-chlorine shock for hot tubs usually comes in smaller containers and is perfectly fine to use in your pool.

Finally, if you have a major pool problem, like algae or bodily waste, you'll want to use chlorine shock because it's way more potent.

4. Don't Worry about Calcium Hardness with Temporary Pools

You may see a calcium hardness reading in your testing kit. But you don't need to worry about adjusting your calcium hardness if you take your pool down every year.

This level only really affects inground pools made of concrete and plaster.

5. Upgrade Your Cartridge Filter

If your pool came with a standard-issue cartridge filter, you may want to consider upgrading it. While it's perfectly functional, you might see improved performance with a different model that has better filtration materials.

6. Backwash Your Sand Filter in Shorter Rounds

If you have a sand filter, you'll still need to backwash it to keep it clean. But smaller or Intex sand filters can benefit from shorter cycles.

Backwash for one minute and then rinse for one minute. Repeat this cycle for three rounds to avoid blowing anything back into the pool.

7. Install a Skimmer Basket

If you don't have a skimmer basket in your pool, it's an affordable investment and easy to install.

Skimmer baskets are critical as the first line of defense for your filter, catching leaves and debris before water flows into your system.

8. Use an Easy Hand-Held Vacuum

There are filter-line vacuums that you can attach to your filter pump system. Water is vacuumed through your filter and out the waste line onto the ground.

However, if you want something easier for weekly pool cleaning, you may want to consider a rechargeable manual vacuum. It uses internal power instead of your pool's filter system to clean.

For bigger jobs, like algae, you may want to have a vacuum that connects to the filter pump to get good suction. But for smaller jobs and weekly maintenance, a "pool dustbuster" is a really handy and easy tool.

9

POOL OPENING AND START-UP

POOL OPENING AND START-UP

Opening your pool is easy to do on your own if you know what steps to take in what order. Even if you open your cover and find an algae infestation, you can get your pool clean and clear in a few days with the right chemicals. And with some simple maintenance tasks right when you open, you can ensure your equipment and filter system run smoothly the rest of the season. In this section, you'll learn about:

1. **When to Open Your Pool:** Learn the right time to open your pool so you can avoid algae issues.

2. **How to Open an Inground Pool:** Learn the correct steps to open an inground pool, including restarting your pump-filter system and what start-up chemicals to add.

3. **How to Open an Above Ground Pool:** Learn the correct steps to open an above ground pool, including proper cover removal and adding start-up chemicals.

When to Open Your Pool

As a general rule of thumb, you should open your pool when the outside daytime temperature stays consistently above 70°F (21°C). This is still a little too cold to go swimming, but it's not too cold for algae to grow.

As the weather starts to warm up, algae can start to grow in your pool water—especially if you use a mesh pool cover and the water is exposed to sunlight. Springtime is also "pollen season," and that can start collecting in your pool with mesh covers.

So to help prevent algae and stop pollen from collecting in your water, open your pool and run your filter and pump when daytime temperatures are a steady 70°F degrees.

How Do You Know if the Weather will Stay Above 70 Degrees?

Start by checking out the historical weather averages in your area. Depending on where you live, you may hit the 70-degree sweet spot sooner than you think.

Most pool owners in the U.S. open their pools between May 1st and May 15th, just before Memorial Day Weekend.

How to Open an Inground Pool

Before you begin, you'll want to make sure you've got all your tools and supplies ready. You'll probably already have some of the items on hand, but you might need to restock some supplies and chemicals. And when it's time to start the pool-opening process, be sure to enlist the help of a friend, neighbor, or family member.

Opening Supplies

- Start-up chemicals or start-up kit
- Pool cover pump
- Soft broom
- Winter cover cleaner or car wash soap
- Pool gasket lubricant
- Thread seal tape
- Skimmer net
- Garden hose with filter
- Pool brush
- Pool vacuum
- Safety goggles
- Chemical-resistant gloves
- Shock
- Test strips

Start-up Chemicals

A pool start-up chemical kit includes everything you need to get your pool ready. But you may already have a lot of the chemicals on hand, and you might not need everything that comes in a kit.

You'll need:

- pH increaser
- pH decreaser
- Alkalinity increaser
- Calcium hardness increaser
- Metal sequestrant
- Water clarifier
- Shock

1. Clean off the Pool Cover

Use a soft broom to sweep away any dead leaves or other large debris from your winter cover. Then use a pool cover pump to remove any standing water from your cover.

Some of these pumps can be a bit slow at removing water, while others will suck up debris and just about anything else that gets in their way. Know what your pool cover pump is capable of so you won't overwork it.

2. Remove Pool Cover

This is when having an extra set of hands will be a big help. You'll need to lay your cover somewhere flat to clean it—and you'll have to move it to that flat spot without dragging it over any rough surfaces. Have your partner stand on the opposite side of the pool from you to help you lift and fold the cover back and forth on itself, like an accordion.

Pool opening is also a good time to inspect your cover to see how it fared over the winter. If it's damaged, now's the time to replace your pool cover so you have a new one waiting for you when you close your pool after the season. And if it's beyond help, you can skip the pool cover cleaning and storing.

3. Clean and Store Your Pool Cover

With your cover folded up, have your friend help you move it to your yard and spread it out flat. That small step will help make your pool cover cleaning easier and go much more quickly. Apply pool cover cleaner or car wash soap and use a soft broom to scrub it gently. Avoid using any abrasive or sharp tools or harsh chemical cleaners, which could destroy your pool cover.

Rinse away all the cleaner or soap with a hose. Dry the cover with a towel or leaf blower before folding it up again. Store the cover inside a storage bag or heavy-duty container with a lid. If you used water weights, empty them and allow them to dry completely before storing.

Protect Your Cover in Storage

Do not store your pool cover on the ground or the floor of your shed or garage. Bugs, rodents, and other pests can damage it over the summer.

4. Skim the Pool

Use a skimmer net or leaf net to grab anything that has fallen into your water. You'll be doing more cleaning later but getting all the big stuff out now will make all the other cleaning you do easier. So remove any large debris that could clog your filtration system when you turn it back on.

5. Remove Winterizing Plugs and Ice Compensator

When you closed your pool for the winter, you likely blew out the pipes and installed winterizing plugs to prevent water from getting back into them and freezing. You'll need to walk around the pool and remove all those plugs.

You should see some bubbles as the pool water flows back into the pipes. This is normal. If you used an ice compensator or a soda bottle inside your skimmer, you'll need to remove it and the winterizing plugs that are in there. Replace the filter basket at this time too.

6. Reinstall Accessories

Do you have a pool ladder, diving board, step rails, slide, or other accessories you removed for the winter? Reinstall all the items you removed at the end of pool season.

This is a good time to lubricate bolts and grease your diving boards hinges.

7. Add Water

You've probably lost a few inches of water over the off-season, even with a winter cover on your pool. Be sure to use a garden hose with a filter attachment.

The filter helps prevent metals and minerals from getting into your pool. Make sure the water level is at least halfway up the skimmer.

8. Set Up and Run Your Filter and Pump

Reinstall the drain plugs in your pump and filter using thread seal tape. Lubricate any O-rings with pool gasket lubricant to protect them. Use the same lubricant on your pump housing O-ring. If you see any cracks in that O-ring, replace it immediately to avoid sucking air into your pump. And if you have a pool heater or automatic chlorinator, these also have drain plugs that need replacing.

Before you start running water through your pool system, take a look at your filter. Wash or replace any filter media, like cartridges, if necessary. Replace the air bleeder, sight glass, and pressure gauge if they were removed for the winter.

Next, open your return side valves. This means water being pulled into your pump has somewhere to go (i.e. it returns to your pool).

Switch your multiport valve to filter. Flip your circuit breaker, then turn on your pump. Once water is flowing through, your pump is primed. If you need help priming your pump, check out the Troubleshooting Section.

If your pressure gauge shows a sudden spike, shut off your pump immediately. Check to make sure nothing is impeding water flowing through your system. If necessary, prime the pool pump again.

You may also need to backwash your filter if the pressure gauge is still too high.

> ### What about Antifreeze?
>
> If you used antifreeze when you closed your pool, you can expel it from your lines by turning your multiport valve to waste. But a little antifreeze may still make it into your pool water. Don't be concerned. The antifreeze made for pools is nontoxic, and the rest of it will be filtered out in subsequent filtering cycles.

9. Brush and Vacuum the Pool

After your filter is running, it's time to brush and vacuum. Brushing can help remove any algae spores clinging to the walls. Vacuuming your pool will help manually pick up any sediment or dirt on your pool floor.

10. Test and Adjust Metal Content in Your Water

While your pool water sat stagnant through the winter, your metal levels may have increased. To avoid the staining and buildup caused by any metal in your pool water, add a metal sequestrant. Unsure what your metal levels look like? You may want to run a water sample over to your pool supply store when you open your swimming pool for the season. This will give you an accurate baseline of the metal content to work from for the rest of the season.

11. Test and Balance Alkalinity, pH, Calcium Hardness

Once you've tested your water, it's time to start balancing your chemicals. Remember, adjust alkalinity first, then pH, and finally calcium hardness. Avoid adding any chemicals you don't need at this stage. And you'll be shocking your water in a later step, so you don't need to worry about chlorine or sanitizer levels yet.

12. Shock Your Water

To kill algae spores, bacteria, and get your water sparkling clean, you'll need pool shock. We recommend double shocking at pool opening. To double shock, you'll use two pounds of chlorine shock (for chlorine or salt systems) per 10,000 gallons of water. Before you add chlorine to your pool, wear safety goggles and chemical-resistant gloves. And be sure to shock at night if you use cal-hypo shock.

What about Algaecide?

Algaecide is effective at tackling early-stage algae growth or as a preventive maintenance measure. However, because you're shocking your pool and balancing the water, you should be able to kill any of the algae spores present and prevent anything from blooming later.

13. Filter for 24 Hours

Leave your filtration system running for at least 24 hours to mix up the shock and filter remaining debris, dead algae spores, and any other gunk.By the next day, your pool should be crystal clear. If it looks a little cloudy, that may be from the shock. You can either wait a little longer for it to dissipate or add a dose of pool water clarifier to clear it more quickly.

Salt Water Pool Owners: Time to Add Salt!

After you've balanced your other chemicals and shocked your water, it's time to add salt and get your salt water system up and working. Be sure to wait until the chlorine levels have dropped back into the normal range after shocking. Check out the Salt Water Pool Maintenance Section for more information on how much salt to add.

14. Retest Water and Adjust CYA

Be sure to retest your chlorine levels to make sure they're in the correct range (1 to 3 PPM). Add sanitizer to your pool, like chlorine tablets, and set your automatic chlorinator or floater.

And before you start using your pool, test and balance your CYA levels (cyanuric acid) so your chlorine doesn't get destroyed by the sun. If you're using stabilized chlorine that already contains CYA (like chlorine pucks), you likely don't need to add any additional CYA.

Final Cleanup and Safety Inspection

To ensure everyone's safety in and around your pool, here are some precautions to take after you've opened it:

- Spray your pool deck down thoroughly with a hose to rinse away any chemicals that may have spilled where swimmers could step in them.

- Be sure to test all the safeguards around your pool area, such as gate locks and door alarms. If anything isn't working properly, fix it as soon as possible.

- Store your chemicals safely and out of reach of children and pets. Keep them in a cool, dry place in their original packaging. Be sure the containers are closed properly and chemicals are not stored mixed or too close to each other.

How to Open an Above Ground Pool

Once you learn how to open an above ground pool, the process will become easier every year. All you need is the right supplies, a little elbow grease, and at least one other person to help. The basic supplies for opening your pool are probably ones you already have on hand. But make sure you have everything you need before starting the opening process.

Opening Supplies

- Start-up chemicals or start-up kit
- Pool cover pump or sump pump
- Soft broom
- Winter cover cleaner or car wash soap
- Skimmer net
- Garden hose with filter
- Pool brush
- Pool vacuum
- Safety goggles
- Chemical-resistant gloves
- Shock
- Test strips

Start-up Chemicals

A start-up chemical kit includes everything you need to get your pool ready. But you may already have a lot of the chemicals on hand. And you might not need everything that comes in a kit. You'll need:

- pH increaser
- pH decreaser
- Alkalinity increaser
- Calcium hardness increaser
- Metal sequestrant
- Water clarifier
- Shock

1. Clear Your Winter Pool Cover

Whether you have a pool safety cover or a winter cover, your first priority is removing the water, leaves, and debris. A pool cover pump makes short work of any excess water. You can also use a regular sump pump if you don't have a pool cover pump.

Then remove leaves and other debris with a soft broom. Be gentle since sharp equipment or overly enthusiastic sweeping can damage your cover. Try to remove as much of the debris as you can. The more you remove now, the less you have to worry about falling into the water when you remove the cover.

2. Remove Winter Pool Cover and Air Pillow

With another person's help, carefully remove the cover. Don't drag it across the ground, and take care to keep any lingering debris from falling into the pool.

If you've installed a pool air pillow with your cover, be sure to remove it along with your cover. You can deflate the air pillow once it's safely out of your pool.

3. Clean and Store Your Winter Pool Cover

Find a large flat area, like your lawn, deck, or driveway, and spread the cover flat. Make sure the area is clear of sharp objects and other potentially damaging items.

Wash your cover with water, cover cleaner (or car wash soap), and a scrub brush or soft broom. Scrub it thoroughly but gently. Make sure you allow your cover to dry thoroughly before storing it to avoid damage from moisture and mold.

Stash your winter cover in a durable tightly sealed plastic tub or other large storage container during the off-season. This will keep critters from damaging it while it's stored away.

4. Remove Winter Pool Plugs, Ice Compensators, Skimmer Plate

Start removing your winterizing pool plugs. Carefully check all around your pool, and remove plugs from all openings, including the return jets (also called eyeball fittings) and skimmer bucket. If you use an ice compensator or soda bottle in your skimmer bucket, be sure to remove that too.

Reinstall all your skimmer baskets and return jets. If you used a skimmer plate (also called a skimmer cover) over the winter, make sure you remove it.

A skimmer plate is designed to keep water out of your skimmer during the winter while allowing you to keep your pool filled. Once it's gone, water can flow easily when you reactivate your pool's filter system.

5. Add Water To Your Pool

Depending on how you closed your pool, you may need to add water. When you add water, use a hose filter to screen out impurities. Make sure your pool is filled to the halfway mark of your skimmer's opening.

6. Reinstall Your Deck Equipment

Reinstall your deck gear. This includes ladders, steps, or lifts. Double-check each component for rust or other damage. If anything seems flimsy, damaged, or worn out, now's the time to replace it.

7. Set Up Your Pump, Filter, and Other Equipment

It's time to get your pool equipment running. First, put back all the plugs in the drains and pressure gauges to your pool filter system, pump, and other equipment. Don't forget to make sure the ground wires are properly connected to the pump. Next, attach your system's hoses to your equipment, and double-check the connections.

1. Connect the skimmer to the pool pump.

2. Connect the pump to the filter.

3. Connect the filter to the heater, chlorinator, and any other extra filter equipment. If you don't have any, attach the hose directly to the return inlet.

8. Start Your Pump and Filter

If you have a multiport valve, make sure it's turned to the filter position. And make sure any valves, including the return valves, are open so water can flow through all the plumbing. Then turn on the system. Make sure the system starts and check for any leaks or drips.

If you find your system is running dry, you may need to prime the pool pump. (See Troubleshooting Section.)

If your pressure gauge shows a sudden spike, shut off your pump immediately. Check to make sure nothing is impeding water flowing through your system. If necessary, prime the pool pump again. You may also need to backwash your filter if the pressure gauge is still too high.

9. Clean Your Pool

Brush your pool, including the walls and any hard-to-reach nooks and crannies. This will remove any algae spores and contaminants clinging to the surfaces. And skim the surface of the water to collect any floating leaves, bugs, or other debris that may have snuck in while you've been busy doing everything else. If you have a lot of sediment at the bottom of your pool, you'll need to vacuum your pool as well.

10. Add Start-up Chemicals

Break out your test kit and test your pool water to make sure all the chemicals are properly balanced. If you want to establish a baseline reading to follow through the rest of pool season, you can take a sample of your pool water to your nearest pool dealer and have them test it for you. Once you've tested your water (either at the pool store or with your own test kit), it's time to start balancing your water. Remember, adjust alkalinity first, then pH, and finally calcium hardness. You'll be shocking your water in a later step, so you don't need to worry about chlorine yet.

11. Shock Your Pool

Once you've got your water balanced, you'll want to shock your pool. Use two pounds of pool shock for every 10,000 gallons of pool water. This is a double shock, giving your pool twice the dose of shock to kill any contaminants in the water. Don't forget to shock at night or at dusk to keep sunlight from burning off the shock too quickly.

What about Algaecide?

Algaecide is effective at tackling early-stage algae growth or as a preventative maintenance measure. However, because you're shocking your pool and balancing the water, you should be able to kill any of the algae spores present and prevent anything from blooming later.

12. Filter for 24 Hours

Once you've shocked your pool, let your pool pump run for at least 24 hours. Then retest your pool water. It may be cloudy at this point, which is a sign that there's dead algae in the water.

You can use a flocculant or clarifier to speed up the process.

Salt Water Pool Owners: Time to Add Salt!

After you've balanced your other chemicals and shocked your water, it's time to add salt and get your salt water system up and working. Be sure to wait until the chlorine levels have dropped back into the normal range after shocking. Check out the Salt Water Pool Maintenance Section for more information on how much salt to add.

14. Retest Water and Adjust CYA

Be sure to retest your chlorine levels to make sure they're in the correct range (1 to 3 PPM). Add sanitizer to your pool, like chlorine tablets, and set your automatic chlorinator or floater.

And before you start using your pool, test and balance your CYA levels so your chlorine doesn't get destroyed by the sun. If you're using stabilized chlorine that already contains CYA (like chlorine pucks), you likely don't need to add any additional CYA.

Final Cleanup and Safety Inspection

To ensure everyone's safety in and around your pool, here are some precautions to take after you've opened it:

- If you have an above ground pool deck, spray it down thoroughly with a hose to rinse away any chemicals that may have spilled where swimmers could step in them.

- Be sure to test all the safeguards around your pool area, such as gate locks and door alarms. If anything isn't working properly, fix it as soon as possible.

- Store your chemicals safely and out of reach of children and pets. Keep them in a cool, dry place in their original packaging. Be sure the containers are closed properly and chemicals are not stored mixed or too close to each other.

10

~~~

POOL CLOSING AND WINTERIZING

POOL CLOSING AND WINTERIZING

You can save a lot of money by learning how to properly close and winterize your pool. Not only can you avoid paying a service company to do the work, but you'll also properly protect your equipment so it will last for years to come. With the right chemicals and closing sequence, you can prevent winter temperatures from damaging your cover and plumbing. In this section, you'll learn about:

1. **When to Close Your Pool:** Learn the right time to close your pool so you can protect your equipment from cold temperatures.

2. **Pool Closing Kits:** Compare the chemicals in pool closing kits with what you actually need.

3. **How to Winterize an Inground Pool:** Learn the correct steps to close an inground pool, including blowing out the lines and protecting your equipment.

4. **How to Winterize an Above Ground Pool:** Learn the proper steps to close an above ground pool, including protecting your pool from collapsing in the off-season.

5. **How to Winterize a Temporary Small or Intex Pool:** Learn how to properly take down and store a temporary pool.

When to Close Your Pool

The timing of winterizing your pool is crucial. If you live in a colder climate, wait until the temperature falls and stays below 65°F (18°C). Lower temperatures are inhospitable to algae and can help the water stay cleaner longer. Otherwise, if it's still too warm out, you risk incubating algae underneath the cover.

But what if you live in a climate that sees several warm days over the winter? If temperatures reach 65°F (18°C) or more after you close, you might need to add an algaecide underneath the cover.

Finally, if you live somewhere without freezing temperatures, you won't need to take any freeze prevention measures we mention later on. Be sure to check out the Off-Season and Year-Round Pool Maintenance Section.

How Do You Know if the Weather will Stay Below 65 Degrees?

Start by checking out the historical weather averages in your area. Depending on where you live, you may hit the 65-degree sweet spot sooner than you think.

Most pool owners in the U.S. close their pools between September 15th and October 1st, just around the start of autumn (fall).

Pool Closing Kits: Are They Worth It?

Winter pool closing kits usually come with everything you need to keep your pool protected and algae-free in the off-season. But you might already have a few of the chemicals on hand. Here are the three winterizing chemicals that are worth adding to your water when you close:

Winter Algaecide

Most closing kits market their algaecide as a "winter" formula, so you might already have the right kind of algaecide on hand. Look for a 60% polyquat algaecide. This is non-copper based with a powerful enough concentration to kill algae in the off-season. It's more expensive than a copper-based algaecide, but it won't stain or foam.

Slow-Release Winter Ball or Winter Pill

A winter ball or winter pill slowly releases a blend of enzymes, clarifiers, and stain and scale prevention into your water during the off-season. And it won't affect the rest of your water chemistry. So if you have water with high metal content or if you struggle with stains, scaling, or scum lines in the spring, this product can help.

And it's a convenient, easy-to-use alternative to buying enzymes, clarifiers, and stain remover separately. This is considered extra insurance.

Stain and Scale Preventer

In addition to an all-in-one winter pill, many pool closing kits come with a separate chemical for stain removal and scale buildup prevention.

But the best stain protection for your pool? A solid winter pool cover that keeps debris out of your water. And if you completely clean your pool before closing, you shouldn't need additional stain and scale prevention.

How to Winterize an Inground Pool

The supplies you'll need to winterize your pool will also vary a bit depending on your climate, what types of pool accessories you have, and whether you've been balancing your water chemistry right up until closing day—which makes the closing process much easier. Be sure you have everything on hand before you start the closing process.

Closing Supplies

- Tools for removing pool accessories, such as ladders
- Air compressor
- Test kit or test strips
- Chemicals (pH, alkalinity, chlorine, calcium hardness, etc.)
- Polyquat 60 algaecide
- Winter pill or ball
- Shock
- Stain and scale preventer
- Winter pool cover or safety cover
- Water tubes
- Rubber plugs
- Gizzmo
- Pool brush
- Skimmer Net
- Pool Vacuum

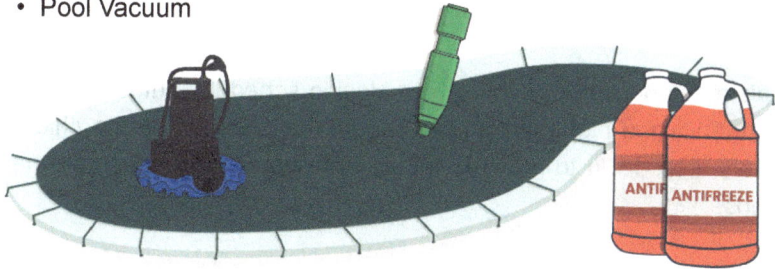

1. Clean Your Pool

Before you do anything else, clean your pool. Remove anything floating in the water with a skimmer net. Then brush your pool walls and floor, getting into the nooks and crannies as best you can. This will help kick up any sediment hanging around, as well as disturb the beginnings of any algae spores. If you have any symptoms of algae, use an algae brush and be especially thorough.

This breaks up the algae so it can be vacuumed up. It also disturbs any blooms so they're more susceptible to the treatment chemicals you'll be adding. Finally, manually vacuum all the stuff you kicked up while brushing.

2. Test the Water and Adjust Chemicals

After vacuuming, test the water. It's important that the levels (pH, alkalinity, etc.) are properly balanced before closing. This will help protect the pool from corrosion and scale buildup that can occur while it's closed.

Make sure the chlorine level is within normal range at this stage. If it's too high, it may destroy the other additives you put in before they have a chance to work.

3. Shock Your Pool

A few days before closing or the night before putting on the cover, shock your pool one last time. If you notice any green water or algae blooms, add double or triple the amount of shock, depending on the type and severity of the algae problem. Then run the pump overnight to distribute the shock throughout the pool and circulation system.

This may add a day or so to your closing schedule, but it'll save you from an algae nightmare in the spring. Just make sure the chlorine levels drop down to normal range before you proceed with the next steps.

4. Add Winterizing Chemicals

Once the other levels are correct, it's time to add winterizing chemicals. This includes winter algaecide and enzymes or a winter pill. If you have high metal content, a stain and scale preventer can also help.

- **Winter Algaecide:** Add one dose to prevent spore growth throughout the off-season. If your cover has a mesh panel or other way for dirt, leaves, and debris to enter the water, use a double dose of algaecide (and consider adding another round under the cover in early spring).

- **Winter Pills or Balls:** Designed to be left under your pool cover, these contain sanitizer and clarifier and dissolve slowly over several months. And the enzymes in these balls can help take some of the burden off the algaecide by attacking organic contaminants. They also contain stain and scale prevention, so you won't need to add a separate product for that.

- **Stain and Scale Preventer:** If your water has high levels of metals, add this when closing. This suspends any metals in the water so they can't settle onto your pool surfaces, oxidize, and eventually cause stains.

What about Antifreeze?

If you blow out your lines properly, you shouldn't have to worry about them freezing. But if you want some extra insurance, you can use antifreeze. Choose an antifreeze designed specifically for pools. This type is nontoxic, unlike the car version of antifreeze. And use one that's rated down to 10°F (-12°C). If your winter temperatures are colder than that, check the temperature rating on the antifreeze you buy. Most manufacturers recommend 1 gallon of antifreeze for every 10 feet of pipe. If you blew out all or some of your pipes, use less antifreeze. And always refer to the manufacturer's instructions around dosing.

5. Lower Your Pool's Water Level

If you live in a warm, dry climate, you can skip to the next step! The reason for removing some water at the end of the season is to prevent freeze damage and possibly overflow.

Ideally, your water level should be below the tile border or the bottom edge of the skimmer if you don't have a tile line (or whichever is lower if you have both). If you have thaws or a rainy winter, it's a good idea to check the water level while the pool is closed.

The exact level to drain the water down to is determined by which type of cover you'll be using and the type of pool surface you have.

The water helps support your cover and the weight of any snow or debris that ends up on top. So it's important to follow the manufacturer's recommendations too.

- **Vinyl Liner:** Bring the water to one inch below your skimmer opening or tile line, whichever is lower.

- **Plaster or Non-vinyl Pool Liner:** If you're using a solid cover, lower the water to 6 inches below the skimmer or tile line. When using a mesh cover, lower the water to 18 to 24 inches below the skimmer or tiles. If you have an automatic pool cover, be sure the water is no lower than the bottom of the skimmer.

Be sure to check with your local guidelines for disposing of any pool water that's been treated with chemicals.

6. Clean the Filter and Pump

The last thing you want to do is leave a bunch of nasty debris and bacteria sitting in your filter all winter. Now's the time for a deep filter clean so you can start the next pool season on the right foot.

- **Cartridge Filter:** Remove the cartridge and wash it with pool filter cleaner or muriatic acid, then rinse it and allow it to dry thoroughly before you store it. Or you may choose to replace it with a new one altogether.
- **Sand Filter:** Use a cleaner made for sand filters to clean the sand itself.
- **D.E. Filter:** You can use a cleaner made for D.E. filters or use a solution of muriatic acid to wash the grids or fingers before storing.

At this point, be sure to drain all water out of the pump, filter, pool heater, automatic chlorinator, etc. Toss the plugs into your skimmer basket for storage.

7. Blow Out the Lines

If you live in a warmer climate where the temperature doesn't get below freezing and you want to avoid blowing out your lines, just using antifreeze will be fine.

But if you experience freezing temperatures regularly, you'll need to remove every last bit of water from your lines, pump, and filter. This will prevent fractures caused by ice in the lines and equipment. Blowing out the lines means you won't need to add antifreeze, either.

Your pool plumbing is not built to withstand excess pressure, so purging the lines of water is a delicate process. Because it involves blasting air through the plumbing, you could inadvertently do serious damage.

Blow out the lines only if you're confident you know what you're doing.

We highly recommend hiring a pool professional just for this step if you're anything less than absolutely certain of your ability to do it yourself.

Screw this part up, and you could be in for thousands of dollars in repairs.

How to Blow Out Your Lines

1. Remove all the return fittings and skimmer baskets.
2. Remove all the drain plugs from your filter system.
3. Set the multiport valve to recirculate.
4. Set the valve in front of your pump to the skimmer line.
5. Attach your air compressor or Shop-Vac to the pump's drain plug opening. You may need an adapter.
6. Blow air through the system, watching for bubbles from the return lines and skimmer.
7. Use your Shop-Vac to remove the water being blown out of the skimmer until it's dry.
8. Insert a rubber plug or Gizzmo in the hole in the bottom of the skimmer.
9. Install rubber plugs in each return line as you see air bubbles escape from them. If you live somewhere cold, you may need to use straight pressure plugs in the return lines.
10. Turn the valve in front of your pump to the main drain setting to move air in that direction.
11. Watch for bubbles from the main drain in the deep end. Let it run for about a minute.
12. Turn the pump valve back to the skimmer line, then shut off your air compressor.
13. Put a plug inside the pump in case the valve leaks.

Winterize Your Salt Water System

If your pool uses a salt water system, switch the chlorine generator to the "winter" setting if it has one. If it doesn't, most chlorine generators have a removable electrolytic cell you can access by unscrewing the end caps. Remove the cell, or your entire salt system if you prefer, and store it inside for the winter. Take a few moments to clean the cell before storing. It'll prolong its life and help reduce the risk of hardware problems when it's time to reopen your pool.

8. Remove Any Pool Accessories

Leaving things installed around your pool like ladders and rails means they can rust and interfere with your pool cover.

Remove your accessories, then clean and dry them thoroughly before storing them in a clean, dry place. Keep them out of direct sunlight to minimize potential weather damage.

Also be sure to remove the fittings from the return lines, including the line for your automatic cleaner if you have one. Then pull out and clean your skimmer baskets.

You can toss the fittings into the clean skimmer basket to help you keep track of them.

9. Install a Winter Cover

You have a couple choices for covering your pool in the off-season, depending on your weather and your budget:

Solid Winter Cover

This will protect your pool from contaminants and keep all the chemistry work you've done nicely under wraps. Use water tubes or pool cover weights to keep it from sinking into your pool over time. The tubes and weights will also prevent any gaps along the edges of your pool. The cover manufacturer's instructions may suggest how many tubes to use, so read them carefully.

And be sure you have a pool cover pump to remove pooling water from the cover, both to protect the cover and any people or animals who could become trapped or drown in that pooled water.

Protect your pool cover by keeping it clean, but don't use anything sharp like a shovel or rake. A regular push broom works well to remove leaves and even a few inches of snow at a time. You can also use a rubber broom with a squeegee to help remove water. Even though you don't need to clean your pool daily when it's closed, it's good to check on the cover regularly.

Pool Safety Cover

A more expensive option than standard covers, a pool safety cover can help protect your pool from the elements while also keeping people and animals from falling into the water. They're often solid but are also available in mesh as well as hybrid versions that have a mesh panel to let water drain into the pool.

If you use a mesh or hybrid safety cover, you may need to lower the pool water level again during the winter if you get rain or snowmelt.

How to Winterize an Above Ground Pool

Learning how to winterize your pool helps you avoid green and stagnant water in the spring, protects your pool from freeze damage, and saves you money by not hiring a service company.

If you leave your pool uncovered, you'll likely have to deal with significant debris, contaminants, and algae. And not only are your pipes, filter, and pump susceptible to damage, your pool walls are at risk of collapse.

Before you winterize your above ground pool, make sure you've got the necessary equipment and chemicals on hand. You'll also want to enlist the help of a friend to lift and secure the cover.

Closing Supplies

- Tools for removing pool accessories, such as ladders
- Test kit or test strips
- Regular chemicals (pH, alkalinity, chlorine, calcium hardness, etc.)
- Polyquat 60 algaecide
- Winter pill or ball
- Shock
- Stain and scale preventer
- Winter cover
- Cover winch and cable
- Cover clips
- Water bags (if you have a walk-around deck)
- Pool antifreeze (if necessary)
- Pool air pillow
- Winterizing plugs
- Return line plugs
- Skimmer plate or skimmer cover
- Pool brush
- Skimmer net
- Pool vacuum

1. Clean Your Pool One Last Time

Before you close up, you need to clean your pool. That means skim the surface, brush down the walls, and vacuum the entire pool. A little prep now will save you from some potentially nasty surprises when you open your pool next spring.

And a clean pool makes it much easier to properly balance your water in the following steps.

2. Test and Balance Your Water

Test your water and adjust your pH, alkalinity, and calcium hardness levels. Remember, your goal is a pH reading between 7.4 and 7.6, and an alkalinity reading between 100 and 150 PPM.

Also make sure the calcium hardness is between 175 PPM to 225 PPM. You'll be shocking your pool soon, so don't worry about the chlorine levels yet.

3. Shock Your Pool

Once your levels are balanced, it's time to shock your water. You can use a fast-dissolving, non-chlorine shock before you put the cover on instead of a more powerful shock. But if you've got stagnant, cloudy, or greenish water, you'll need to use a more powerful shock.

A few days before closing or the night before putting on the cover, shock your pool with a chlorine-based shock (for chlorine or salt water pools). And if you have significant algae issues, add double or triple the amount of shock. Then run the pump overnight to distribute the shock throughout the pool and circulation system.

This may add a day or so to your closing schedule, but it'll save you from an algae nightmare in the spring. Just make sure the chlorine levels drop down to normal range before you proceed with the next steps.

4. Add Winterizing Chemicals

Once the other levels are where they need to be, it's time to add the winterizing chemicals. This includes winter algaecide and enzymes or a winter pill. If you have high metal content, a stain and scale preventer can also help.

Winter Algaecide

Add one dose to prevent spore growth throughout the off-season. If your cover has a mesh panel or other ways for dirt, leaves, and other debris to enter the water, use a double dose of algaecide (and consider adding another round under the cover in early spring).

Winter Pills or Balls

Designed to be left in a closed pool, these contain sanitizer and clarifier but dissolve over several months under the winter cover. And the enzymes in these balls can help take some of the burden off the algaecide by attacking organic contaminants. They contain stain and scale prevention, so you won't need to add a separate product for that.

Stain and Scale Preventer

If your water has high levels of metals (for example, if your water comes from a well), add stain and scale prevention when closing. This suspends any metals in the water so they can't settle onto your pool surfaces, oxidize, and eventually cause stains.

5. Clear and Store the Lines

Just like the plumbing in your house, your pool lines can be damaged by freezing temperatures and expanding ice. Even if winters are mild in your area, clearing, removing, and storing the lines will make for easier setup next spring. Make sure the valves are closed to prevent water coming from your pool, then disconnect the lines and allow all the water to run out. Let them air dry before storing them in a dry place out of direct sunlight. Drying is crucial unless you want to find mold in them next season.

6. Protect Your Skimmer

You have a couple of options when winterizing your skimmer. The first step is to remove the skimmer basket and store it somewhere safe and dry for the winter.

You can then decide whether you'd like to cover your skimmer for the season or not. A winter skimmer cover is a plate that covers the entire skimmer, sealing out the elements. If you use one of these, you won't have to drain your pool below the skimmer line, saving you a bit of time and hassle.

If you choose not to cover your skimmer, keep an eye on your skimmer during the winter to make sure water can drain out if it rains. Keep the bottom of the skimmer free and clear—don't plug it up.

If water accumulates in your skimmer over the winter and then freezes, the expanding ice can cause your skimmer to crack. Also, if the snow or water load is too great, the weight could compromise your skimmer wall. This is when a skimmer cover is handy.

7. Winterize Your Filter and Pump

The best way to protect your filter and pump is to pack it away for the winter. Moving your hardware indoors after you disconnect is the best way to protect it from freezing temperatures. But it may not be possible with all types of equipment. So be sure to remove any and all water from your equipment regardless.

Completely remove all drain plugs on your pool pump, chlorinator (if you have one), and all the hoses. Store all the drain plugs (including the ones from the filter) in the pump basket so that you keep them all together and you won't have to go hunting for them in the spring. Keep the pump, chlorinator, and hoses indoors to prolong their life.

Depending on the type and size of filter you have, you may or may not be able to bring it inside.

Sand Filter

Set your multiport valve to winterize and remove the drain plug at the bottom to allow the filter to drain completely. If your multiport valve has a bleeder valve and a sight glass, remove those, too, and store them in the pump basket for easy retrieval next season.

Bring your filter indoors for winter storage. If the weight of the sand makes this too difficult, you can leave it outside if you remove all the drain plugs. With the plugs removed, freezing water or condensation that builds up inside the filter tank won't crack it.

D.E. Filter

Drain the filter, then rinse off the grids (or fingers) with a hose to remove excess D.E. Leave the valves open.

Cartridge Filter

Drain the filter, then rinse off the cartridge with a hose. Leave the valves open and store the cartridge indoors for the winter.

Winterize a Salt Water System

If your pool uses salt water system, switch the chlorine generator to the "winter" setting if it has one. If it doesn't, most chlorine generators have a removable electrolytic cell you can access by unscrewing the end caps. Remove the cell, or your entire salt system if you prefer, and store it inside for the winter. Take a few moments to clean the cell before storing. This will prolong its life and help reduce the risk of hardware problems when it's time to reopen your pool.

8. Clean and Stash Your Accessories

Don't forget to remove any ladders, toys, fountains, or other detachable accessories connected to your pool. Leaving them in the pool can damage the items or, even worse, your pool. They could puncture the lining or start to rust. Corroded metal can contaminate your water and cause serious hardware problems.

Gather up all your accessories, then give them a good cleaning with a multipurpose pool surface cleaner. Let them dry. Then store them in a clean, dry place, away from direct sunlight, until spring.

9. Lower the Pool Water (If Necessary)

Whether or not you need to drain any water in your pool depends on how you protect your skimmer. If you're concerned about freezing and cracking and don't use a winter skimmer cover plate, then you should drain the water level below the skimmer and returns.

But if you use a winter skimmer plate, you won't need to drain out any water. Simply remove the hose from your skimmer so it can drain properly and install the plate.

Also, keeping the water level at its normal level is better for your winter cover. If you have a solid cover, draining the water below the return lines can put added pressure on your cover when rainwater and snow collect on top. You'll need to keep draining water off the cover with a pump or siphon to protect it from damage.

Don't Empty Your Pool!

Never drain an above ground pool completely when winterizing! Your vinyl liner can dry out or the pool walls could collapse.

POOL CLOSING

10. Install an Air Pillow

In cold climates, placing an air pillow under the cover protects the sides of the cover and the walls of your pool from damage. Even if you don't live in a cold climate but you close and cover your pool, you can use an air pillow to keep water and debris off to the side of the pool for an easy spring cleanup.

Inflate the air pillow to around 50% or 60% of its capacity. This allows the pillow to compress without immediately popping after the first substantial snowfall. Then place the air pillow in the middle of the pool. You can use a thin rope to secure it to either side of the pool so that it stays in the middle. Some pillows also come with built-in grommets to allow you to secure them on all four corners for easy centering.

While you don't absolutely need the pillow to stay centered all winter, doing so protects your pool cover and walls from ice more effectively. You can prolong the life of your pool pillows by sealing the seams and valves with duct tape once you've inflated the pillows. This will reduce air loss due to leaks and bolster the pillows' strength.

11. Install the Pool Cover

Place the pool cover over your pool—and the air pillow—and secure it by using a cable and winch or a combination of winter cover clips and a cable. If your pool has a walk-around deck, you can also add water bags to help secure your cover. Throughout the winter, keep an eye on your cover and do your best to keep it dry. Brushing off snow or using a cover pump will help remove excess water and keep your pool cover in good shape.

Don't Use Bricks or Stones to Secure Your Cover!

These might damage your liner if it were to fall into the pool.

How to Winterize a Temporary Small or Intex Pool

There's a huge time investment involved in breaking down and setting up your Intex pool every season. If you want to winterize your Intex pool without breaking it down, you can follow the steps in the section about closing an above ground pool. This is especially true if you live in a region with a warmer climate and milder winters.

But just remember that Intex and smaller pools are more susceptible to ice damage. If you live in a colder climate where temperatures drop below 41°F (5°C) in the winter, you should break down and store your pool.

Supplies for Winterizing an Intex Pool

The supplies necessary to winterize Intex pools will vary by climate. Regardless, the first item on your tool list is your owner's manual. If yours is lost, you can usually download it from the manufacturer's website.

- Owner's manual
- Skimmer
- Vacuum head and telescoping pole
- Garden hose
- Drain connector (comes with your Intex pool)
- Soft cloth
- Warm water
- Mild all-purpose cleaner
- Talcum powder or cornstarch
- Replacement filter cartridge

Supplies for Keeping Pool Up in Winter

- Owner's manual
- Skimmer
- Vacuum head and telescoping pole
- Garden hose
- Winterizing chemicals
- Water testing kit
- Intex 12-foot frame set pool cover

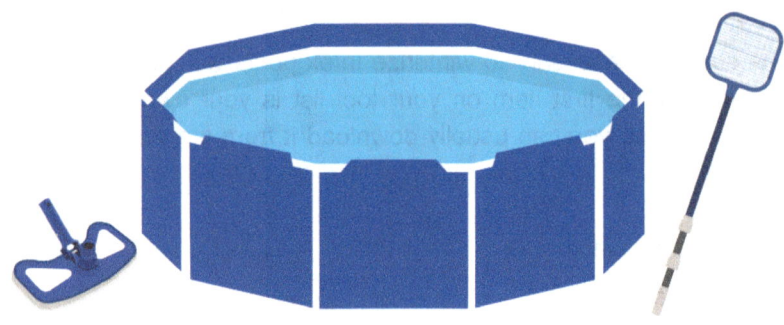

Do You Have an Intex Salt Water Pool?

If you're using an Intex salt water system, you can use the breakdown instructions without any changes for storing your pool. If you're keeping your pool up over the winter, just make sure the winterizing chemicals you use are compatible with salt water pools.

1. Clean and Prepare to Drain Your Pool

You don't want to clog up your pipes with stray debris, so thoroughly clean your water and vacuum the sides and bottom of your pool. Always check before you drain to make sure you don't violate any local ordinances. And before you start draining your pool, disconnect it from all power sources. If you have a skimmer, ladder, or any attached accessories in the pool, remove them. Clean and dry the parts before storing in a clean, dry area for the winter. If your strainer grid—the screwed-in portion connecting your pool to your filter—is exceptionally dirty, remove and replace it.

For Keeping Your Pool Up in Winter (Warm Weather Instructions)

Make sure any inflatable parts are properly inflated. Clean any debris from the water and vacuum the sides and bottom of the pool. It's going to be sitting covered for several months, so you don't want anything gross stewing all the way till spring. Once it's clean, balance the water chemistry (pH, alkalinity, etc.).

2. Attach Hose to Drain Connector

Whether you have an inflatable or metal frame, the same simple draining instructions apply. Check the drain plug on the inside of the pool to make sure it's plugged in. Do not unplug it. The water will take care of it later. Find the drain connector that should have come with your pool. Attach the female end of the hose to the thin end of the drain connector. (The female end of the hose is the part you attach to a faucet or spigot.)

Once the hose is securely connected, point the other end of the hose away from your house and any other structures. Emptying water near a building's foundation can cause some serious structural damage, so it's critical the flow of water is directed away from any structures.

3. Connect the Drain Connector to the Drain Valve

Remove the cap from the drain valve, but don't attach the drain connector and hose just yet. Do one last check to make sure your hose is in the proper draining position because the pool will start to drain the second you attach the connector. When you're sure everything is set, push the drain connector into the valve. It will disrupt the inner drain plug, and the water will begin to flow. Tighten the connector to the valve to ensure it doesn't come loose while draining.

4. Allow Your Pool to Drain

A tiny garden hose plus a big pool means a long drain time. Check in on your pool's progress occasionally to make sure the connector is still tightly secured. Keep an eye on the hose while the pool is draining to make sure it doesn't move and remains directed away from your home and other structures. This is a good time to get a head start on cleaning. As the water level goes down, you can start cleaning the pool walls with a mild all-purpose cleaner and soft cloth. Do not use any strong or abrasive cleaners on your lining.

5. Finish Draining

The water will eventually lower to a point where it's unable to reach the drain. Help the rest along by carefully lifting the side of the pool away from the drain until the pool is completely empty.

Warm Weather Instructions

Add winterizing chemicals to the clean water. Using slow-release chemicals (like a winter pill) will help disperse chemicals evenly while the pool is covered. You can also add non-chlorine shock and a winter algaecide at this stage. Allow the chemicals to circulate for a day before adding the cover.

6. Reattach Loose Parts

Remove the drain connector and your garden hose before replacing the inside drain plug and the outside drain valve cap. These get folded up along with the wall, so this is the best way to store the parts without losing them.

Warm Weather Instructions

Depending on your pool model, you either need to close your inlet and outlet valves or plug in the inlet and outlet fitting to the inside of the pool wall. If you're unsure how to do this, refer to your owner's manual. You can skip to the warm weather instructions in Step 12.

7. Clean Your Pool

Wipe down the inside of your Intex pool with a soft cloth, warm water, and mild cleaner. Thoroughly rinse and drain any leftover water.

8. Deconstruct Frame and Let Liner Dry

If your model has a frame, reverse your owner manual assembly instructions to take it down. Clean and dry the frame pieces before storing in a dry and secure location. Let your liner air dry completely. Once the water has evaporated, sprinkle a little talcum powder or cornstarch on the liner to absorb leftover water and prevent excessive sticking.

9. Fold the Liner

The process is kind of like folding a fitted sheet. The goal is to bring in the sides of the circle and keep folding it in on itself. Refer to your Intex owner's manual for specific instructions. But even if your folding is messy, just make sure the liner is completely dry. Fold it as neatly as you can so you can put it away without it taking up too much space. Once you have the liner folded, you can store it in its original packaging.

10. Drain and Clean Your Accessories

Leaving water in your filter parts and pump can lead to mold and bacteria later. Make sure all the water is out of your accessories, clean them up, let them air dry, and store them in a clean, dry area.

11. Store Filter

Now's the time to discard your filter cartridge. Iit's really not worth the effort to clean and reuse your Intex pool filters. Just make sure you have replacements on hand for next season. If it only needs a light clean, you can use a filter cleaner. But once you can't get it fully clean anymore, it's time to replace. If you have a sand filter, it's a good idea to clean it with a sand filter cleaner.

12. Properly Store Your Pool Parts

Keep your liner, frame, pump, and filter hoses indoors in a dry area that is not exposed to freezing temperatures. To make setup easier next season, make sure you keep all attachments together so you're not digging through the garage or attic for a missing piece.

Warm Weather Instructions

Turn off your pump and filter. Remove the hoses attaching them to the pool as well. Clean, sanitize, and drain the pump, filter chamber, and their hoses. Ensure they are completely dry before storing indoors in a dry, temperate location. The last thing you need to do is cover your pool to keep leaves and dirt out of your water. Once that's done, your Intex pool is officially winterized. Be sure to regularly clear any standing water from the cover when you get a lot of rain. **Warning:** Intex pool covers are not pool safety covers, which means they won't keep wayward animals or adventurous children from climbing across and falling in. Take appropriate measures to prevent accidents.

11

~~~

OFF-SEASON AND YEAR-ROUND POOL MAINTENANCE

OFF-SEASON AND YEAR-ROUND POOL MAINTENANCE

Unfortunately, the responsibilities of pool ownership don't end when swimming season is over. It's important to continue caring for your pool during the off-season (fall, winter, and early spring) to ensure a successful and clean opening.

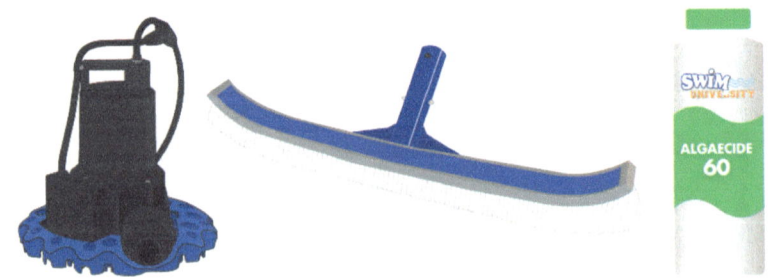

1. Add a Midwinter Algaecide

Use an algaecide or algaestat (preventive), particularly one that stays in the water for a good length of time. On the last day of your pool being open, add this to the water and run the pump for 24 hours to fully circulate. Then shut down the circulation system for the winter.

If you can, you may want to add an algaecide under the cover if you expect warmer temperatures during the winter or early spring. By keeping the green stuff away as long as possible, your pool start-up will be much easier.

2. Check Your System to Prevent Freezing

As winter approaches and you plan to close the pool, remember to check your pipes and motorized parts. As the temperatures begin to dip to freezing levels, any excess water in these parts can freeze. If that happens, the pipes can crack, which can cost serious money in the long run.

3. Keep Your Pool Cover Clean

You should absolutely have a winter cover for your pool. A dirty but safely covered pool beats a sparkling clean but uncovered pool any time. Remove any water that has accumulated on top of your pool cover to keep it from freezing.

You can use a sump pump or a winter cover pump. And brush any snow off the top of your pool cover to prevent it from sinking or collapsing.

4. Add Chlorine to Your Pool to Ensure a Clean Opening

If you have a safety cover on your pool, we recommend adding chlorine a few different ways to protect your water in the off-season:

- In the fall, make sure to add chlorine and algaecide to your pool to protect your water over the winter. Don't add too much chlorine though. If the chlorine level is too high over the winter, you can bleach the liner.

- As soon as the water thaws in the spring, pop open a corner of the cover and add liquid chlorine to the pool (about 1–2 gallons for an average inground pool). You can do this yourself or hire a professional to do this for you.

- If you find your pool is pea-soup green in the spring, add more liquid chlorine, allow your filter to do its work, and monitor the progress. Be patient. If you don't see progress in several hours, repeated doses of chlorine and algaecide may be in order, and your pool may benefit from an extra vacuum session.

5. Check that Your Safety Cover is Properly Fitted

Having clean, clear water in the spring makes your life much easier. One key element in achieving that is a properly fitted safety cover. If your pool cover doesn't fit, it's an invitation for dirt, debris, and even small animals to find their way into your pool.

If you notice debris or fine sediment when you open your pool, vacuum your water on waste. If you try to vacuum the sediment from the bottom of the pool and run it through the filter system, you may find that the sediment is so fine that it goes right through your filter.

6. Pay Attention to Weather

If the fall has been mild and warm, it's a good idea to check the pool and add more chlorine and algaecide just ahead of the colder season.

If you live in an area that has heavy rains in the fall and you use a mesh cover, much of the winterizing chemicals you use may become diluted. Just before the first big freeze hits, charge up the chemicals to help ensure the water makes it through to spring start-up without an algae bloom.

7. Use an Enzyme Midwinter to Break Down Contamination

Using an enzyme product during the off-season (even poured through a mesh cover when the water is not frozen) will help to break down nonliving organic contamination. This includes bird droppings, pollen, or even contaminants from swimmers left over from your pool season.

An off-season enzyme will help prevent the waterline ring that can occur through the winter, which would normally require a lot of scrubbing in the spring.

8. Keep Your Winter Cover Free of Debris

If leaves, sticks, and other junk accumulate on your pool cover throughout the winter, you can end up with a nasty stew of stagnant water, which is a mess to remove and some of it often ends up in the pool.

Using an air pillow connected to the cover in the center of the pool not only protects your pool from snow and ice damage, but it also disperses water and debris to the sides of the pool, making cleaning easier. You want to keep some water on the cover to help stabilize the cover in the wind, but you don't want any debris.

9. Keep an Eye on Your Air Pillow and Cover Cables

Periodically check your cover cable to make sure it's tight. If the cable becomes loose, the cover might slip into the pool. Check your air pillow to make sure it still has air in it. If you see it going flat, get another one, slip it under the cover, and blow it up.

10. Protect the Water and Open Early

The challenge in cold environments is that water is not being circulated, the pool is covered, and a typical sanitizer like chlorine will degrade and disappear during the long winter.

This is why many winterization products include algaecides that are stable and will stay in the water for extended periods. Most algaecides will survive the winter and slow or stop algae growth; some of these products may even slow bacterial growth.

Finally, open the pool before the weather and water gets too warm. If you wait until later in the spring to open the pool, you'll likely have more algae growing under the cover.

Keeping Your Pool Open All Year

Thinking about keeping your pool open all winter? If you don't want the hassle of winterizing your pool equipment or you don't like the look of a winter cover in your backyard, there are a few precautions you need to take to keep your pool open in the colder months.

Luckily, pools are easier to maintain in the winter. Algae has a hard time growing in temperatures below 60°F (or 16°C). So if you keep your pool open in the winter, you'll need less chlorine or sanitizer. And after all the leaves fall, you'll get less organic debris falling into your water in the winter—and that's less work for your sanitizer. Finally, because it's cooler out, you won't lose as much water and chemicals to evaporation.

However, your equipment could be damaged by a freeze. You'll need to keep your water constantly moving whenever temperatures get close to freezing. But if your pump accidently shuts off because of a power outage, your plumbing and pool equipment could be seriously damaged. So if you want to keep your pool open, follow these steps to keep your pool protected in the off-season months.

Heads Up: Salt Chlorine Generators and Heat Pumps Don't Work in the Cold!

Heat pumps stop working well when it's below 50°F outside. And salt chlorinators don't generate chlorine when your water temperature drops below 60°F. This means you'll need to use an alternative sanitizer method, like a chlorine floater, in the cooler months.

1. Keep All the Valves Open

Your pool valves need to be at least partially open to keep water moving freely through your plumbing. Water that isn't moving is at risk of freezing and damaging your equipment. This means keeping valves partially open in all skimmer lines, cleaner lines, drains, returns, water features, and attached spas.

2. Keep the Pumps Running

The goal during the winter is to keep your water moving to prevent freezing. Keep your pump running whenever temperatures start dropping below 40°F (4°C). Even if the surface water freezes, the water in your pipes won't freeze if the pumps are running and the valves are partially open. You should also run your pump in the fall if leaves or other debris are getting into your pool. But if you don't have a lot of debris and if you aren't experiencing freezing temperatures, you only need to run your pump for a few hours a day in the milder months.

3. Keep the Water Warm, Especially in Cold Climates

If you live in an area where temperatures drop and stay well below freezing, running your pump won't be enough. You'll need a pool heater to keep your water at 40°F or above to prevent your plumbing from freezing. Regardless of where you live, you can help retain heat in your water with a pool cover. If you live in a warmer climate and use your pool occasionally in the winter, use a solar cover to help trap in heat. And if you're not using your pool, consider a more permanent cover to keep in heat and keep out debris.

4. Install a Freeze Sensor

If you don't want to run your pool pump 24-7, you can use a freeze sensor. These sensors monitor air temperature and/or water temperature and will turn on your pump when temperatures drop too low. Some newer pump models actually come with built-in freeze protection control.

5. Winterize Your Water Features

If your pool has fountains, waterfalls, or deck jets, consider winterizing and closing the valves and turning them off to reduce the risk of freeze damage.

6. Keep the Pool Clean

It takes much less work to maintain a pool during the winter, especially after the leaves fall. But it still takes consistent cleaning, especially if your pool is left uncovered.

Skim your water at least twice a week or more often if leaves are falling. Brush the walls once a week and vacuum at least once per week. If you have lots of leaves in your pool, you may want to consider buying an automatic pool cleaner that's built for picking up leaves.

7. Keep the Water Balanced

While you may need less chlorine in the winter, you still want to maintain good water chemistry to prevent damaging your pool equipment and surfaces.

Make sure your pH, alkalinity, calcium hardness, and cyanuric acid levels are in the proper ranges.

- Test and balance total alkalinity and pH at least once a week while your pool is open.

- Test CYA levels. Normally, these should be between 30–50 PPM. But you shouldn't need to add more CYA to your pool in the winter, especially if you're still adding stabilized chlorine to your pool.

- Test chlorine. You won't need much chlorine in the winter because there's less algae and less evaporation. You can keep your chlorine levels at 1 PPM during the winter months. Once temperatures start to rise to 60°F or higher, you may want to increase your chlorine levels to 3 PPM or start shocking your pool once a week.

255

8. Monitor Your Water Level

Make sure that your pool's water level is at least halfway up the skimmer so that your pump and filter system can run without sucking in air.

What Happens If Your Pump Accidently Shuts Off in the Winter?

If your filter or pump fails while the outside temperature is at or below freezing, you'll need to act fast to prevent damage.

- Turn off the breaker to power down the pump and heater in case the power turns back on.
- Immediately loosen all the drain plugs on the pump, heater, filter, and any other equipment.
- Close the line valves.
- Open the filter air pressure release, a.k.a. the air bleeder valve.
- If you live in a colder climate where freezing temperatures are common, it might be easier to close and winterize your pool altogether than worrying if your equipment will fail or freeze in cold weather. But regardless of where you live, always have a backup plan in case of power failure.

Vacation Pool Care

If you're going out of town, there are a few things you must do to protect your pool while you're away. Otherwise you could come back home to an algae infestation, or even a burned-out pool pump.

Here's a step-by-step guide on how to prep your pool before you go on vacation.

1. Check Your Water Level

Make sure your water level is a little above normal to help offset evaporation when you're away. If your water dips below your skimmer while the pump is running, your system could overheat.

2. Remove Debris from Water

Make sure you skim any debris out of your water before you leave. Anything left to decompose in your pool can contribute to cloudy or green water.

And consider running your filter system all day before you leave town to help pick up smaller contaminants. Finally, if you haven't backwashed or cleaned your filter in a while, now would be a good time.

3. Remove Anything from the Skimmer

You don't want anything blocking the flow of water while you're gone. So remove any debris, skimmer socks or panty hose from the skimmer. And empty your pump baskets too.

If you're gone for more than a week, ask a neighbor to empty the skimmer basket periodically.

4. Test and Balance Your Water

Make sure your pH, alkalinity, and free chlorine are within range. Your pH can be on the lower side since you'll be adding chlorine shock in the next step, and that can elevate your pH levels.

5. Shock Your Pool

Depending on how long you'll be away, add a single or double dose of chlorine shock to your water. This will help prevent algae and contaminants from building up while you're away. Just be sure to let the filter run for a few hours after you've added it. And if you've used an unstabilized shock like cal-hypo, you'll want to add it at night.

6. Add Extra Chlorine Tablets

Add several extra chlorine pucks to your floating dispenser or chlorinator to help keep your water continuously sanitized while you're away. If you usually add tablets directly to your skimmer, that can be risky if your pump shuts off when you're out of town, so consider using a floater in the interim (or investing in a chlorinator).

7. Keep Your Pump and Filter Running

Ideally, you'll want to run your filter 24 hours a day to keep everything circulating and sanitized. But you'll want to run your filter at least 8 hours daily while you're gone. So make sure you've set up your automatic timer. Also turn off other components like your heater.

8. Remove Solar Blankets and Install Your Safety Cover

Set up your automatic cover or safety cover while you're away to keep your pool water protected. And be sure to lock and secure any gates or security devices around your pool perimeter.

After you get back from vacation, be sure to retest your water and adjust your alkalinity, pH, and chlorine if necessary. If your water is over chlorinated, wait to swim until your chlorine levels have returned to normal.

If your pool isn't over chlorinated, shock your pool to kill any contaminants that might have built up while you're away, and refill your chlorine supply in your chlorinator or floater.

12

~~~

TROUBLESHOOTING
WATER ISSUES

TROUBLESHOOTING WATER ISSUES

Whether you're dealing with cloudy water, an algae infestation, or pool foam, we'll walk through how to tackle the most common pool water issues. In this section, we'll be covering:

1. Algae and Green Water

2. Cloudy Water

3. Pool Foam

4. Pool Stains

5. Low Chlorine, Chlorine Lock, or Chlorine Demand

6. Water Bugs

7. Pink Slime or Pink Algae

8. White Water Mold

Algae and Green Water

Unfortunately, a regular amount of chlorine will not kill pool algae. And running your pool filter will not eliminate algae spores. But knowing what type of pool algae you have will help you treat it. So the first step is to determine what color algae is in your pool.

Teal Green
2x shock

Dark Green
3x shock

Black Green
4x shock

- **Green Algae:** The most common and easiest algae to kill. Getting rid of green algae involves vacuuming and brushing your pool, then shocking and filtering your water. Green algae will vary in severity from teal green to dark blackish green.

- **Yellow Algae (Mustard Algae):** This is a rarer form of algae found in humid climates. It looks like globs of pollen or sand that cling to the shady corners of your pool. It is chlorine-resistant. Killing mustard algae involves multiple rounds of brushing your pool surfaces and adding extra shock to your pool water.

- **Black Algae:** This is actually bacteria. Its roots dig into concrete surfaces, making it extremely tough to kill. Getting rid of black algae requires several rounds of deep cleaning, and it will grow back quickly if you aren't thorough.

What About Pink Algae?

Pink algae is a slime, not algae! This pink slime found on pool surfaces is actually airborne bacteria.

How to Kill Algae with Chlorine

You can get rid of algae quickly by vacuuming and brushing your pool, balancing your pool's water chemistry, and then shocking and filtering your pool water.

Just be thorough as you clean your pool surfaces. If you leave behind even a small number of algae spores, it won't be long before they regrow and bloom again.

1. Vacuum Your Pool Manually

Automatic or robotic pool cleaners aren't well suited for cleaning algae. You'll need to manually vacuum your pool on your filter's waste setting. This allows you to bypass your filter, preventing contaminated, algae-filled water from recirculating back into your pool.

When you vacuum your pool manually, pay special attention to areas with algae. And be sure to refill your pool's water as you vacuum, maintaining your water level at least halfway up the skimmer.

2. Brush Your Pool Walls and Floor

Scrubbing the algae off your pool walls helps chlorine get deeper into the remaining algae. It also loosens up contaminants so they can be killed and filtered out.

Using a stiff pool brush on a telescopic pole, brush the walls and floor of your pool. Pay special attention to corners, crevices, and shady areas where algae is usually worst. As you go, your water will become cloudy, obstructing your view, so brush the tougher spots first.

If you have a concrete or gunite pool, use a pool brush with stainless-steel bristles to remove algae from your pool walls. Otherwise, we recommend using a nylon bristle pool brush.

3. Test and Balance the Water

Use test strips or a liquid test kit to test your alkalinity and pH. Balancing your chemistry now ensures your sanitizer will be effective against the algae. High pH or low alkalinity will especially inhibit pool shock.

4. Shock Your Swimming Pool

Adding shock to your pool superchlorinates your water. And this extra dose of sanitizer will kill algae growth. The more serious your pool algae problem, the more shock you'll need.

We recommend using calcium hypochlorite shock, or cal-hypo shock, as an effective algae treatment. Follow the package instructions to determine the dose for your pool size, then multiply that by two, three, or four, depending on which type of algae you have.

- **Green Algae:** Double dose of shock (x2)
- **Yellow or Dark Green Algae:** Triple dose of shock (x3)
- **Black Algae:** Quadruple dose of shock (x4)

Use the entire contents of the bag when opened. If any granules settle to the bottom of the pool, use a brush to disperse them. Add the right dosage of this product during evening hours while the filter pump is running.

Remember to shock your pool at dusk or night. If you shock during the day, the sun will eat up most of the chlorine before it has a chance to kill the algae. And put your cleaning equipment, like your vacuum head or pool brush, in the shallow end of your pool so your tools will get sanitized while the shock is in the water.

Be sure to run your filter for eight hours or overnight to circulate the shock. If there's still a significant amount of algae in your pool, repeat the brushing and shocking process again.

5. Filter Out the Pool Algae

After your shock treatment kills the algae, it'll turn your water a cloudy blue. Don't panic! That's just dead algae.

When algae dies, it turns from green to gray, and the dead, gray algae particles need to be filtered out. Run your filter continuously for at least 8 hours or until the water clears up. You can use our water clarifier to speed up the process.

6. Test Your Pool Water Again

Make sure your water chemical levels are balanced and your chlorine is back to normal before anyone gets back into the water. Adjust your alkalinity, pH, and chlorine levels as needed.

You may also want to test your cyanuric acid and calcium hardness levels since you've removed water from your pool and replaced it with fresh water.

7. Clean Your Pool Filter

Your filter just processed a lot of contaminated water. And the last thing you want is your dirty filter slowly adding microscopic algae spores back into your pool.

Deep clean your filter cartridges by soaking them in diluted muriatic acid or by replacing them entirely. If you have a sand or D.E. filter, now's the time to backwash.

8. Repeat As Necessary

If you have very stubborn dark green or black algae, you may need to repeat the vacuuming, brushing, shocking and filtering process one or two times.

The last thing you want is any leftover algae to grow back into a big problem, so it's worth getting rid of it the first time around!

Can You Use Algaecide to Get Rid of Pool Algae?

Technically, you can use an algaecide to kill algae. But we don't recommend using it to get rid of a large algae problem. Algaecide is very expensive compared to chlorine. And it can introduce a lot of copper to your pool water. However, algaecide is effective for early-stage algae growth, small amounts of algae, or as a preventive measure. Algaecide is also handy for killing off lingering algae after you've cleaned your pool. Once you're done vacuuming, brushing, and shocking your pool, wait for your chlorine levels to fall below 5 PPM. Then add a dose of algaecide. Brush your pool to loosen any last bits of algae you can't see. The algaecide will help kill remaining algae particles before they're filtered out.

How to Remove Early-Stage Algae with Flocculant

You can use pool flocculant to treat the early stages of algae growth. This additive bonds to floating algae particles, making it easier to vacuum them out of your pool. But if you have anything more serious than a mild green algae problem, we recommend you follow the full cleaning plan.

Here's how to use pool flocculant to get rid of early-stage algae:

1. If you have a multiport valve on your filter, shut off your pump and turn the valve to recirculate or recycle. This will mix the flocculant around without filtering the water.

2. Add the recommended dosage of flocculant to your pool.

3. Circulate your water for 2 hours, then shut off your pump and let it sit overnight. The floc will bind to the algae, then settle on the pool floor.

4. Turn the multiport valve set to waste so dirty water doesn't blast back into your pool through your return lines when you vacuum.

5. Hook up your backwash hose to the backwash/waste port. Direct your wastewater appropriately.

6. Vacuum your pool. Work slowly to make sure you get all the thick sediment off the bottom. If the water gets too cloudy, you may need to stop and allow the particles to settle again before continuing to vacuum.

7. Add water while you're vacuuming to maintain your pool's water level.

8. Double shock immediately after vacuuming to eliminate any remaining algae. You may also want to brush the pool sides and floor before shocking.

9. Run your filter until the water clears.

Cloudy Water

Cloudy pool water is caused by four common pool issues: poor filtration, low chlorine levels, poor water chemistry, or contaminants in the water. Here's how to troubleshoot each one of these issues and clear up your pool.

Root Causes of Cloudy Water

1. Poor Filtration

Filter problems are the main cause of cloudy pool water. If your filter isn't functioning properly, then it can't remove the tiny contaminants that cause cloudy pool water.

Keep your pool's circulation system flowing with regular cleaning, maintenance, and run times. Check for the following filtration issues:

- **Your Pool Filter Has a Clog or Buildup:** If you haven't cleaned your filter in a while, it's time to backwash your sand or D.E. filter, clean your D.E. filter grids, or clean the cartridge in your filter.

- **Your Skimmer Basket or Pump Basket is Full of Debris:** Remove any leaves, twigs, or other debris in your skimmer or pump basket.

- **Your Pool Filter Media Needs Replacing:** If your filter media is worn out or damaged, it won't be able to capture contaminants that cause cloudy water. So every 5 years, change your filter sand or replace your cartridge filters every 2–3 years. If you have a D.E. filter, add fresh diatomaceous earth powder or replace your D.E. grids.

- **You're Not Running Your Filter Long Enough:** To fix a cloudy pool, all your pool water must run through the filter system at least once a day. That means you need to run your filter system for at least 8 to 12 hours a day.

- **Your Pool Pump or Filter Needs Replacing:** As it gets older, your pool filter system can start to fail, and you may need to replace major pieces of equipment.

2. Low Chlorine Levels

Pathogens, bacteria, and cloudy water form when there's not enough chlorine to sanitize your water. Chlorine levels can drop if there's lots of debris like leaves in your pool. Bodily contaminants like sweat or sunscreen can use up your chlorine quickly.

Finally, chlorine can drop if your water is exposed to the sun's UV rays and your chlorine is not properly stabilized. Here's how to balance your chlorine levels:

- **Test Your Free Chlorine Levels:** "Free Chlorine" is the amount of chlorine that's available to sanitize your pool water. If you have a chlorine or salt water pool, your free chlorine should read between 1 and 3 PPM.

- **Calculate Your Combined Chlorine Levels:** If your free chlorine levels are lower than your total chlorine levels, you have combined or used up chlorine. Your combined chlorine should be below 0.5 PPM.

- **Shock Your Pool with Cal-Hypo Shock.** To quickly bump up your free chlorine levels and remove chloramines, shock your pool using calcium hypochlorite shock.

- **Test and Add Cyanuric Acid if Needed:** Make sure you have the proper levels of cyanuric acid in your water. This will help prevent the sun's UV rays from breaking down your chlorine too quickly. Your CYA levels should be between 30 and 50 PPM.

4. Contaminants, Like Debris or Algae

Contaminants, particles, and small debris in your pool can cause cloudy water. This is common in the spring. Early-stage algae growth may also cause cloudy pool water. Here's what to do:

- **Treat Algae:** If you have visible algae growth, you'll need to get rid of the algae before you treat the cloudy water. To remove algae, you'll need to skim, brush, and vacuum your pool. Be sure to bypass the filter by vacuuming on the waste setting. Then you'll want to shock your pool.

- **Test, Balance, and Clean Your Pool after a Rainstorm:** Storms can blow dirt and debris into your pool, and the rain can dilute your pool water. That means your chlorine levels can drop, which we know can lead to cloudy water. So test, balance, skim, brush, and vacuum the pool as needed.

If you've tackled these common problems and you want to fix cloudy pool water fast, you can use either a pool clarifier or pool flocculant (a.k.a. pool floc).

However, your cloudy pool water will return if you don't correct the underlying causes. So be sure your filter system is running smoothly, your chlorine levels are correct, your water is balanced, and you've eliminated any algae growth.

Clarifier and flocculant both help clear up cloudy water, but both work differently and require different equipment.

How to Use Pool Clarifier to Clear Cloudy Water

Pool clarifier uses your pool filter system to clear up the cloudy water. This is the easiest method for clearing cloudy pool water, but it takes a few days depending on your pool filter system's power.

A pool clarifier works with any filter type and works best with milder cloudy water issues.

1. Skim, Brush, and Vacuum Your Pool

Remove large debris with a heavy-duty skimmer. Brush your walls well with a stiff pool brush, then vacuum manually. Do not use an automatic pool cleaner. It won't properly suck up finer debris.

But if you think you've got an algae problem, you need to address that first.

2. Test and Balance Your Water

Test your water with test strips or a liquid test kit. Test strips are easier and quicker to use but are less accurate than a good liquid test kit. Or you can take a water sample to your local pool store.

Then adjust your pH and alkalinity as needed until your water is balanced.

3. Shock Your Pool

To eliminate any contaminants or chloramines in your cloudy pool water, add a high dose of chlorine by shocking your pool. If the cloudy water in your pool is due to an algae bloom, you'll have to double or triple shock depending on the type of algae you have. Always shock your pool at dusk or night for maximum effectiveness.

Run your filter and let the shock dissolve overnight or for at least 8 hours. Then retest your water.

4. Run Your Filter 24-7

You'll need to continuously run your filter over the next few days to help clear up the cloudy water. Then you can return to regular filter run times once your water is clear. Your pool will clear faster depending on the type of filter you own. D.E. filters, for example, filter out extra fine particles and will clear up cloudy water more quickly. If you have a cartridge filter, it will take a bit longer. If you have a sand filter, it will take the longest.

5. Increase Your Pool Circulation

Your skimmer located at the surface of your pool can't get to the debris or cloudy water at the bottom of your pool. To help all your pool water pass through your filter, you can increase your pool's circulation.

- **Position your return jets.** Point your return jet(s) down at a 45° angle and all in the same direction. This will help churn the cloudy water up from the bottom of the pool to the top where your main skimmer can get it into your filter system.

- **Use your bottom drains.** If you have an inground pool, make sure the main drain at the bottom is on and is pulling water from the bottom of the pool into your filter system. This will speed up filtering and clear the pool water faster.

- **Turn your vacuum upside down.** If you have an above ground pool with no main drain, you can hook up your manual vacuum cleaner and turn it upside down at the bottom of the pool to mimic a bottom main drain.

6. Add Pool Water Clarifier

After your pool has circulated and shock has dissipated, it's time to add your clarifier. Clarifier helps bind tiny particles into bigger particles that your filter can capture. Be sure to read the manufacturer's instructions to make sure you're adding the correct amount for your size pool. Add it every other day as your filter runs until your water clears. If you have extremely cloudy water, you need to use a pool flocculant.

How to Use Pool Flocculant to Clear Cloudy Water

Pool flocculant (a.k.a. pool floc) causes particles to coagulate together, creating large clumps that sink to the bottom of your pool.

It's much faster and more powerful than a pool clarifier, but it takes much more work and requires a lot of manual vacuuming.

The coagulated particles cannot be removed by your filter, so you must be able to vacuum the water out of your pool while bypassing your filter media (i.e. the waste setting).

1. Balance Your pH

Test your water's pH levels with test strips or a liquid test kit. Then adjust your pH as needed, either with a pH increaser or pH decreaser.

2. Add Pool Flocculant (Floc) Your Water

Pool flocculant binds the contaminants that cause cloudy pool water. Those large clumps then sink to the bottom of your pool.

Be sure to read the manufacturer's instructions to make sure you're adding the correct amount of flocculant for your size pool.

3. Circulate Your Water

Circulate the pool water with your filter system for 2 hours. If you have a multiport valve, set it to "recirculate" to bypass your filter.

After circulating the pool chemical for 2 hours, shut off the filter system for the next 8–12 hours to let the particles settle to the bottom of the pool. Make sure your automatic timer doesn't turn on in the middle of the night.

4. Vacuum Water Out of Your Pool

You should now see a big cloud at the bottom of the pool. This means the pool flocculant collected all the particles that were making the water cloudy and sank them to the bottom. And that means it's time to vacuum.

If you vacuum your water through your filtration system, it'll just blow right back in through the return jets. Instead, you have to vacuum the water out of your pool.

To do this with a multiport valve on your filter, set it to waste. This will send the pool water out of the backwash port as you vacuum. Keep a garden hose in your pool to refill your water while you vacuum. If you don't have a multiport valve, open the drain port on your filter and let it drain out as you vacuum. Use a backwash hose to direct the water coming out of your pool.

Move the vacuum slowly along the bottom of the pool or else you'll kick up the cloudy water. You may have to do this multiple times. Let the cloud resettle before continuing.

5. Test and Balance Your Water

Because you've removed water from your pool, you'll need to rebalance your water chemistry. Test your pool water using test strips or a liquid test kit and adjust your alkalinity and pH. Once you get those levels balanced, add your chlorine.

Now that you've gotten the cloudy water out of the pool, you can start running your filter system normally (8–12 hours a day or however long it takes your water to cycle through your filter at least once).

Pool Foam

Chemical imbalances, high levels of organic contaminants, or low calcium can all create pool foam. In some cases, shocking the pool will solve it. In others, you may need to balance the water chemistry or change the pool chemical brands you're using.

1. High Levels of Organic Contaminants

Even small amounts of personal care products like hairspray, soap, lotions, and shampoo can introduce organic contaminants into your pool and cause foam problems. Be sure to rinse off before you swim. Shock your pool, preferably with chlorine shock. The superchlorination will eradicate the contaminants and help bring your pool water back to its normal, clear state.

2. Pool Chemistry Issues (Especially Calcium Hardness)

If your chemistry is off-balance, especially your sanitizer, you can end up with pool foam. This can also happen if you buy extremely cheap pool chemicals (like chemicals sold in bulk at big-box stores). Balance your pool water. Test the water, then start by balancing the alkalinity and pH. Next, adjust the sanitizer levels. Finally, be sure to check your calcium hardness levels. When the calcium level drops too low, the water becomes too soft, and that leads to foam production. Once the water is balanced, wait a few hours to see whether the pool foam dissipates. If it doesn't, you'll need to shock your pool.

3. Algaecide Issues

When algaecide isn't used correctly, it can cause foaming. Even higher quality algaecides can cause foam if you use too much, though they tend to foam less than cheaper versions. Why does it cause foam? The molecules in algaecide can react and get agitated, causing the water to froth. But it usually breaks down over time. Wait several days, and it should dissipate on its own. While you're waiting, you can also skim the foam from the surface of the water to speed up the process.

Pool Stains

Before you can apply the correct pool stain remover, you need to determine what stained your pool. The most common pool stains generally fall into two categories:

- **Organic:** Leaves, berries, and other organic debris can leave stains if they're allowed to settle and sit on your pool's surfaces.

- **Metal:** Several types of metal can accidentally be introduced into your pool. Maybe your primary water source is a well, or maybe you have corroded copper pipes in your water system. Rusted metal accessories, parts, and equipment can also cause stains.

Once you determine what type of stain you have, you can decide which type of pool stain remover to use. The best way to figure that out is by the stain's color:

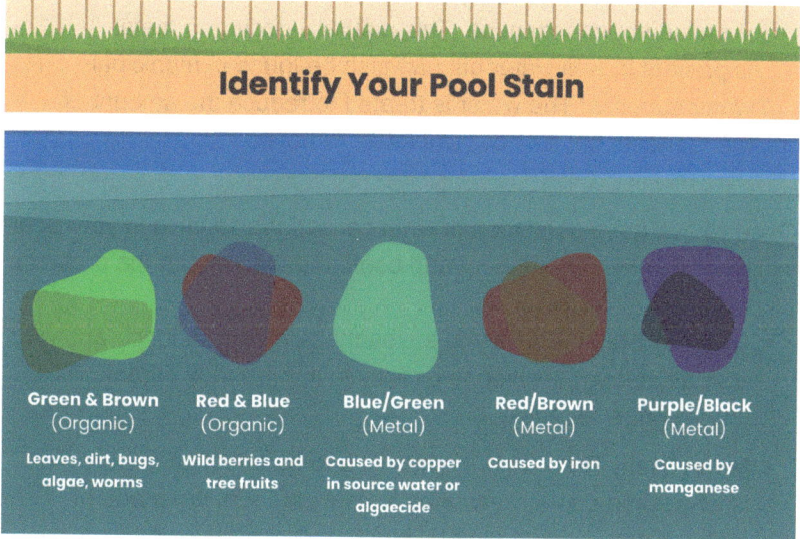

Identify Your Pool Stain

Green & Brown (Organic)	Red & Blue (Organic)	Blue/Green (Metal)	Red/Brown (Metal)	Purple/Black (Metal)
Leaves, dirt, bugs, algae, worms	Wild berries and tree fruits	Caused by copper in source water or algaecide	Caused by iron	Caused by manganese

- **Greenish-Brown Stains:** These are most likely organic stains caused by leaves or other plant matter.

- **Reddish-Blue Stains:** These are more than likely from brightly colored berries. If you have berry-bearing trees or bushes near the pool, they're the most likely culprits.

- **Blueish-Greenish-Black Stains:** These could be caused by organic matter like leaves or berries. But if there's nothing like that around your pool, they were likely caused by copper, which can be present in well water. Or if you have copper piping anywhere in your plumbing system, they may be corroded, which can also cause stains.

- **Greenish-Brownish-Red Stains:** This combination is an indication of iron in the water. If you fill your pool with well water, it's highly likely that it contains iron. Or perhaps you have iron somewhere in your pool area, such as a fence. If it rusts and the rust makes its way into your pool somehow (when it rains, for example), you can end up with stains of these colors.

- **Brownish-Blackish-Purple Stains:** This dark color combination is caused by manganese. This naturally occurring metal is present in well water but can also be found in municipal water supplies. The water is treated to reduce the amount of manganese, but it's not completely removed.

Once you've got a good idea of what caused the staining in your pool, you'll need to test your theory and confirm the source of the problem:

- **Organic Stain Test:** If you suspect an organic stain, try applying a small amount of chlorine directly to it. If it's truly organic, it should go away easily.

- **Metal Stain Test:** Chlorine has little to no effect on metals. This is why some pool accessories such as ladders are made of metal. If you suspect a metal stain, apply some ascorbic acid— vitamin C—powder to the stain. If the stain is removed or at least lightened by the powder, it was caused by metal.

How To Get Rid of Organic Pool Stains

As the identification test indicated, chlorine is the solution here. But because the amount you use for regular sanitizing isn't enough to remove stains, you'll need to superchlorinate the water with shock.

1. **Test and Balance the Water:** Use test strips or a liquid test kit to ensure that the alkalinity is between 100 PPM and 150 PPM, with 125 PPM being ideal, and that the pH is between 7.4 and 7.6, with 7.5 being ideal.

2. **Shock the Pool:** If you're dealing with just one small stain, a regular dose of shock should take care of the problem. But if you have multiple or large stains, to get rid of them with just one round of shocking, use a triple dose. This means adding 3 pounds of calcium hypochlorite shock for every 10,000 gallons of water.

3. **Brush the Pool:** Use a stiff pool brush to thoroughly scrub the stains. It's OK if you don't remove them completely at this point.

4. **Run the Pump:** Allow the shock to circulate throughout the pool for at least eight hours or overnight.

5. **Brush the Pool Again:** During those 8 hours or the next day, scrub the stains again.

6. **Check the Stains:** If stains are still visible, repeat the process.

How to Get Rid of Metal Pool Stains

Metal stains can be a little more difficult to get rid of, but it's not impossible.

1. **Test the Water for Metals:** It's a good idea to find out what kind of metal has stained your pool. It can make a difference in the type of pool stain remover you need to get. Some home test kits will test for metals, but your best bet is to take a sample of your pool water to your local pool store and ask them to test it for you.

2. **Get a Metal Pool Stain Remover**: Look for one that targets the type of metal that's stained your pool.

3. **Follow the Instructions:** Each pool stain remover will work a little differently, so follow the manufacturer's instructions to ensure the best results.

> ## A Metal Sequestrant is Not a Metal Pool Stain Remover
>
> It can help prevent stains by making it easier for metals to be removed from the water. But once you have a metal stain, a sequestrant will not remove it.

Low Chlorine, Chlorine Lock, or Chlorine Demand

If your free chlorine level is lower than 1 PPM, then you need to take action to raise your chlorine levels. Chlorine levels at or below 1 PPM mean your pool water isn't sanitized, which can lead to algae growth and bacteria buildup.

But what if you've added chlorine tablets or granules, and the levels won't change? How do you raise free chlorine in a pool if you've already added chlorine?

If your chlorine levels are low (1 PPM) or you're not getting a chlorine reading at all (0 PPM), shock your pool water with a chlorine-based shock. But if your chlorine levels continue to remain low, even after shocking, you may have a high chlorine demand issue. First, you need to understand the different chlorine readings:

- **Free Chlorine:** This is the amount of chlorine that's available to sanitize your pool water. In other words, it's the chlorine that hasn't been used up and is still free to kill contaminants. If there isn't enough free chlorine in your water, bacteria and other harmful microorganisms can build up. Your free chlorine levels should be between 1 and 3 PPM.

- **Combined Chlorine (a.k.a. Chloramines):** This is chlorine that's already been used up to fight contaminants in the water. Your combined chlorine level should be no more than 0.5 PPM. If the amount of combined chlorine gets too high, your chlorine will stop working effectively, and it will produce that classic chlorine smell.

- **Total Chlorine:** This is the sum of free chlorine and combined chlorine. If the total chlorine levels are the same as the free chlorine levels (like 3 PPM), it means none of the chlorine has been used up (combined chlorine), and it's available to work as a sanitizer.

Root Causes of Low Free Chlorine Levels

The first step in raising the free chlorine in your pool is knowing what caused it. And there are several factors that can contribute to sudden or chronically low free chlorine levels.

1. High Chlorine Demand

Chlorine can only sanitize so much. If you have a high bather load or a lot of debris in the water, you'll need more chlorine to sanitize the water effectively. The more contaminants you have to fight in the water, the more chlorine your pool water will demand.

Chlorine demand is most common when your pool water sits untreated and stagnant for the winter. Heavy rainfall can also lead to chlorine demand, especially if you experience runoff from your yard.

If you just added chlorine or a chlorine-based shock to your pool and you still have a low chlorine level, there's a chlorine demand problem. In order to cure chlorine demand, triple shock your pool with calcium hypochlorite or cal-hypo shock.

2. Heavy Pool Use

The more swimmers you have in the pool and the more often you use it, the more contaminants your chlorine will need to fight. Things like sunscreen, dirt, and even the oil from your skin can cause your chlorine to work overtime.

Shock your pool weekly, especially after parties, to keep your free chlorine levels high and your water sanitized.

3. Sunlight and Low Cyanuric Acid Levels

If you're using unstabilized chlorine (like liquid chlorine or bleach) to sanitize your water, your chlorine levels will drop in the sunlight. That's because the sun's rays will break down your chlorine if it doesn't have any stabilizer (a.k.a. cyanuric acid). Test your cyanuric acid levels regularly and use a chlorine stabilizer to keep your chlorine from breaking down in the sunlight.

4. Very High Cyanuric Acid Levels

When your CYA levels are too high, it can hamper your chlorine's effectiveness. High CYA will weaken your chlorine's ability to sanitize your water. If you use three-inch chlorine tablets (trichlor pucks), it will consistently raise your cyanuric acid. Regularly test your CYA levels and make sure that it stays within the correct range of 30 and 50 PPM.

5. Increased Organic Contaminants

A heavy rainstorm can increase the contaminants in your pool water. That can quickly use up your free chlorine, as it binds to everything in an effort to sanitize the water. Be sure to clean debris from your water after a storm and shock your pool, especially if you've experienced runoff.

6. Refilling the Pool with Fresh Water

If you've just added fresh water to your pool, it could disrupt your water chemistry. More fresh water means less sanitized, balanced water with the proper amount of pool chemicals.

7. Not Adding Enough Chlorine

One of the simplest reasons behind low free chlorine levels is that there's not enough chlorine regularly added to the water. If you're adding chlorine tablets to your skimmer but your pump shuts off, that chlorine won't get into the water. And if you use a chlorine floater, make sure you have enough chlorine in it to cover your surface area.

8. Not Enough Salt in Your Salt Water Pool

If you use a salt water generator and your chlorine levels are low, your pool may not have enough salt. Your salt cell needs a certain level of salinity to function.

Test your pool salinity every month to make sure your salt levels are within range. And be sure to regularly inspect your salt water generator to make sure it's working properly.

How to Raise Free Chlorine Levels

If you've not cleaned your pool yet and there's a lot of debris, your free chlorine level is likely low because it's busy working on cleaning all those contaminants. Clean your pool and remove debris, then test the chlorine level.

Next, test your water's pH, alkalinity, and cyanuric acid levels. You'll want to make sure these are within the recommended ranges.

Once your pool is free of debris and your other levels are balanced, it's time to shock your water.

When you shock your pool, you're adding enough chlorine to reach a "chlorine breakpoint." This raises your pool's free chlorine levels to 10 times or more over the normal amount.

Don't Use a Non-Chlorine Shock!

Using a non-chlorine shock will decrease your combined chlorine but it will not raise your free chlorine level. That's because the oxidation in a non-chlorine shock helps break up contaminants without adding chlorine. Use cal-hypo shock or sodium dichlor shock.

Troubleshooting Chronically Low Free Chlorine

If your free chlorine levels are still low after shocking your water, there are several root causes:

- **Other Pool Chemicals are Out of Balance:** Without the right amount of pH or cyanuric acid in your water, your chlorine levels can fluctuate. So make sure these are balanced before shocking.

- **High Contaminant Load:** You may have a buildup of bacteria or algae that requires a more aggressive shock treatment. If your pool looks dusty on the bottom or clouds up when you brush it, it's likely mustard algae.

However, if you find that you're consistently getting low chlorine readings, you might have other more pervasive issues:

- **Check Your Cyanuric Acid Levels:** Low CYA means that your chlorine is susceptible to the sun's UV rays. So your chlorine will burn up faster. On the other hand, if your CYA levels are too high, your chlorine may be less effective, and you may need to partially drain and refill your pool.

- **Watch for High Chlorine Demand:** Your chlorine's effectiveness is finite. So if there are lots of swimmers or debris and organic contaminants in the water, more chlorine is required to properly sanitize the water. At a certain point, your chlorine gets used up faster than you can add it and your levels remain low. Again, shocking your pool can help fix this.

- **Inspect Your Salt Water Generator:** If you have constantly low chlorine levels in a salt water pool, you might need to add more pool salt or clean or replace your salt cell.

Water Bugs

Exactly as the name suggests, water bugs are insects that live in or on water. Usually, you'll find water bugs in ponds and other natural bodies of water. But two types in particular—water boatmen and backswimmers—seem to love swimming pools. Here's how to get rid of each one:

1. Water Boatmen

Water boatmen are oval-shaped and are usually brown or greenish brown in color. They have large eyes and usually don't grow more than half an inch long.

Their rear-most legs are longer than the others and are fringed with hairs that help them stay afloat and paddle, hence their name. Those legs usually extend forward, past the second set of legs. They also have wings, and yes, they can and do fly.

Because they eat algae, mosquito larvae, and other water microorganisms, water boatmen are considered beneficial insects. They're not poisonous, and they don't bite. But you still don't want them in your pool.

These particular water bugs are likely there because there's also algae in your pool. Remember, water boatmen eat algae. They also lay their eggs in algae.

Don't See Any Algae in Your Pool?

It could be that it just hasn't bloomed to the point where it's visible yet. But algae spores are microscopic, so if you see water boatmen in your pool, it's because they know there's algae there before you do.

1. **Remove the Water Bugs in Your Pool with a Net:** The easiest way with a leaf net. Remember, they fly, so they may just take off as soon as you scoop them out of the water.

2. **Vacuum the Pool:** Manually vacuum the pool. Be sure to vacuum on the waste setting to keep the dirty water from returning to the pool.

3. **Brush the Pool:** Scrub down the surfaces of your pool—including ladders and steps—to loosen any algae clinging there. This will move it into the water so the shock you're about to add kills it all.

4. **Test the Water:** Adjust your alkalinity and pH levels as needed. This will ensure the chlorine shock works the way it should.

5. **Shock the Pool:** Use a double dose of pool shock, preferably something as powerful as cal-hypo shock. If the water is a darker green, you may need a triple or even quadruple dose.

6. **Run the Pump:** Now you need to get the shock evenly distributed and allow it to dissipate so you can use the pool again. Run the pump for at least 8 hours, preferably overnight. And if you triple or quadruple shocked, run it for 24 hours. Test the water to make sure chlorine levels have returned to normal before you swim again.

How Do You Keep Water Boatmen from Returning?

Clean your pool on a regular basis and keep your chlorine (or other sanitizer) level where it's supposed to be. This'll keep algae out of your pool, which and keep the water boatmen out as well. If algae can't grow in your pool, there's nothing for the water boatmen to eat, and they'll go somewhere else. For a really quick fix to keep bugs from returning, just use a solar pool cover on your pool when you're not using it. The cover floats on top of the pools so bugs can't.

2. Backswimmers

These water bugs are long, thin, and a light- to medium-brown color. Backswimmers' back legs are longer than their other legs and are fringed to help them skim across the water. They also have wings and fly. While they don't grow more than half an inch long, they do bite!

Backswimmers' most distinctive characteristic is that they swim upside down, which is why they're called "backswimmers."

They're often mistaken for water boatmen. So if you see water bugs in your pool and you're not sure what they are, check to see whether they're upside down. If so, you have nasty backswimmers to deal with.

Backswimmers are predators, so they eat other bugs, including water boatmen. So just as you probably have water boatmen because you have algae, you probably have backswimmers because you have water boatmen.

The best way to get rid of backswimmers is to remove their food supply. That means getting the water boatmen out of the pool, which also entails getting rid of algae. While backswimmers don't eat algae like water boatmen, they do lay their eggs in it.

The same procedure you use to keep water boatmen from returning will also keep backswimmers from coming back. As long as there are water boatmen in your pool, there will also be backswimmers looking for a meal.

Pink Slime or Pink Algae

If you have orangish-pink streaks or spots around your pool's water line, it's likely pink slime. Pink slime is bacteria that's sometimes mistaken for algae. You've probably seen pink slime in your bathroom, like around shower curtains or toilet bowls. It's airborne bacteria that feeds on mineral and fatty deposits.

Just like any other bacteria, pink slime is organic and naturally occurring. But it means your pool isn't clean, and the water isn't properly balanced. The best way to prevent pink slime is to keep your pool sanitized.

Unfortunately, this pink bacteria is resistant to most of the chemicals you use to clean and sanitize your pool—even chlorine. So the usual cleaning processes and sanitizer doses won't kill it.

1. Clean the Filter

If there's pink bacteria in your pool, it's probably in your filter. So before you do anything else, clean the pool filter. Backwash your sand or D.E. filter or spray your cartridge with a hose.

2. Balance the Water

The most important level to balance is the pH. Make sure it's between 7.4 and 7.6, with 7.5 being ideal.

3. Turn Off the Pump

You'll be adding some chemicals to the water, and you don't want them to circulate just yet.

4. Brush the Pool

Using a stiff pool brush, thoroughly brush the bottom and walls of your pool. The goal is to brush as much of the pink bacteria off the surface as possible. Get into the crevices, like around your skimmer, return jets, and ladders.

5. Add a "Pink Algaecide"

Pink slime is bacteria and not algae. But because so many people call it pink algae, you may need to look for products called "pink algaecide."

6. Shock the Pool

A regular dose won't be enough to kill chemical-resistant pink bacteria. You'll need to triple or quadruple shock your pool with chlorine shock. That means adding 3 or 4 pounds of calcium hypochlorite shock per 10,000 gallons of water. Test the water between each application of shock. And remember to shock your pool at dusk or night so it doesn't burn off in the sun. Then, with the pump still off, let the pool sit overnight.

7. Vacuum the Pool

You'll need to manually vacuum the pool. Be sure to vacuum on the waste setting, meaning the water will bypass your filter. And don't allow the water line to drop too low. Have a garden hose handy to refill as necessary.

8. Clean the Filter Again and Run the Pump

Use a filter cleaner to clean your sand or D.E. filter. And use a chemical soak for a cartridge filter. Then run the pump as you normally would.

9. Keep the Chlorine Level High

During the following week, keep your chlorine level at 5 PPM. You'll want to test the water every day to make sure it's this high.

10. Balance the Water

After a week, allow the chlorine level to drop back to 3 PPM, then balance the water as you normally do, bringing all levels to where they should be. You'll want to closely monitor your pool for a week to make sure the pink bacteria doesn't return. It can help to run the pump as often as you can and to brush and vacuum the pool every other day during this time.

White Water Mold

Does it look like there's mucus floating in your water or covering your pool surfaces? You've likely got a white water mold problem. White water mold is actually a fungus. And it means your pool surfaces aren't clean and the water isn't properly balanced. So the best way to prevent it is by keeping your pool sanitized. When it comes to removing the fungus, be thorough. Even the smallest bit of white water mold left behind can multiply again.

1. Clean the Filter

If there's white water mold in your pool, it's probably in your filter. So before you do anything else, backwash your sand or D.E. filter or spray your cartridge filter with a hose.

2. Balance the Water

The most important level to balance is the pH. Make sure it's between 7.4 and 7.6, with 7.5 being ideal.

3. Shock the Pool

A regular dose of shock won't kill white water mold. You'll need to triple or even quadruple shock your pool with chlorine shock. That means adding 3 or 4 pounds of calcium hypochlorite shock per 10,000 gallons of water.

4. Brush the Pool

Using a stiff pool brush, brush your pool and get as much of the white water mold off the surface as possible. Check around the skimmer and return jets, behind ladders, and around other hidden, shady spots.

5. Run the Pump

Run your pump overnight or for at least 8 hours. The idea is to get all the mold you brushed from the pool into the filter, so give it longer than 8 hours if you can.

6. Brush the Pool Again

Think you got all the mold the first time around? Think again. If you leave any mold in your pool, it'll come right back. So brush the sides and bottom of the pool again, and then let everything settle to the bottom.

7. Vacuum the Pool

An automatic pool cleaner won't be enough for this job. You'll need to manually vacuum the pool. Be sure to vacuum on the waste setting and refill your pool if the water line drops significantly.

8. Clean the Filter Again

This time, you'll want to be extra thorough. Use a filter cleaner for a sand or D.E. filter, or a chemical soak for a cartridge filter.

9. Test and Balance the Water

Use test strips or a liquid test kit and bring the pH, alkalinity, and chlorine back to the right levels.

Now that you've done all that work, you'll want to closely monitor your pool for the next week to make sure the white water mold doesn't return. During that time, run the pump as much as you can. You may also want to brush and vacuum the pool every other day.

13

~~~

TROUBLESHOOTING POOL EQUIPMENT AND PLUMBING

TROUBLESHOOTING POOL EQUIPMENT AND PLUMBING

At some point, something will go wrong with your pool equipment. Whether your pump isn't pumping or your filter isn't filtering, there are several very common equipment and plumbing issues that most pool owners face. In this section, we'll be covering:

1. Priming a Pump
2. Pump Stops Working or Makes Noises
3. Air Bubbles from Return Jets
4. Clogged Skimmer Line
5. Pool Leaks
6. How to Repair a Vinyl Liner
7. Filter Pressure Too High or Too Low
8. Sand or D.E. in Pool

Priming a Pump

If your pump is running dry or you don't have water flowing steadily through your pump, it's time to prime. Priming a pool pump means getting water flowing through your pump before you let it run for an extended period. If you turn on your pump and it's not full of water, the whole thing can overheat. It can even melt your pump seals and damage your pool plumbing.

Always prime your pump when you're opening your pool, since your system has been full of air during the off-season. And prime your pump anytime you suspect your pool has been pulling in too much air or you notice your pump housing is dry.

1. Turn Your Multiport Valve to Recirculate

This will direct the water into the filter head, and then right back out to the pool.

2. Remove Your Pool Plugs

This is important if you're opening your pool. You'll need water to be able to flow into the pump, so remove any plugs you may have in the skimmer or return jets before you turn any equipment on.

3. Fill the Pump with Water

Remove the pump's lid and check the inside. If it's dry, you'll need to add some water. This will help fill the pipes and create suction in the pump. Even if it's not completely dry, adding more water can help.

Turn the pump off, remove the lid, and add water to the pump housing with a garden hose. Let the hose run for 2–3 minutes. Just be sure you turn the pump off before this step. Removing the lid while the pump is running will prevent the suction you need to get the pump working properly.

4. Turn the Pump Back On

Once you've filled the pump housing, replace the lid, turn the pump back on, and watch for the housing to (hopefully) fill with water. It may gurgle and sputter a little, and it may take a little time. But eventually, you should see water filling the pump housing. Once it's full of water, the pump is primed. Now it may take a couple of tries to get it primed, depending on how long your pump has been sitting dry. But there are some instances when the pump just won't prime—no matter how many times you try. If you're having issues, here are some troubleshooting tips:

1. **Check Your Water Level:** Keep an eye on your water level. If it drops below the skimmer, the pump will start pulling in air.

2. **Check for Blockages in the Skimmer:** If your skimmer basket is full of debris or you have something stuck in your skimmer, it can block the flow of water and dry out the pump.

3. **Add Water through the Skimmer:** You could have an air pocket blocking the water from moving through the system. Place a garden hose in your pool's skimmer. Adding water from this direction may loosen things up. When trying this method, you'll need your pump on. Water will enter the skimmer and make its way to the pump only if the system is running.

4. **Check for Air Leaks:** If, after several tries, your pump still won't prime, you could have an air leak in the pump housing. Turn the pump off, remove the pump cover and inspect the O-ring for cracks and worn-out spots. You may need to lubricate it with silicone lubricant or buy a new O-ring. Make sure the O-ring is seated when you close the lid so it creates a tight seal. You'll also want to check the rest of your pump, fittings, and connections for any cracks, damage, or spots where air might be getting in.

5. **Check for Clogs in Your Pump's Impeller:** If the pump's impeller is clogged with debris, your pump will lose suction. Turn off your pump, check your impeller and clean it out if necessary.

Pump Stops Working or Makes Noises

If your pump has stopped working or it's making loud noises, you may actually be able to fix it yourself. Here are several common pump issues and how to troubleshoot each one:

1. Pump Isn't Turning On or It's Turning Off While Running

If your pump doesn't turn on at all or if it shuts off quickly after it's started, it's probably an electrical problem. Check your breaker box for blown fuses. Then check your connections to make sure nothing is loose or damaged. If you don't know what you're doing, be safe, and hire a qualified electrician.

If your motor overheats and shuts down after it's started, it could be an overloaded circuit. Make sure you've got the right voltage for your pump. Also, check the motor's vents to make sure nothing is blocking the fan. If the motor shaft isn't rotating, check to see if the motor is jammed with debris.

Finally, if the pump turns on but isn't running full steam and you hear a humming noise, check your capacitor. The capacitor starts your pump with a jolt of electricity. This is one of those parts that are best replaced by a professional.

2. Pump Runs, But It Isn't Pumping or the Flow Rate Is Low

Your pump likely needs to be primed because something has interrupted its suction or water flow.

Be sure to check out the section on priming a pump. If priming the pump doesn't solve the issues, there could be something blocking it, a dirty pool filter, or too much air in the system.

If there's something blocking your pump's suction, check your filter gauge. If it's 10 PSI above the normal reading, clean your filter. This will reduce pressure and reset your pump's flow. Then check your pump basket and impeller for debris.

If there's air in the system, it's probably coming through the skimmer or a leaky O-ring. Be sure to inspect your pump unions, lid, and housing for air leaks.

Finally, make sure your water level isn't too low and check your skimmer basket for debris.

3. Pump Is Leaking

If you have a leaky pump, look for any seals that need replacing, like O-rings in the impeller housing, the thread sealant, or the shaft seal. If your pump is constantly leaking or losing suction, it might be time to get a new pool pump.

4. Pump Is Sucking in Air

Your pump can start sucking in air for a number of reasons:

- A loose pump lid
- A crack in the pump
- A faulty thread sealant
- Faulty O-rings and gaskets
- An air leak in the suction line
- A leaky valve stem
- A plumbing issue on the suction side of the pump.

Look for cracks, leaks, or bad fittings and replace the part. Can't find the air leak? Spread shaving cream on those possible problem areas. If there's a leak, it will suck in the shaving cream, leaving an indent.

5. Pump Is Making a Lot of Noise

If your motor is really rattling, your pool pump may just need better water flow. Clear any blockages out of a plumbing line, look for air leaks, and prime your pump.

However, If your motor has a high-pitched screech, your pump could have bad bearings. Unfortunately, that means you'll need to call a professional to take apart the motor and replace the bearings.

6. Pump Basket Isn't Filling with Water

If the basket isn't filling with water, your pump could be sucking in air or your filter or pump basket could be clogged.

Clean the filter and pump basket. Then check the water level in your skimmer. If it's low, that could be your air problem. Finally, use the shaving cream test to check for other air leaks. Add a bit of shaving cream over the areas where you suspect a leak. If there's a leak, it'll suck in the shaving cream, and you'll see an indent.

7. Pump Is Humming and Won't Start

First, check the impeller for blocking debris. Turn off the pump and remove the screws on the pump housing. Pull out the pump assembly and remove any gaskets away from the impeller. Then remove any debris you see and put the pump back together.

If you hear a buzzing or humming noise, it's coming from the pump motor. This means power is reaching the motor but is having trouble starting it. It could be a bad capacitor, centrifugal switch, or a buildup of rust in the motor. It could also mean the impeller is stuck.

Time to Replace Your Pump?

A well-made pool pump should last about 8 to 10 years with proper maintenance. But here are a few signs that your pump is on its last legs:

1. You have consistently low filter pressure (even when the filter is clean).

2. Your pool pump is constantly leaking (even when it's turned off).

3. Your pump always loses its prime.

Air Bubbles from Return Jets

Do you have air bubbles shooting out of your pool's return jets? You've likely got air in your system. And usually it's because air is entering through the suction side of your pool. This is especially common when you open your pool in the spring.

There are three places you need to check to figure out how you're getting air in the plumbing:

1. Check Your Skimmers

This is where water is supposed to enter the filtration system. But if there's a problem with the skimmer, there's probably a problem with air in the system.

If your pool doesn't have enough water, your skimmers might be pulling in air, which is why you'll see bubbles in the pool. Be sure your pool's water level sits in the middle of the skimmer's opening.

Then check the skimmer baskets. Make sure the skimmer baskets are not damaged and are seated properly to ensure good water suction.

Finally, check your weir. This is the skimmer flap or door on the front of the skimmer. It's there to trap large debris from entering the filtration system. It also regulates water flow into the system. Sometimes it can get jammed, so make sure it's moving freely. And if your skimmer doesn't have a weir, it's a good idea to install one.

2. Check Your Pump

If everything seems to be okay with the skimmer, the problem may be with the pump itself. First, check the pump lid. If it's cracked, that's the problem. However, the most common issue is usually the lid's O-ring. Turn the pump off, remove the lid, and check the O-ring for cracks. Just bend the O-ring between your fingers, around the whole O-ring, to check for any signs of cracking.

If it looks like the O-ring is splitting or dry-rotted, it needs to be replaced. If there are no signs of cracking, add a Teflon-based O-ring lubricant to help keep it from drying out.

Then check the pump basket. If the basket is cracked, it won't sit correctly in the housing. Replace the broken pump basket, make sure you clean it frequently, and keep it properly seated so the lid seals properly.

Finally, check the drain plugs. On the pump housing, you'll find a drain plug or two. Make sure the drain plugs are not loose or leaking. You can apply some pipe thread sealant tape, a.k.a. plumber's tape, for a tighter seal.

3. Check Your Plumbing Unions

If you have an inground pool, you might have some unions in the plumbing. These are threaded connectors between piping that allow you to easily replace your filter equipment without having to cut your pipes.

Inside the union, check the O-ring for damage. If you see cracks in the O-ring, replace it. If not, make sure the O-ring is properly seated inside its groove. If the O-ring isn't in its groove, it won't create a proper seal and will allow air to get into the system, which will create air bubbles in the pool.

Clogged Skimmer Line

Think there's something stuck inside of your skimmer line? A random tennis ball or a pile of debris can clog up the inside of your plumbing. Be sure to check and clean out your skimmer basket at least once a week. But if your skimmer basket is debris-free and you still think there's an issue, here are a few signs your skimmer line might be clogged:

1. Pool Pump Is Pulsing or Loud and the Pressure Is Low

If water is surging or pulsing in your pump, this may be a sign of a clogged pipe. But first, you have to rule out other potential problems, like air leaks. Check the O-ring on your pump lid. Then check to see if the impeller inside your pump is clogged. Be sure the pump is off when you check this. It may also be time to backwash or clean your filter if you haven't done that in a while. And if you have just cleaned your filter, that may have caused an air pocket to form (check out the section on priming your pump).

2. Water Intake into Your Pump Is Slow, Even If the Skimmer Basket Is Empty

If water is slowly coming into your pool pump, check the skimmer door to make sure it isn't stuck. Also, make sure your pool's water level is halfway up the skimmer. If the skimmer door and water level look good, you may have a clog in your skimmer line.

To find out which pipe is blocked, run your pool pump and check each line one at a time. You can do this by using your pool diverter valve, a.k.a. a Jandy Valve. Switch the valve between the skimmers and the main drain lines. If one line has low pressure or your pump loses suction, that means it's clogged with an air pocket or debris. As you test these lines, be sure to always leave one line open. You never want to run your pump with all the intake valves closed and no water flowing.

If you've determined that there's a clog in your skimmer line, here are two ways to try to unclog it yourself. If you're not comfortable handling your pool plumbing on your own, be sure to call in a professional.

1. Move Pool Diverter Valve Back and Forth

Opening and closing the pool diverter valve while the pump is running may dislodge whatever is blocking your skimmer line. Shimmy the diverter valve back and forth between the lines for several seconds each time. After several rounds of opening and closing the skimmer valve, you may remove the air pocket or dislodge the debris into the pump strainer basket. Be sure to always leave one line open during this process so there's water flowing to your pump as it runs.

2. Clear the Blockage With a Drain Cleaning Bladder

Drain cleaning bladders attach to your garden hose and are then inserted into the clogged line. When the hose is turned on, the bladder expands and pushes pressurized water down the pipe.

First, shut off your pump completely. Make sure your diverter valve is turned to the skimmer line. Then remove your skimmer basket. Insert the hose with the bladder attachment into the suction hole of your skimmer. Push it in as far as it will go. When you turn on the hose, the bladder will expand while it's in the pipe. That pressurized water will push any debris and air to the pump. If that doesn't work, try using the drain cleaning bladder in the pump.

Make sure the pump is still off and the diverter valve is set to the skimmer line. Remove the pump basket and insert the hose with the bladder into the pump's intake pipe that flows back toward the pool. This will force pressurized water back into the skimmer. Keep an eye out for debris that blows back to the skimmer. You will also want to use the bladder in the pump if you have a clog in your main drain line. Just make sure the diverter valve is turned to the main drain when you do this. Keep in mind that it can take several rounds of diverting water or using the bladder to unclog your lines.

Pool Leaks

Pool leaks can occur anywhere in your pool. But before you start searching for a leak, you'll need to rule out a few issues like evaporation or a crack in the filter system plumbing.

Before you run any tests inside your pool, you'll need to make sure the leak isn't happening somewhere inside your plumbing or pool equipment.

Start by checking your entire filter system area. That includes your pool pump, filter, heater, chlorinator, and any O-ring or connections where you might be losing water. Luckily, these leaks are easy to access.

However, there's a chance there could be a leak in a part of your plumbing you can't see. And if you have an inground pool, leaks can happen in cracked piping underground.

Regardless, even if you're not sure if you have a plumbing leak, you'll first need to test your pool to make sure that you're not losing water to evaporation. Then you'll narrow down the source of the leak. You can do this with the bucket test or the ink test.

1. Bucket Leak Test

This DIY method is easy. You likely already have all the supplies you need: a 5-gallon plastic bucket and a waterproof marker or duct tape.

1. **Place and Fill the Bucket:** Put your empty 5-gallon bucket in the water on the second step of your pool. Fill the bucket with water to match the pool's water level. Use the marker or duct tape to mark this level inside the bucket.

2. **Turn Off the Pump:** Turn off the recirculating pump as well as any other auto-refill device you may have.

3. **Compare Water Levels:** Wait 24 hours and compare the pool water level to the level of water in the bucket. If both have gone down but remain even, your pool is losing water due to evaporation. But if the swimming pool level is now lower than the level in the bucket, you likely have a leak.

4. **Repeat with Pump On:** To narrow down the possible source of the leak, repeat the test for another 24-hour period, this time with the pump on.

5. **Compare New Results:** If the water loss in the pool is greater with water circulating under pressure, the leak is most likely somewhere in your pool's filter system or plumbing.

2. Dye Leak Test

This method will help you find the exact location of the leak, but it's a little more involved. You'll need to purchase a leak finder dye to add directly to your pool water. It's also handy to have some waterproof tape on hand for marking potential leaky spots in your pool.

1. **Check the Ground and Walls Around the Pool for Wetness:** If the ground is wet where it shouldn't be, your pool is likely leaking somewhere near that area and seeping somewhere in the ground. Keep narrowing it down as much as possible before using the leak finder dye.

2. **Turn Off the Pump and Water Features:** You'll need the water to be as still as possible before using the dye to help find the location of the leak. This will also help you detect leaks in or near the skimmer.

3. **Use the Pool Leak Detection Dye to Pinpoint the Leak:** Go to the edge of the swimming pool in the area where you think the leak might be. Without touching the water, squirt the dye in the water close to the surface and the wall. If the leak is near, you will see the dye move toward the exaction location of the leak like a current.

4. **Mark the Spot for Patching:** Use waterproof tape to mark the spot where you spotted the leak detection dye moving toward. This is to help you remember where you need to patch the leak.

If you suspect your leak is at the bottom of your pool, you'll need to swim to the bottom to perform the leak finder test. But you'll need to be as still as possible when you run the test so the dye doesn't go everywhere.

If you have a concrete pool or gunite pool and it's developed cracks, especially where the plastic skimmer meets the pool wall, you'll need some plaster repair. But if your pool has a vinyl liner, you can repair the patch yourself. Check out the section on how to repair a vinyl liner.

How to Repair a Vinyl Liner

Leak repair is fairly straightforward in a vinyl liner pool, and a well-placed quality pool patch can last for years. But no matter what method you use to repair your pool's liner, patches are temporary. And the bigger your tear, the more likely it will snag or peel off over time.

So before you do any repair, decide if your liner is worth trying to patch or if it's time to replace it altogether. The older the liner, the thinner it's become and the more prone it is to spring leaks in the future. And keep in mind that any area close to the stairs or near your pool's fittings is being pulled by the weight of your pool water. They're under more duress than other areas of your pool, so patches there may be less likely to hold up in the long run.

If you do want to repair the leak, there are three methods to choose from, and all of them can be used underwater or dry. Do not drain your pool to fix a leak. You shouldn't need to drain any of your water to apply a patch to a leak. Draining out too much water in an above ground pool can cause the walls to collapse. And emptying out any pool with a vinyl liner will dry it out, making the liner brittle. So plan to patch the liner underwater unless the leak happens to be dry and above the waterline.

1. Waterproof Tape

Similar to duct tape, this tape is clear, waterproof, and resistant to UV rays. You can overlap this tape if you need to patch large sections. It's the lowest cost option and the easiest to redo if you make a mistake. But it's best for smaller leak repair, as it tends to peel over time.

2. Peel-and-Stick Patches

These patches are made of real vinyl and are designed specifically for pools. Some patches are precut into round shapes, making them less likely to peel around the edges. They're also inexpensive and easy to use: simply remove the backing and press of the leak. But they're also best used on smaller tears or punctures.

3. Vinyl Patch Kit

If you have a larger hole to repair or you want a longer-term solution, use a vinyl patch kit. These kits come with large chunks of blue or clear liner and special underwater vinyl adhesive. These are more complicated to use, but they'll last longer than waterproof tape or a peel-and-stick patch.

Filter Pressure Too High or Low

Your pool filter pressure gauge is one of your most valuable pieces of equipment. Just like a check engine light, it can alert you to a potential problem with your filter system before things get out of hand. The filter pressure gauge is attached to the top of your filter. It's a small dial with numbers and an indicator "hand" that moves up or down to indicate whether the pressure level is too low, too high, or just right. Your pool filter needs a certain amount of pressure inside the tank to function. This pressure is measured in pounds per square inch or PSI.

When water is flowing through normally, the filter pressure is normal. When your water flow increases or decreases, the pressure inside the filter and the reading on your filter gauge will change. If that pressure gets too low or too high, the filter won't work properly. And that can damage your pool equipment.

What is Normal Filter Pressure?

Average filter pressure ranges from 10 PSI to 25 PSI. What's "normal" for your filter will depend on a few factors like the filter size, your pump size and power, and how clean or dirty the filter is. But you can set a baseline number for what's normal for your filter. Right after you clean or backwash your filter, take note of the PSI reading on your pool filter pressure gauge. That's your normal pressure level. You may even want to mark this on the gauge itself. Then check your pressure gauge once a week as part of your regular pool maintenance routine. Now there is a chance your pressure gauge is faulty or has worn out over time. If you turn the pump motor off and the pressure gauge doesn't drop, that might mean it's time to replace it. Luckily, it's not that expensive. Another good indicator of normal water pressure is the flow out of your return jets. If your water flow is fine but your pressure gauge is off, that might be another sign your gauge is faulty.

How to Fix High Filter Pressure

When your pool filter pressure gauge starts to read higher than normal, it's not necessarily a bad thing. As your filter gets dirty, the PSI will naturally start to rise. But as weird as it sounds, your filter is actually a little more effective when it's a bit dirty. As dirt and debris start to build up, they can help grab even more dirty particles as they pass through the filter media.

So a slight rise above normal pool filter pressure is okay, especially if your water flow is good. But when the pressure reads 10 PSI above normal, it's time to take action. Usually, this means cleaning your cartridge filters or backwashing your sand or D.E. filter. If cleaning or backwashing the filter doesn't bring the pressure level down or if the pressure rises rapidly after you've cleaned it, it may be time to replace your cartridges or grids.

Another way to fix high pool filter pressure? Your air relief valve. Air in your pool circulation system can cause high pressure. This could happen if your pool's water level is too low and it's sucking in air.

Air can also get in the system if you've turned the pool off and then on again, say for vacation or to clean it. When water begins to flow through the system, it pushes any air that's built up back through the system. Left too long, air can damage your equipment, especially the pump which must contain water to function properly.

So that's where the air relief valve can help manually release the air from the system and bring the pressure back down. This valve is usually a tiny handle near the filter pressure gauge or the top of your filter.

How to Fix Low Filter Pressure

If the pool filter pressure gauge starts to read 5 PSI or lower than normal, it means water isn't reaching the filter quickly enough. The most common cause is a blockage located somewhere before the filter. This means it's time to check the skimmers, pump basket, pump impeller, and drain covers for anything blocking your circulation.

- **Check the Skimmers:** Again, your pool water level should reach halfway up the skimmer. Make sure the skimmer basket is seated properly to ensure good water suction. And make sure your skimmer flat door, a.k.a. the weir, is moving freely.

- **Check the Pump Lid and Pump Basket:** Turn off your pump-filter system and take off your pump lid. Make sure the O-ring inside the lid is fitted properly and that your lid isn't cracked or damaged. Then remove the pump basket and empty it if it's full of debris.

- **Check the Pump Impeller:** Your pump impeller sits behind the pump basket in the impeller housing. And it's the only moving part of your pump that propels water into your system at a very high velocity. That means if it's clogged, your pressure might be low. You can easily unclog it by using a screwdriver or even a wire hanger to check inside and make sure the impeller is spinning freely. Just make sure your system is off before checking it.

Now there is a less common but more serious cause for a low pool filter pressure, and that's a leak somewhere in the system like the pool pump. Examine the pump carefully for any signs of a leak. If the pump is the problem, you can repair it yourself, hire a professional, or replace the pump entirely.

Just remember if your filter is clean, there's no blockages in your system, and your pressure gauge still says something's wrong, it might be a problem with the gauge itself.

Sand or D.E. in Pool

If there's sand at the bottom of your pool and you own a sand filter, you likely have to fix and replace some parts in your filter. But if you don't own a sand filter, and live nowhere near sand, chances are it's not sand. In fact, it might be yellow (mustard) pool algae.

To test, brush it up. If it forms into a cloud, you have yellow pool algae. Be sure to check our Troubleshooting Section about Algae and Green Water. So how did the sand get outside of your filter and into your pool? Inside your sand filter is a pipe that runs down the center of the sand. At the bottom of that pipe are laterals.

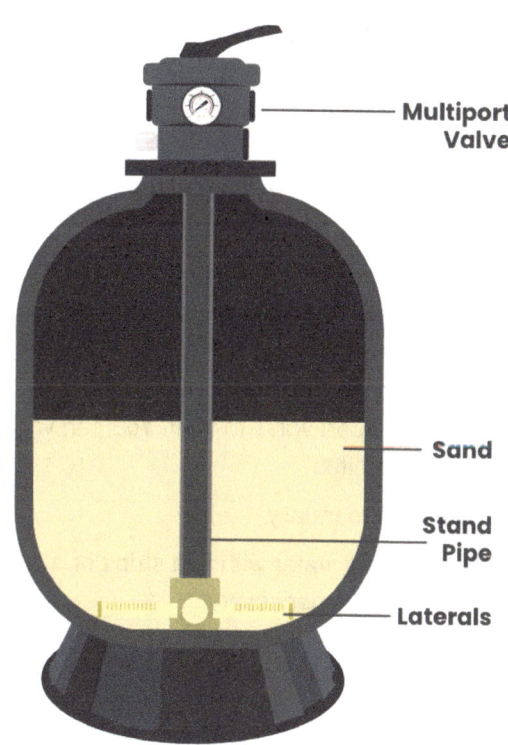

Multiport Valve

Sand

Stand Pipe

Laterals

Either your standpipe or your laterals may be cracked. Chances are, it's one or more of the laterals located at the bottom of the standpipe since the standpipe is pretty thick and harder to crack than the laterals. Only one of the laterals needs to crack in order to leak sand into your pool.

Laterals can crack if the filter got moved and shifted the standpipe or if the laterals were weak or old and cracked under the heavy weight of the sand. No matter how it happened, you need to fix it.

Before removing any sand from your pool, you'll have to fix your sand filter standpipe or laterals. Otherwise, more sand will just end up in your water.

Take apart your sand filter, remove all the sand and replace whatever piece is broken. Once you've replaced the broken parts and put your filter back together, you can move on to addressing the sand in your pool.

How to Get Sand Out of Your Pool

If your sand filter breaks and starts dumping sand into the pool, it will be fairly concentrated below the pool returns. That makes it fairly easy to remove.

1. Use a pool brush to push all the sand to one area, or at least to a few concentrated areas.
2. Set the filter's multiport valve to filter. You can vacuum the sand back into the filter.
3. Vacuum your pool manually.
4. Test and balance the water with test strips or a liquid test kit, and add chemicals as necessary.

How to Get D.E. Out of Your Pool

Just like with a sand filter, when you find D.E. powder in your pool, it means something is broken inside your filter. And it's probably your filter grids.

1. Shut off your pump and open your D.E. filter to expose the grids.

2. Remove the grids and rinse off the caked-on D.E. powder with a hose.

3. Remove the top manifold and take out each grid and rinse them down again.

4. While you have each grid separated, examine them with a close eye. Look for rips and tears in the fabric around the grids. Feel for any broken ribs. Also, check the pipes and manifold for any cracks.

5. Replace any broken or ripped pieces, then put the grid manifold back together and in the tank.

6. Close up the tank and turn the filter system back on. Don't forget to add more D.E.

7. Vacuum up the D.E. in your pool once your filter is fixed.

14

GLOSSARY OF TERMS

Acid: Liquid (muriatic acid) or dry granular (sodium bisulfate) substance used to lower the pool's pH (toward a more acidic condition) or to lower total alkalinity levels.

Air Relief Valve: Located on the top of the filter and sometimes accompanied by a pressure gauge, this is opened to release air trapped in the filter. Also called a bleeder.

Algae: Over 20,000 species known to exist. Algae may form on pool surfaces or may bloom in suspension. We typically know algae to be green, but it may also be yellow (mustard algae), black, blue-green, or any shade in between. It may form in separate spots or seem to grow in sheets. Pink algae is not algae at all but a form of bacteria. Algae are living, breathing organisms that need warmth, sunlight, and CO_2 to thrive.

Alkalinity: Alkaline refers to the condition where the water's pH is above 7.0 (neutral) on the pH scale. It is the opposite of acidic. Alkalinity is the amount of carbonates and bicarbonates in the water, measured in "parts per million" (PPM) of total alkalinity.

Automatic Pool Cleaner: A device which agitates or vacuums debris from the walls and floor of the pool.

Backwash: The process of thoroughly cleaning the filter medium and/or elements by reversing the flow of water through the filter to waste.

Balanced Water: Balanced water exists when all your chemical parameters are where they should be. The key components of water balance are pH, total alkalinity, calcium hardness, and temperature, as measured using the Langelier Index of water balance.

Ball Valve: A device with a hollowed-out ball inside which can be turned with an external handle to decrease or increase flow.

Biguanides: The name for a certain class of sanitizers which use the polymer PHMB, the only nonhalogen sanitizer available for pool and spa use.

Bicarbonate: An intermediate form in the deprotonation of carbonic acid.

Bleeder: See Air Relief Valve.

Booster Pump: Secondary to the filter pump, a booster pump is used to power an automatic pool cleaner.

Breakpoint Chlorination: When you shock your pool, the goal is to reach a high enough level of free chlorine, measured in PPM, to break apart molecular bonds, specifically the combined chlorine molecules. When breakpoint is reached with sufficient additions of chlorine, everything in the pool is oxidized.

Bromamines: A combined bromine-ammonia molecule. Unlike chloramines, which are strong-smelling and offer no sanitizing properties, bromamine compounds continue to sanitize.

Bromine: A member of the halogen family, commonly used as a sanitizer in spas because of its resistance to hot water with rapid pH fluctuations.

BTU: British Thermal Unit. A unit of measurement for the use of gas by a gas appliance. Pool heaters are rated by their consumption.

Buffer: A base such as sodium bicarbonate (baking soda). When added to your pool, it will increase alkalinity, which increases the buffering capacity of the pool. It is your pool's resistance to pH change.

Calcium: A soft gray alkaline earth metal.

Calcium Carbonate: Known as scale, crystalline deposits of calcium may form on your pool surfaces, equipment, or even line your pipes. Properly balanced water can prevent this.

Calcium Chloride: This flaked calcium salt is used to raise levels of calcium hardness in your pool water. Also good for melting snow.

Calcium Hardness: The level of the mineral calcium dissolved in the pool water, as measured by a titration test.

Capacitor: The capacitor is the battery for your pump motor. It provides the energy needed while starting, reaching 3,450 RPM quickly. Replace your capacitor when the shaft can be spun freely with a wrench or by hand. When powering the motor, you'll hear a buzz or a hum from the motor, but no impeller movement. Replace your old capacitor with an exact match to the MFD number on the new capacitor.

Carbon Dioxide: A gas, which when present in the water, provides necessary food for the growth of algae.

Cartridge: A type of filtration where the cartridge is a pleated, porous element through which water passes.

Cavitation: A general term used to describe the behavior of voids or bubbles in a liquid. Cavitation is usually divided into two classes of behavior: inertial (or transient) cavitation and noninertial cavitation. Inertial cavitation is the process where a void or bubble in a liquid rapidly collapses, producing a shock wave. Such cavitation often occurs in pumps and impellers. Noninertial cavitation is the process where a bubble in a fluid is forced to oscillate in size or shape due to some form of energy input, such as an acoustic field. Such cavitation can be observed in pumps.

Channeled Sand: When water has worked open "holes" in the sand and is streaming right through (without really going through the sand).

Check Valve: A one way flow device.

Chelator: A chelating agent is a water-soluble molecule that can bond tightly with metal ions, keeping them from coming out of suspension and depositing their stains and scale on pool surfaces and equipment. Similar to sequestering agents.

Chloramines: The chlorine molecule is strongly attracted to nitrogen and ammonia. When these two combine they form a chloramine, which are undesirable, foul-smelling, space-taking compounds. Shocking the pool will get rid of these compounds.

Chlorine: A member of the halogen family of sanitizers, its use in swimming pools is in the elemental form of a liquid, granular, or tablet compound. When added to water, it acts as an oxidizer, sanitizer, disinfectant, and all-around biocidal agent.

Chlorine, Free Available: Free available chlorine is chlorine which is active, not combined with an ammonia or a nitrogen molecule, and ready to react to destroy organic material.

Chlorine, Combined: That portion of total available chlorine left over when free available is subtracted. It's the measure of chlorine which has already attached itself to other molecules or organisms. Most of this is made up of chloramines.

Chlorine, Total Available: The sum of combined and free chlorine levels. With a DPD test kit, one determines free available level, then total available. The difference, if any, is the level of combined chlorine.

Chlorinator: Device which allows for the safe, controlled introduction of chlorine into the water.

Chlorine Demand: The quantity of free available chlorine removed during the process of sanitizing. The amount of organic and inorganic material contained in the water will demand a certain level of oxidizer to be destroyed.

Circuit Breaker: A switch which allows manual override of an electrical circuit. It also automatically breaks the circuit when current fluctuations are detected.

Circulation System: The circuit of plumbing that continuously carries the water out of the pool, through the pump and filter, then returns it to the pool.

Clarifier: A clarifier is a chemical used as a coagulant for suspended microparticles. It helps the filter by clumping smaller particles into filterable sizes.

Coagulant: The properties of a chemical used in the assemblage and precipitation of suspended material, which may make the pool appear cloudy.

Conduit: A pipe, usually gray PVC or flexible PVC, designed to carry wires from a source (time clock) to a load (pump motor).

Contaminants: Any microparticle or organism which reduces water clarity or quality and may present a health hazard. All our filtering, circulating, and sanitizing is directed toward killing contaminants.

Coping: The capstone on top of the bond beam which finishes the edge around a pool or spa. It may be precast concrete or brick. On vinyl liner pools, prefabricated coping is usually part of an integrated system for the wall, vinyl liner, and deck.

Copper: An effective algaestat and algaecide. Elemental copper is used in many pools in products.

Corrosion: The effects of an acidic pool environment—one in which the pH and/or alkalinity are very low. Corrosion results in the form of etching, pitting, or erosion of pool equipment and surfaces.

Coupling: A plumbing fitting designed to join two pieces of pipe.

Cover, Automatic: Solid, reinforced vinyl which rolls onto a reel on one end of the pool and attaches on the sides into small aluminum tracks. It can be motorized or hand-crank style. Some models may snap the sides into small anchors placed into the deck, providing more shape flexibility. It also provides debris protection, as well as heat, chemical, and water retention.

Cover, Hard: A cover which rests on the edge or coping of the spa or small pool. Provides a barrier to debris and possibly people, while keeping the heat trapped in.

Cover, Solar: Sometimes called a thermal blanket, this cover floats on the surface, magnifying the sun's rays to warm the water. It also prevents chemical, heat, and water evaporation.

Cover, Winter: A barrier to sun and debris, winter covers secure the pool from contamination. These are subdivided below.

Cover, Mesh: These stretch tightly across the pool like a trampoline. They are the only covers which can be called "safety covers" in that the mesh polypropylene allows precipitation to pass through.

Cover, Solid: These are usually made of some form of plastic or vinyl and are secured around the edges, either by aqua blocks, similar weight, or the edges attach to anchors set in the concrete or wood deck.

Cyanuric Acid/Conditioner/Chlorine Stabilizer: Also called conditioner or stabilizer, cyanuric acid (or CYA) provides a shield from the sun around the chlorine molecule, extending the efficacy of your chlorine.

Diatomaceous Earth (D.E.): The filtering medium of the D.E. filter, this dry powder is the fossilized remains of an ancient plankton diatom.

Dichloro-S-Triazinetrione: A chemical compound. It is an oxidizer, bactericide, algicide, and cleaning agent that reacts with water to form hypochlorous acid, which is related to bleach.

Disinfectant: Chemicals or processes which work to destroy vegetative forms of microorganisms and other contaminants. Examples are chlorine, bromine, and ionizers. Also includes copper and silver algaecides.

Diverter Valve: Used in a twin-port skimmer, a diverter allows the operator to manipulate the amount of flow from the main drain and skimmer to the pump.

DPD: A method of testing for chlorine levels in the pool water. Unlike OTO, DPD testing allows determination of total and free available chlorine levels which, through subtraction, gives us combined levels.

Drain: Also called the "main drain," this plumbing fitting is the start of one suction line to the pump and is usually situated at or near the center bottom of the pool.

Dry Acid: Sodium bisulfate, a granular form of acid used to lower pH and alkalinity in the water. It is safer and less caustic than muriatic acid. Usually available as a pH decreaser.

Effluent: The water that flows out of the pump on its way through the filter, heating, treating equipment, and then returning to the pool. Also known as the pressure side.

Elbow: A 90- or 45-degree plumbing fitting used where your pipes take a turn.

Enzymes: Used in swimming pool formulations designed to break down and digest oils in a pool or spa, similar to the way enzymes are used in oil spill cleanup efforts.

Fill Water: Used in filling or adding to the water level. Whether from the hose or from a well, your fill water brings its own chemical makeup and water balance (or lack thereof).

Filter: A device used to remove particles suspended in the water by pumping water through a porous substance or material.

Filter Element: A device inside a filter tank designed to trap solids and direct water through a manifold system to exit the filter. Cartridge filter elements and D.E. filter grids are two examples.

Filter Media: A fine material such as sand, diatomaceous earth, polyester fabric, or anthracite coal that removes suspended particles from water passing through it.

Filter Pump: The device that pulls water from the pool and pushes it through the filter on its way back to the pool.

Filtration Rate: The rate of water pumped through a filter, in gallons per minute (GPM).

Foaming: A term used to describe surface foam on your water, especially in spas or hot tubs. Foaming is caused by high TDS levels working in combination with soft water and oils. Certain low-grade algaecides can foam when added to a pool or spa. Use enzymes for foam control.

Flocculant: Essentially the same as a coagulant, this chemical (such as alum) is used to combine suspended alkaline material and/ or algae into a heavy gel, which sinks to the bottom for vacuuming to waste.

Flow Rate: The quantity of water flowing past a specific point in a specified time (i.e., the number of liters flowing through the filter in one hour).

Gas Valve: An electronic valve in the pool heater that directs gas flow from the meter to the pilot and the burner tray.

Gasket: A gasket is a mechanical seal that fills the space between two objects, generally to prevent leakage between the two objects while under compression. Gaskets are commonly produced by cutting from sheet materials, such as gasket paper, rubber, silicone, metal, or a plastic polymer.

Gunite: A dry mixture of cement and sand mixed with water at the "gun," hence the name. A gunite operator "shoots" the pool's rough shape and finishes with a trowel.

Halogen: A member of the family of elements fluorine, bromine, chlorine, and iodine.

Hard Water: Water which is high in calcium hardness and other salts.

Heater: A device used to heat the water. It may be electric, fuel-operated, or solar-powered.

Heat Exchanger: A set of eight or ten ribbed copper tubes that absorb the heat produced below it and transfer it to the water cycling through its tubes.

Heat Pump: The antithesis of the air conditioner, the heat pump's cooling coil removes heat from the air while the condenser coil transfers it to the water cycling through it.

Horsepower (hp): The name of several non-metric units of power. The most occurring conversion of horsepower to watt goes 1 horsepower = 745.7 watts.

Hypochlorite: A family of chlorine compounds, such as calcium hypochlorite and lithium hypochlorite (both granular), and the liquid sodium hypochlorite. When these compounds contact water, they release hypochlorous acid, the active sanitizing agent.

Impeller: The rotating vanes of a centrifugal pump that create the flow of water. The impeller is shaft-driven by an electric motor.

Influent: The water coming in and up to the impeller from the suction lines. These pipes are under vacuum pressure.

Ionizer: An ionizer is a device mounted on your return line and through which water flowing will receive charged metal ions. Manufacturers may use a copper anode and/or silver. Copper is an algaecide and algaestat, while silver is known for its properties as a bactericide.

Iron: Usually introduced into the water from iron plumbing or from well water, ferric iron can stain surfaces, while ferrous iron will turn your water a clear green color.

Ladder Bumpers: Rubber caps or inserts that protect the pool plaster or vinyl liner from the sharp steel ends of the ladder.

Laterals: Elongated capped plastic nipples at the bottom of a sand filter, which are slotted to allow for water passage while keeping the sand in the filter tank.

Magnesium: A light, ductile, silver-white, metallic element. Its presence in high non-chelated concentrations can lead to stains and scale when conditions are right.

Minerals: Calcium, manganese, magnesium, nickel, copper, silver, iron, cobalt, or aluminum. Their presence in high non-chelated concentrations can lead to stains and scale when conditions are right.

Microorganism: A living, breathing creature in your pool. The purpose of disinfectants is to remove such infectants.

Mechanical Seal: A seal behind the impeller which prevents water from running out along the shaft of a motor. Also known as a pump seal.

Motor: A machine for converting electrical energy into mechanical energy. Your motor is known as the dry end of the filter pump. It drives the impeller, which moves the water.

Multiport Valve: A four- or six-position valve that combines the functionality of several valves into one unit, revolutionizing pool plumbing.

Muriatic Acid: The liquid dilution of hydrochloric acid used to lower pH and alkalinity and to remove mineral stains and scale. Extremely caustic and corrosive.

Nitrogen: When combined with chlorine, nitrogen creates chloramines, which do not belong in your pool. Nitrogen can be introduced to pool water through swimmers' wastes (perspiration, suntan oil, etc.) or by organic material.

Non-chlorine Shock/Oxidizer: A granular form of potassium peroxymonosulfate used to oxidize materials such as microorganisms, contaminants, or chloramines.

O-ring: A loop of elastomer with a round (O-shaped) cross section, used as a mechanical seal or gasket. Designed to be seated in a groove and compressed during assembly between two or more parts, creating a seal at the interface.

OTO: Another method of testing for free available chlorine levels in your pool, as in an OTO test kit.

Oxidation: The "burning up" of organic waste and compounds in the pool water. It also refers to what you may see on your metal pool surfaces if your water is corrosive. Rust is a form of this kind of oxidation.

pH: The scale of relative acidity or alkalinity, expressed in logarithmic numbers from 0.0–14.0, with 7.0 being neutral. What's really being measured is the hydrogen ion concentration. Some would say pH stands for Power of Hydrogen.

Plaster: A common type of interior finish applied over the concrete shell of an inground swimming pool.

Plunger: The sliding disc assembly that changes valve position in a push-pull valve. For example, up for backwash and down for filtration.

Potassium Permonosulfate: See non-chlorine shock.
Polymer: An algaecide/algaestat made up of repeating polymer molecules. Used for green algae and available in varying strengths.

PPM: Parts per million. A method of assigning value to certain concentrations of chemicals in the water. For example, chlorine should be kept at around 3 parts per million, by weight and in relation to the water it's dissolved in.

Precipitation: To precipitate is to come out of solution or become insoluble by result of chemical action. Material forced out of solution, purposely or accidentally, will then settle, stain or scale, or remain suspended in the water.

Pressure Check: A test for the rate of water flow. Also a test for leaks in plumbing by placing a line in question under pressure and waiting for the pressure to drop.

Pressure Gauge: A device indicating pressure in a filter system. Provides a determination of how the system is operating and informs us when service is required.

Pressure Side: The return side of the plumbing. The section from the pump impeller toward the pool.

Pressure Switch: A switch used in pool heaters which opens when the flow rate is insufficient for safe heater operation. This disrupts the circuit in the heater, preventing it from firing.

Pump: A mechanical wet end, powered by an electric motor, which causes hydraulic flow and pressure for the circulation of the pool water.

Pump Strainer Basket: A device placed on the suction side of the pump, which contains a removable strainer basket designed to trap large debris in the water flow without causing restriction. Sometimes called a pump leaf trap.

Push-Pull Valve: A two-position valve used for backwashing sand or D.E. filters.

PVC: Polyvinyl chloride, which is used to make flexible and rigid PVC pipe used for pool plumbing.

Rate Of Flow: Quantity of water flowing past a designated point within a specified period, measured in gallons per minute (GPM).

Reagent: The chemical indicators used in testing water balance. (All the little bottles or tablets in your test kit.)

Residual: Usually refers to free available chlorine levels remaining in the pool after initial treatment or activity with contaminants.

Restricted Flow: The term used to describe a condition preventing full flow of water. Restriction can occur with full skimmer or strainer baskets, obstructions in the plumbing, dirty filter, undersized plumbing or equipment, or placing devices like heaters, cleaners, or fountains in the circulation system. Restriction on the suction side creates higher vacuum (or suction). On the pressure side, it creates higher pressure.

Salt Water Generator/Salt Water Chlorinator: Also known as a salt system or a salt water chlorinator, a salt water generator uses sodium chloride (salt) to create chlorine.

Sand Filter: A filter tank, usually fiberglass or ABS plastic, filled with sand and gravel. The pump diffuses water over the top of the sand bed, forces it through the sand, and into the laterals on the bottom.

Sanitizer: A chemical agent used to remove unwanted contaminants.

Scale: Usually whitish in color, scale forms on pool surfaces and equipment when mineral salts are forced out of solution. A scaling condition is one in which calcium hardness, pH, and/or alkalinity levels are out of balance.

Sequestering Agent/Metal Sequestrant: A sequestering agent ties up minerals tightly in solution, preventing their precipitation, which colors the water and/or stains the pool. Synonymous to chelators, these are commonly called stain and scale chemicals.

Skimmer: A surface skimmer is a plumbing fitting set at water level, containing a weir mechanism and a debris basket. The skimmer is part of the suction side of the circulation system.

Skimmer Basket: Beneath the lid, the basket strains debris as the first line of defense in filtering the water.

Skimmer Net: Attached to a telescopic pole, a skimmer net is a very useful tool in keeping the pool clean. Also called a skimmer net are the flat "dip and flip" nets, which aren't so useful.

Shock: This term describes the products used in shocking, such as hypochlorites, potassium permonysulfate, or hydrogen peroxide. "Shocking" describes the act of bringing the sanitizer level up so high that breakpoint chlorination is reached. When breakpoint is reached, the water is "shocked," tearing apart molecules and slashing through cell walls.

Shotcrete: A different type of application of the concrete and sand mix which is used to "shoot the shell." Gunite is pumped dry and mixed with water at the gun, whereas shotcrete is pumped wet.

Soda Ash: A base used to counteract an acidic condition by raising pH.

Sodium Bicarbonate (Baking Soda): Another base; however, its properties will increase alkalinity more than pH. Used to raise total alkalinity levels.

Sodium Bisulfate: A granular form of acid used to counteract a scaling condition by lowering pH and/or alkalinity.

Sodium Hypochlorite: Liquid chlorine used in pools that is identical to yet stronger than bleach.

Sodium Dichlor: A granular form of chlorine that is stabilized with cyanuric acid. Used for shocking and superchlorination.

Soft Water: Water that has low calcium and/or magnesium content.

Stabilizer: See cyanuric acid. Stabilizers, also called conditioners, can be added directly to your pool to extend your chlorine efficacy. Cyanuric acid is already added to certain "stabilized" products such as trichlor tablets and sodium dichlor.

Standpipe: Vertical pipe that carries water from the hub and lateral assembly to or from the multiport valve on a top-mount sand filter.

Strainer Basket: The second line of defense in removing debris from your pool is the pump basket. The holes are smaller than those in a skimmer basket and prevent the pump impeller from clogging up.

Suction Side: The plumbing prior to and carrying water to the pump. This side is under vacuum pressure.

Superchlorination: Applying 7–10 times the normal amounts of chlorine to the pool as an added "boost" for contaminant removal.

Test Kit: A method used to test the water balance and sanitizing level of your pool water.

Timer: A mechanical device that controls the timed operation of your electrical equipment, primarily your filter and booster pumps.

Total Alkalinity: The "buffering" capacity of the water or the ability of the pool water to resist changes in pH. Additions of sodium bicarbonate will increase total alkalinity, expressed in PPM.

Total Dissolved Solids (TDS): A measure of everything that has ever dissolved in the water (i.e., all the matter that is in solution). High TDS levels can oversaturate your water, causing all sorts of reactions.

Trichloro-S-Triazinetrione: A chemical compound used as an industrial disinfectant, bleaching agent, and reagent in organic synthesis. This white crystalline powder, which has a strong "chlorine odor," is sometimes sold in tablet or granular form.

Turbidity: Cloudy, dull, hazy water, due to microparticle suspension.

Turnover: The amount of time it takes your pump to move all the water in your pool through the filter and back again. Usually, pools are designed for an eight-hour turnover.

Ultraviolet Light: Ultraviolet (UV) light is electromagnetic radiation with a wavelength shorter than that of visible light, but longer than soft X-rays. It is so named because the spectrum starts with wavelengths slightly shorter than the wavelengths humans identify as the color violet (purple).

Underdrain: The lower collection system in a filter which directs filtered water back toward the pool. It also distributes water in reverse during backwashing. See laterals.

Vacuum: The low-pressure condition created in the suction line. And the cleaning process of sucking leaves, algae, and debris from the pool floor.

Valves: A device placed in the plumbing line that restricts or obstructs water flow to create desired hydraulics or may permit flow in one direction only (as in a check valve).

Vinyl Liner: One type of interior pool finish. The liner is draped over a sand or cementitious floor and locked to the top of the pool's wall.

Weir: The device in a skimmer that controls the amount of water coming into the skimmer and keeps debris inside. It's the moving door at the mouth of the skimmer.

We Simplify Pool and Hot Tub Care for Everyone

Pool and spa maintenance can be difficult. And it's hard to find a trusted source of information you can rely on. We get it. And it's the reason Swim University® exists.

Matt Giovanisci, the founder, started in the industry at age 13. He was a stock boy and water tester for a local pool store on the weekends. He continued working in the industry, and moved to bigger pool companies along the way.

Matt was helping thousands of pool owners every year. But he wanted to share his knowledge and unique teaching style on a larger scale. So he launched Swim University® in 2006.

Since then, Swim University® has made pool care easy for millions of homeowners. And each year, we continue to help more people with water chemistry, cleaning, and troubleshooting.

We're a Family-Owned Small Business

What started as a solo project has grown into a tight-knit family team, committed to producing the best pool care content out there. And we're proud to have our entire team and product line based in the USA.

We're always posting new articles and videos to help you keep your pool and hot tub clean and clear.

Visit us online for more pool care information:

www.SwimUniversity.com